ORGANISATION FOR ECONOMIC CO-OPERATION AND DEVELOPMENT

Urban
travel
and
sustainable
development

EUROPEAN CONFERENCE OF MINISTERS OF TRANSPORT

ORGANISATION FOR ECONOMIC CO-OPERATION AND DEVELOPMENT

Pursuant to Article 1 of the Convention signed in Paris on 14th December 1960, and which came into force on 30th September 1961, the Organisation for Economic Co-operation and Development (OECD) shall promote policies designed:

- to achieve the highest sustainable economic growth and employment and a rising standard of living in Member countries, while maintaining financial stability, and thus to contribute to the development of the world economy;
- to contribute to sound economic expansion in Member as well as non-member countries in the process of economic development; and
- to contribute to the expansion of world trade on a multilateral, non-discriminatory basis in accordance with international obligations.

The original Member countries of the OECD are Austria, Belgium, Canada, Denmark, France, Germany, Greece, Iceland, Ireland, Italy, Luxembourg, the Netherlands, Norway, Portugal, Spain, Sweden, Switzerland, Turkey, the United Kingdom and the United States. The following countries became Members subsequently through accession at the dates indicated hereafter: Japan (28th April 1964), Finland (28th January 1969), Australia (7th June 1971), New Zealand (29th May 1973) and Mexico (18th May 1994). The Commission of the European Communities takes part in the work of the OECD (Article 13 of the OECD Convention).

Publié en français sous le titre :
TENDANCES DU TRANSPORT EUROPÉEN ET BESOINS EN INFRASTRUCTURES

THE EUROPEAN CONFERENCE
OF MINISTERS OF TRANSPORT (ECMT)

The European Conference of Ministers of Transport (ECMT) is an inter-governmental organisation established by a Protocol signed in Brussels on 17th October 1953. The Council of the Conference comprises the Ministers of Transport of 31 European countries.[1] The work of the Council of Ministers is prepared by a Committee of Deputies.

The purposes of the Conference are:

a) to take whatever measures may be necessary to achieve, at general or regional level, the most efficient use and rational development of European inland transport of international importance;

b) to co-ordinate and promote the activities of international organisations concerned with European inland transport, taking into account the work of supranational authorities in this field.

The matters generally studied by ECMT – and on which the Ministers take decisions – include: the general lines of transport policy; investment in the sector; infrastructural needs; specific aspects of the development of rail, road and inland waterways transport; combined transport issues; urban travel; road safety and traffic rules, signs and signals; access to transport for people with mobility problems. Other subjects now being examined in depth are: the future applications of new technologies, protection of the environment, and the integration of the Central and Eastern European countries in the European transport market. Statistical analyses of trends in traffic and investment are published each year, thus throwing light on the prevailing economic situation.

The ECMT organises Round Tables and Symposia. Their conclusions are considered by the competent organs of the Conference, under the authority of the Committee of Deputies, so that the latter may formulate proposals for policy decisions to be submitted to the Ministers.

The ECMT Documentation Centre maintains the TRANSDOC database, which can be accessed on-line via the telecommunications network.

For administrative purposes, the ECMT Secretariat is attached to the Secretariat of the Organisation for Economic Co-operation and Development (OECD).

---

1. Austria, Belgium, Bosnia-Herzegovina, Bulgaria, Croatia, the Czech Republic, Denmark, Estonia, Finland, France, Germany, Greece, Hungary, Ireland, Italy, Latvia, Lithuania, Luxembourg, Moldova, the Netherlands, Norway, Poland, Portugal, Romania, the Slovak Republic, Slovenia, Spain, Sweden, Switzerland, Turkey and the United Kingdom. (Associate Member countries: Australia, Canada, Japan, New Zealand, the Russian Federation and the United States. Observer countries: Albania, Morocco.)

FOREWORD

Following a decision made by the OECD Group on Urban Affairs and the ECMT Committee of Deputies in November 1990 a Project Group on Urban Travel and Sustainable Development was set up in May 1991. The mandate given to the group was to:

- review urban travel and the problems associated with its growth;
- identify policies capable of influencing the demand for urban travel and, in particular, car use;
- propose measures which could contribute to sustainable development; and
- indicate the economic, environmental, social and political consequences of such measures.

This publication is the result of a three-year inquiry by this Project Group. It has included the analysis of transport-environment policies in 20 countries and 132 cities. Some of the results were presented at a Conference held in Düsseldorf (Germany) in June 1993. The publication examines:

- the role of economic incentives and disincentives;
- the role of land-use planning;
- the potential of traffic calming and other new approaches to traffic management; and
- the use of marketing, telematics and other innovations to improve public transport.

The importance of combining in coherent, reinforcing packages land-use planning, economic incentives and traffic management is particularly stressed.

The Conclusions and Executive Summary were approved by the OECD Group on Urban Affairs and by the ECMT Committee of Deputies, in April 1994. The publication is derestricted on the responsibility of the OECD and ECMT Secretaries-General.

ACKNOWLEDGEMENTS

The OECD and ECMT would like to thank a number of people and organisations who helped to complete this report. Firstly, we are indebted to the national delegates and the Chairman of the joint Project Group on Urban Travel and Sustainable Development, Mr. Peter Güller (Switzerland), who provided many inputs. Mr. Vernon Webster was the main consultant for the project. He was helped by Mr. Terence Bendixson. The Transport Research Laboratory in the United Kingdom, and especially Ms. Mira Dasgupta undertook the analysis of the questionnaire answers from the cities. Mr. Richard Oldfield assisted in the modelling work and with the mathematical calculations. The consulting firm ECOTEC drafted the chapter on land-use planning. The preparation of this report was overseen by Mr. Ariel Alexandre (OECD) and by Mr. Jack Short (ECMT).

TABLE OF CONTENTS

Part 1
BACKGROUND TRENDS AND PROBLEMS

Part 2
POLICY ANALYSIS

Part 3
POLICIES FOR THE 1990s AND BEYOND

8

LIST OF FIGURES

LIST OF TABLES

PRINCIPAL CONCLUSIONS

Present land-use and transport policies in OECD/ECMT countries are leading to excessive travel by car in cities and their immediate surroundings.

Such policies are the cause of growing congestion, air pollution, noise, acid rain, and the risk of global warming. These trends are increasingly seen as unacceptable by Member Governments.

Some governments and municipalities have recognised the need for change and are aiming to reduce car travel for trips to city centres and ensure accessibility by other means. Finding ways to reduce dependency on cars for travel in the suburban and outer parts of metropolitan regions is more difficult and work on it is only beginning. Large scale road investment is no longer seen as a solution.

Bringing about a shift away from post-1945 urban development and travel trends will take time. The location of jobs, travel habits and lifestyles will all have to change.

This OECD/ECMT study underlines that strategies to bring about such changes are necessary and that their benefits – economic, environmental and social – will greatly outweigh their costs.

Car dependency in cities can only be reduced by the combined effect of land-use and transport policies. The goals of such policies will need to be openly stated. Their implementation will need to be steady and long term. An integrated policy approach is essential; three main strands of such a policy package can be identified.

- *Best Practice:* raise the effectiveness of current land-use planning and traffic management measures, including parking control and provision/encouragement of other means of transport, to the level of those in the best managed cities. This strand is a necessary part of a coherent strategy, but will be insufficient to bring major benefits on its own.
- *Innovations:* develop new policies to shape urban developments into less car-dependent forms and apply congestion pricing to traffic management, with the objective of bringing demand for car travel into balance with road capacity.
- *Sustainable Development:* introduce repeated annual increases in motor fuel taxation to promote more economical vehicles, shorter and fewer car trips, a shift in travel away from solo driving and greater use of environmentally-friendly modes.

All three strands of the policy package are necessary to reduce car travel, especially in cities, to improve accessibility for those without cars and to achieve sustainable urban development. Together they could reduce substantially the economic, environmental and social costs of travel in OECD countries, currently estimated to be equivalent to about 5 per cent of Gross Domestic Product (GDP).

All levels of Government have responsibilities to bring about change. Central governments and international organisations have key roles in setting the standards and the framework within which cities can operate. Acceptance by the population of the needed measures has to be won through providing information on the problems and through consultation on the measures to be applied.

EXECUTIVE SUMMARY

1. Current situation

Key urban trends

About three quarters of the population of OECD/ECMT countries now live in urban areas. Settlement patterns are becoming more complex and the continuing suburbanisation of population and jobs is one of the major features.

Travel by car has increased in almost all countries and at a rate which, fifty years ago, would not have been thought possible. This has been due to long-term annual increases of 2 to 3 per cent in national wealth, a general lowering in the real costs of using a car and the emergence of more car-dependent lifestyles.

Trip length both by car and public transport has been increasing as activities have become more dispersed. Suburb-to-suburb journeys have shown the fastest growth. At the same time, there has been a shift from walking and cycling to mechanised modes.

Car ownership has conferred on a large and increasing public a freedom to travel anywhere at any time and enabled jobs, shops and services to relocate to peripheral areas. It has also allowed more people to enjoy living in spacious surroundings, which may be considered as a positive trend in some cases.

Industry has not been slow to take advantage of the freedom offered by road movement. The ease with which goods can be transported from anywhere to anywhere has allowed innovations, such as ''just-in-time'' production and a reduction in warehousing facilities. Firms of all kinds have, at the same time, tended to move to edge-of-town sites to exploit the increased personal mobility of their car-owning customers and employees.

Such innovations in road haulage practice, coupled with increases in consumption of goods, have caused road freight traffic to grow at nearly 5 per cent p.a. over the last 20 years – even faster than car traffic (3.3 per cent p.a.).

15

Costs of key trends

All these changes have been associated with economic growth, but they have not been without their costs:

- almost all large towns and cities are congested in the central and inner areas for much of the day and along the main arteries at peak times. Many are becoming increasingly congested in the suburbs at certain times of the day. The cost of road congestion in OECD countries is estimated to be equivalent to about 2 per cent of the GDP;
- fringe areas of cities are difficult and costly to serve by public transport;
- those without access to a car are becoming increasingly isolated from jobs and services;
- deaths and injuries on urban roads occur in unacceptable numbers, do untold damage to those who are bereaved and maimed and create an aura of fear. The costs of road accidents are estimated to be equivalent to 1.5 to 2 per cent of GDP in OECD countries;
- inner and many outer parts of cities are dominated by road traffic. Neighbourhoods are severed by roads and noise affects to a serious extent almost half the urban residents in most countries. The cost of noise pollution in OECD countries might well be equivalent to about 0.3 per cent of GDP;
- air pollution is present in almost all parts of cities. Exhaust emissions, in addition to contributing to smog, are associated with a wide range of health problems. Local air pollution is estimated to cost the equivalent of about 0.4 per cent of GDP in OECD countries;
- not all the effects of traffic are local. Smog and acid rain are regularly exported from cities to their surroundings and even to adjacent countries. Carbon Dioxide (CO_2), which is emitted whenever fossil fuels are burnt, spreads to the upper atmosphere and contributes to global warming. The costs of non-local pollution are estimated at 1 to 10 per cent of GDP.

Resource implications of world-wide economic growth

Increasing use of energy for transport, industrial and domestic purposes has important economic and ecological implications:

- the demand for oil is gradually using up the world's readily-available reserves. Most of this consumption is by a relatively small proportion of the world's population. Urbanisation and rising car use in developing countries will put further pressure on world oil supplies; but, more importantly;
- these trends will increase the risk of global warming.

Before considering what might be done to combat these problems, it is necessary to look at what has already been tried and how successful the measures have been.

2. Lessons from past experience

Practice in different countries varies and, even within countries, different cities have pursued different policies. This has provided a wealth of experience.

Measures to increase transport capacity

Building more and more roads in cities and conurbations has enabled more people to travel by car, but has not reduced peak-period congestion to any noticeable extent. As soon as new road space becomes available in large cities, it is quickly filled. Even city regions with the most extensive road networks have high congestion levels. Attempts to solve the congestion problem in this way, especially in Europe, would change cities beyond all recognition, the cost would be prohibitive and congestion would still not be eliminated.

While congestion might spread in cities which make little or no attempt to increase road capacity in line with demand, such cities will not "grind to a halt". People and firms adapt. Travellers change either mode or destination. Firms do not locate in areas which they feel are not suitable, if there are others which are. But the resulting solution may be far from optimal: cities need a network of high-quality roads for essential traffic and to allow historic and other sensitive areas to be protected from unwanted traffic and the problems associated with this.

Improving public transport has been the main weapon in most cities' armouries. It has added to transport capacity and made travel easier and more pleasant for its users. It has enabled city centres to remain compact and be able to attract the specialist activities and services which people expect to find in them. It has enabled them to compete more effectively with peripheral shopping and service facilities.

But improved public transport has not, in general, attracted car users in sufficiently large numbers to affect congestion levels. The users of the improved services have tended to come from cycle, walk and car passenger modes and any car drivers who have transferred to public transport have been quickly replaced by new car drivers as a result of the suppressed demand for car travel in peak periods in most large cities. It is possible that new rail systems have been more successful in attracting car drivers than road-based systems, but even so, the effect on congestion has been slight.

Priority measures which attract travel from low-occupancy to high-occupancy modes have been successful in many cities and have increased the *passenger-carrying* capacity of the road network significantly. Cities like Zurich, which have included such measures as an integral part of a comprehensive package, have achieved a high use of public transport and economic success also.

Measures to restrain car use

Constraints on the supply of public parking spaces, and congestion itself, have had the effect of limiting urban traffic, though using a scarce resource (people's time) to ration another scarce resource (street capacity) is inefficient. Charging higher fees for public parking (while limiting the supply) is more efficient, since it uses money to ration street space (this is a transfer payment, which can then be used for other purposes). Even so, commuters with free parking or company-paid spaces are not affected and no impediment is put in the way of through traffic. Higher charges also tend to increase the turnover of parking spaces and hence the amount of road traffic.

Despite all the problems, parking controls of one sort or another are still the most common means of restraining traffic in most OECD/ECMT countries: they seem to be accepted by both public and politicians and are reasonably enforceable. In some countries, however, parking control is still a little-used tool.

A novel method of limiting car use is being used in Southern California, where employers who subsidise their employees' parking costs are, in some cases, obliged under new legislation to give their employees the option to take the equivalent cash allowance in lieu of a free space. The number of commuters who drive alone is expected to decline from 70 per cent to 55 per cent as a result.

Taxation of free parking places provided for company employees, and/or other benefits in kind, is becoming more commonplace.

Special lanes for high occupancy vehicles (HOVs) on motorways and at toll booths are used as effective restraint measures in the United States and Australia and are now being tried in Europe (in Amsterdam).

Other types of regulatory measures, such as restricting access to particular parts of cities, are being increasingly used to restrain traffic and protect the urban environment (Milan and Berlin are good examples of this).

So far the use of congestion pricing to promote changes in travel mode has been tried in Singapore only. In some cities (in Norway, for example), low-cost tolls are levied to pay for new roads: such systems have the potential for reducing congestion by charging different amounts at different times of the day. Stockholm is also planning to use charges to reduce traffic. Pricing methods of various kinds are being considered in a number of other cities and a detailed assessment of the likely impact of introducing road pricing in London is being carried out.

Congestion pricing, like parking charges, will have spatial effects and implications for equity, which need to be taken into consideration.

Measures to calm traffic

Traffic calming measures have been successfully introduced in a number of cities in order to reduce speeds and casualties and make the areas more attractive and more suited to the needs of pedestrians and cyclists, but the technique has been used in a relatively piecemeal fashion up to now, so that cities still seem to be largely dominated by road traffic. The most extensive use is in the Netherlands and Germany.

To gain full advantage from such systems, they need to be on an area-wide or even city-wide basis, with clear transport priorities established.

18

Land-use planning measures

Some very large metropolitan areas, *e.g.* Tokyo, London and Paris, have been transformed into multi-centric regions through a combination of market forces and strong regional strategies (including fiscal inducements and disincentives), thereby taking some of the pressure off the principal city centres. Congestion has been eased in some of these cases, but dependence on the car has probably increased as activities have become more spread out.

Such attempts as have been made in the past to locate homes and jobs in closer proximity (for example, in new towns and designated growth areas) have provided no convincing evidence of a lasting saving in travel-to-work distances (though there may have been benefits of a different nature). While travel is relatively cheap, most commuters, when offered the alternatives of travel-time saving or wider choice of job and housing opportunities, tend to choose the latter. The same might be true of shopping and other types of journeys.

The extent of people's adaptability, and that of businesses too, has tended to be underestimated in the past, so that land-use and transport policies have not always worked as intended. People and firms do what is best for themselves and not necessarily what is best for the city, the country or even the planet. Everyone optimising their own situation does not automatically lead to an overall optimum – this has to be reached by careful land-use management and a knowledge of how people respond to changing conditions. Policy makers should therefore try to ensure through a variety of measures, including regulatory and economic instruments, that the rational responses of travellers, residents and firms are compatible with those which lead to more sustainable patterns of urban development.

There have been some successes in revitalising decaying city centres. In Portland, Oregon, for example, a mixture of planning policies to improve the attractiveness of the city centre and bring high-density housing and employment back into the centre, combined with a variety of complementary transport policies, have transformed downtown Portland into a living, vibrant place.

Concentration of attractors of travel, like offices and shops, around railway, tram and bus stations, has been effective in producing a modal shift from car to public transport in a number of cities, *e.g.* Stockholm, Vienna and Toronto. This technique forms the basis of the current land-use planning policy in the Netherlands "The Right Business in the Right Place" and the United Kingdom's Planning Policy Guidance.

Town planners are increasingly considering how development might be shaped to reduce dependence on the private car and the amount of travel in total, using a combination of reinforcing land-use and transport measures. Reducing the need to travel has not previously been seen as an objective – this is a turning point.

Land-use planning has the potential to:

• shape the pattern of urban development and reduce social exclusion and segregation;
• guide the location of major travel-generating uses; and
• ensure a wide range of opportunities are available at the local level.

It is an essential part of the long-term strategy for ensuring more sustainable patterns of urban development and urban travel.

Improvements through technology

Much of the progress towards solving the problems identified in this report has come from advances in technology: these have come about mainly as a result of government regulations (themselves often the result of directives from the European Union or other international bodies).

Changes in behaviour, however, have tended to offset some of the gains made. For example, increases in fuel economy resulting from improvements to engine design have encouraged drivers to trade up to larger and more powerful cars, to drive in a less fuel-efficient manner and to make more and longer journeys, thereby reducing the potential technological gains.

Technology alone is responsible for the progress made in reducing engine noise and noxious emissions from vehicles. Europe has tended to lag behind the United States and Japan, so that air quality improvements have come to Europe more than a decade later. Further progress in this area is constrained by the high-polluting effect of cold starts and the trend for cars to emit more as they get older, but both of these problems are being tackled.

There is a limit to what technology can do on its own, however. People's habits have to change and there is ample evidence that fiscal and regulatory measures can be effective in this respect. But before considering how far policies need to change, it is necessary to examine what is likely to happen if present policies continue in much the same way as they have in the past.

3. A continuation of present policies

Over the next 30 to 40 years, car and goods vehicle traffic is expected to continue growing, if present policies are maintained. Patterns of development will change too: telecommunications will bring to most houses the sophisticated services now available only at the offices of international corporations; vehicles will be transformed; and telematics will bring new levels of sophistication to urban traffic management and public transport systems.

Effects on urban travel and congestion

Policies vary widely in OECD/ECMT countries with different effects on traffic growth: in Switzerland, for instance, the annual growth rate in car travel since 1985 has dropped to roughly half that of public transport travel, but in most countries, car use is increasing much faster than transit use. A continuation of present policies in any of the OECD/ECMT countries will not bring about a reduction in private car travel, which overall is set to double within the next 30 to 40 years in most of these countries. Much of this extra travel will take place in suburban and rural areas, with very little in the inner areas of cities.

This report is concerned primarily with urban travel, but statistics relating to *all travel* are just as relevant; it is difficult to be precise about what is strictly an urban journey, since the activities in urban areas attract commuters and visitors from far and wide and almost all journeys begin or end in urban areas. The same applies to freight movement.

A continuation of past and present policies will not reduce congestion levels in the larger cities and conurbations. Congestion will spread in time and space, though not necessarily getting any worse in areas which are presently highly congested. The increasing use of telematics in traffic and travel information and control systems will bring about smoother travel, but not necessarily any lasting relief from congestion, because of the suppressed demand for car travel.

New and improved public transport systems will continue to benefit the users of these systems, provide a more satisfactory alternative to the use of the private car and strengthen the central areas of cities, by reducing the rate of decentralisation of employment and other activities. These improvements are unlikely, however, to ease peak-period congestion: neither is the financial burden due to capital investment and operating subsidies likely to diminish in most countries.

Restrictions or bans on heavy goods vehicle movements in cities, the establishment of goods distribution centres on the edges of towns and the trans-shipment of consignments to specialised city trucks will help to reduce the impact of heavy lorries on urban traffic and the urban environment. However, increasing use of "just-in-time" techniques will offset such gains to some extent because smaller loads require more frequent trips.

Use of the environmentally-friendly modes of cycling and walking will probably continue to diminish in general, though there will be exceptions in cities and countries which make special efforts to cater for these modes through the provision of more local facilities (Denmark, Germany and the Netherlands, for instance).

Effects on the environment

Pollution levels are falling in many western European cities, mainly as a result of vehicle technology improvements, but it will take some time for the full effects to become apparent because of the large stock of older vehicles still on the roads. In American and Japanese cities, where three-way catalysts have been in use for a decade or more, there is less room for progress through technological improvements.

In the medium term, some emissions may start to rise again due to increasing traffic volumes, bad maintenance, and the ageing of vehicle fleets, but there is every expectation that technology will eventually find a way to allow vehicles to operate in urban areas in a much less polluting way (better performing catalysts, greater use of less-polluting fuels and electric vehicles, etc.).

Noise is a different matter: at best it will improve only marginally as engines become quieter (particularly heavy goods vehicle and motor cycle engines) and tyre/road surface noise is reduced. At worst, the situation will become almost unbearable for many of those living, working and shopping in urban areas, as increasing traffic volumes, accelerations and speeds counteract the gains from technology improvements.

Vehicle-entry restrictions and lorry bans to particular areas of cities (shopping, cultural, historic and residential areas, etc.) will be increasingly used to provide a more pleasant urban environment, with less noise, pollution and hindrance from traffic.

While technology will gradually reduce the specific fuel consumption of vehicles, and therefore the amount of CO_2 emitted from them, the risk to global warming will continue to increase as long as traffic increases and there are no worthwhile incentives (through higher fuel prices, for example) for drivers to trade down to smaller vehicles or drive in a more energy-efficient way.

Effects on safety

Road casualties will probably continue to fall, despite increasing traffic levels, largely due to better protection of vehicle occupants and a gradual transfer from non-mechanised modes to mechanised ones (but not to motor cycles). Changes in behaviour, particularly with regard to drinking and driving are likely to continue, provided there is effective enforcement. Increasing use of pedestrianisation and traffic calming measures will reinforce these improvements.

Effects on urban structure

Decentralisation of both population and employment will almost certainly continue, albeit at a slower rate, with more and more edge-of-city shopping malls; health, leisure and educational complexes; and business and science parks.

City centres, while possibly attracting fewer workers, are likely to remain strong despite the locational changes noted above, at least in European countries. The centres of large cities, in particular, will continue to attract financial institutions (banking and insurance), specialist shopping and service activities, cultural and entertainment facilities and higher-educational establishments. Smaller towns and cities with historic, cultural and architectural interest are also likely to retain their vitality.

4.   What should be done?

Difficult decisions

An overall doubling of car and goods vehicle traffic in many OECD/ECMT countries over the next 30 to 40 years, as forecast, would exacerbate the problems of congestion and traffic domination in towns and cities and impede progress in reducing road casualties and pollution.

There is more uncertainty, however, with regard to the wider problems of energy consumption and global warming from CO_2 emissions. But even if no further progress were to be made towards a Western style of living in the developing world, the current situation would be unsustainable, in the sense that nations would not be able to continue indefinitely to draw on the earth's resources at such a rate: moreover, continual increases in CO_2 emissions increase the risk of irreversible climate changes.

Despite all the advantages to the industrialised nations of the world as a result of the revolution which has taken place in transport during this century, something has to be done, if the problems are to be confronted.

Difficult decisions will have to be made: the planning of development, the cost of travel, the design of vehicles and the management of traffic will all have to change. This will affect the way people live. Changes of such a magnitude can only be brought about slowly. Governments will therefore have to pursue sustainable development by acting on a wide front and over a period of two to three decades, but they will need to start now, especially in cities.

While action is required at all levels of government, international organisations can do much to exert pressure and set standards and targets, which might in some cases be more stringent than individual countries on their own would be willing to introduce. Countries are competing for trade and within any country, individual cities are in competition with each other for new businesses and enterprises. By acting in unison, both cities and countries can avoid being placed at a disadvantage, though evidence is mounting that a good urban environment is a positive factor in the competition between cities.

Policies for the future

Past policies have not been successful in tackling these problems and new approaches are needed. In order to achieve a more sustainable development, integrated approaches are required which combine measures that reinforce each other.

A policy plan with three distinct strands has been identified by the OECD/ECMT joint group. All three are aimed in the same direction, but the more progressive ones would take cities further towards the goals of less congestion, reduced energy consumption, improved access for those without cars, higher environmental standards and reduced overall costs. The whole policy package contains policies and measures aimed at different levels of government and aimed at meeting the needs of cities of various sizes. The implementation strategy will have to take into consideration national and local circumstances, as well as the policies pursued in areas other than transport and the environment.

Strand 1: Best practice

The adoption of best practice in land-use and transport planning, traffic management and the improvement of public transport would involve the wider use of tried and tested measures (most are referred to in this report). Associated with them would be the adoption of standards and targets relating to road safety, environmental quality and social welfare.

The use of best practice everywhere would bring about some changes in travel patterns, but congestion would be little affected outside city centres and travel by car would continue to grow. The most that could be expected is that *rates of growth* in congestion and car travel would be reduced.

Best practice would bring improvements to Central Business Districts, historic and cultural centres and some, but not all, residential areas: it would reduce pollution levels in general, but noise levels only in specific areas. It would do little for people without access to cars and almost nothing to reducing the risk of climate change.

Strand 2: Policy innovations

The second strand is based on innovations in land-use planning and traffic management, some of which are still at the research or development stage. Land-use planning policies would be used to influence the location of jobs and homes so as to widen travel choices. Congestion pricing and telecommunications would be used to bring demand and supply for road space into balance.

The land-use planning measures would be concerned with the types of settlements which should expand, where major developments should locate (in particular, the concentration of major attractors such as offices and shops in areas well served by public transport) and the provision of local facilities. Land uses would be integrated with public transport routes, roads, cycle and walkways. Speed limits would be applied more extensively on through roads and traffic calming would be extended to most residential and school areas.

The integrated package of traffic management measures would include congestion pricing, reductions in city-centre parking, bus priorities, park-and-ride services and investment in transit infrastructure.

Congestion and pollution would be reduced substantially as a result of this innovative package, though noise would continue to be a problem. Safety levels would be improved. People without cars would be able to travel more easily. Car owners not wishing to use their cars would have more acceptable alternatives by public transport, on foot or by bicycle. Dependence on cars would be reduced and traffic growth in urban areas might cease altogether, though overall traffic levels and CO_2 emissions would continue to grow in most OECD/ECMT countries.

Strand 3: Sustainable development

A progressively increasing fuel tax designed to significantly reduce vehicle kilometrage and the amount of fuel used is the essence of Strand 3. The guiding principles of the UN's Framework Convention on Climate Change suggests that this measure should be part of a comprehensive tax on all fossil fuels in order to ensure cost efficiency.

The Intergovernmental Panel on Climate Change states that CO_2 levels must be brought down by fully 60 to 80 per cent if atmospheric CO_2 concentrations are to be stabilised. By way of an example, the Project Group has estimated the likely effects of a 7 per cent p.a. rise in real terms in the price of fuel over the next 20 years. Such a measure would be expected to reduce vehicle-km travelled to about two-thirds of the forecast level 20 years from now and the amount of fuel used to about half of the forecast level. In combination with Strands 1 and 2, vehicle-km would be expected to fall to about 85 per cent of 1991 levels and fuel consumption to about 60 per cent by 2015.

The estimated savings would come about from a reduction in car trip lengths of roughly a quarter, a slower growth in car ownership, a modal shift from car to public transport, cycling and walking, a modest improvement in fuel consumption due to the way vehicles are driven and from trading down to smaller, less powerful vehicles and an improvement in fuel efficiency of nearly a third arising from improved engine design. It should be noted that these calculations are of a preliminary nature: they are based on a large number of assumptions and the results are subject to a good deal of uncertainty.

Other effects of such a policy package would be reduced fuel consumption of goods vehicles arising from increased engine efficiency and fuel-saving changes in production practices and delivery methods (including an increase in return loads). Even with the severe measures of Strands 2 and 3, however, many of the environmental problems due to goods traffic are likely to remain.

Increasing fuel prices would not cause any of the measures in Strand 2 to become redundant, since all the measures operate at different strengths in different areas and on different time scales. City centre restraint measures, for instance, have an immediate effect, whereas a sustained rise in fuel prices is, by definition, a long-term measure. Most of the measures in Strand 2 would become *more* effective under a regime of higher fuel prices.

The taxing of fuel would increase the effectiveness of land-use planning policies designed to bring homes, jobs and shops closer together, since the incentive for people to work near home would be greater when the costs of travel were greater. Under-utilised public transport systems, cycleways and walkways would likewise find more users when car travel costs were raised substantially. And those drivers who found themselves displaced from their cars because of high fuel costs, would have better quality alternatives available to them.

Only Strands 2 and 3 would bring about significant improvements in travel and the urban environment. They would do so by providing greater choice in how to travel and where to live, work, shop and socialise – particularly for those without access to cars. They would also reduce substantially the large social, economic and environmental cost burden. The high fuel cost rises of Strand 3 would take all these improvements further and could significantly reduce this cost burden, currently estimated to be equivalent to about 5 per cent of GDP of OECD/ECMT countries: it is the only one of the three strands of the recommended policy package to actually bring the level of CO_2 emissions down towards the target set by the Intergovernmental Panel on Climate Change.

Introducing and managing change

Governments will be concerned about the possible adverse effects of such policies on transport, on trade and on the economy. There are a number of factors to bear in mind. First, present prices do not reflect real costs and, consequently, the present situation is not optimal. Second, price increases will discharge only marginal users and marginal use. Therefore, the losses in economic terms are likely to be small. Third, those who do travel will be able to do so in a way that is safer, quicker and more comfortable. Fourth, the increased revenues obtained can be used in productive ways, including cushioning the effect on certain businesses if that were believed to be needed.

Governments at all levels have responsibilities to bring about change. Central governments and international organisations have key roles in setting the standards and the framework within which cities can operate and especially in introducing the fiscal measures that contribute most to achieving sustainable development. Acceptance by the population of the needed measures has to be won through providing information on the problems and through consultation on the measures to be applied.

Part 1

BACKGROUND TRENDS AND PROBLEMS

1. INTRODUCTION

1. Towards sustainable development

Context

Car travel and the distribution of goods by road have already caused severe problems in cities all over the world and both car use and road haulage are increasing almost everywhere. This growth was once expected to level out at a point where, given reasonable investment, roads could be provided to accommodate it. While many small towns have been, and still are, able to cope with the traffic they generate, the much higher volumes found in cities are less easily handled. It is possible that they could be accommodated by dispersing city-centre activities and embarking on sustained road investment programmes, as many American cities have done, but, this would have huge costs associated with it, serious resource and environmental implications and no guarantee of eliminating congestion. Moreover, such policies would alter most of our cities out of all recognition. Despite all the drawbacks, dispersion is taking place in virtually all cities – even dense, centralised European ones such as Madrid, Paris and Zurich.

Dispersion encourages more travel by car and necessitates the use of more urban land for roads. New road construction generates more travel and more pollution. Even if technology were able to eliminate most of the toxic vehicle emissions, the problems of noise and CO_2 emissions would still remain. Emissions of carbon dioxide, the principal greenhouse gas, are related strictly to fuel consumption, and on present trends, are set to grow.

Notwithstanding these prospects, policies for urban land use and travel in operation in all OECD countries will lead to increased use of cars and trucks. The same is true of Central Europe, South-East Asia and other developing countries. In all of them, the trend is towards urban dispersal, growing car travel and increasing road goods distribution.

What is sustainable development?

Human settlements – be they cities or single buildings – make demands on land, air, water, fuel and other resources. Settlements that do not consume more than can be replaced have prospects of continuing indefinitely and may be considered sustainable.

Whether or not this is the case with any particular city will depend on the land and other resources (including the upper atmosphere) needed to supply that city's citizens and absorb their wastes. This in turn will depend on lifestyle. The more consumption-based the lifestyle of the citizens, the wider the area and the more resources needed to sustain them and their city.

Sustainability is not, however, based on fixed relationships. Two main variables influence it: one is human aspirations; the other is technology. People can change their ways and technology can reduce the inputs and wastes associated with any given standard of living. Progress towards sustainable cities therefore depends on:

- changes in lifestyles; and
- the application of technology to reduce, for a particular lifestyle, the consumption of resources and the generation of polluting wastes (SERC, 1993).

Cities and sustainable development

Cities are essential. They offer opportunities and experiences unknown in rural economies: the problem is that as citizens get wealthier and their consumption increases, so the impact of their city increases too. Eventually the scale of these impacts becomes global.

This is precisely what is happening in the late 20th century. Thanks to economic development, wealth is increasing in more and more parts of the world and as it does, the zone of impact of more and more cities is expanding. In the case of developed cities, which are large-scale emitters of carbon dioxide – the main greenhouse gas – this expansion has reached the upper atmosphere. Uncertainty exists about how serious a threat this presents, but if current fossil fuel combustion and CO_2 emission trends persist, the outcome could be global climatic change. To reduce this risk, the lifestyles and technology of western countries and the direction of development in the rest of the world will have to change.

The logical place in which to start promoting such changes is in cities. In them is concentrated a high proportion of the economic activity, especially of OECD countries. Progress in the direction of sustainable urban economies therefore promises to make a major contribution to a sustainable world.

2. Urban travel and sustainable development

One quarter of the energy consumed in the life cycle of a car occurs before it leaves the showroom. The production, fuelling, use, servicing and disposal of vehicles all consume resources, occupy land and contribute to air and water pollution. The environmental effects of these processes are mostly local (acid rain and global warming are the exceptions) and appear to be controllable (less so, noise). The final chapter of this report sets out policy proposals bold enough to achieve such control, yet designed and timed to be politically practical.

Defining policies to reduce CO_2 emissions and reduce the risk of further global warming is more complicated. Quite apart from uncertainties about warming itself, transport is not the major source of CO_2, (though it is the fastest growing) and it is emitted by inter-urban as well as urban transport. Nevertheless, as the world's fleet of motor vehicles passes the 500 million mark, as car ownership climbs higher in OECD countries and *as it begins its steep climb in developing countries and countries in transition,* the case for precautionary action to limit car use in cities is strong and getting stronger.

Implementing targets for reducing CO_2 emissions seems likely to be the centrepiece of such precautionary action. And logic suggests that policy-makers should begin with world targets and work down through national targets to ones appropriate to the city or regional level. Targets need to be sectoral as well as global and need to cover not only CO_2, but all other types of emissions also. This will require international negotiation, for which OECD and ECMT are well-placed to take a lead.

2. ECONOMIC, SOCIAL AND URBAN TRENDS

This century has seen dramatic improvements in urban living standards, but these have brought with them many of the problems which are the subject of this report. This chapter looks at the principal trends. It uses published statistics by OECD, the European Union and other bodies, in addition to information from the responses to the OECD/ECMT Questionnaire sent to 132 cities (see Annex 1); the "National Overviews" of transport and land-use policies prepared by each of the participating countries (see Annex 2); and twelve "case studies" of cities carried out specifically for this project (see Annex 3).

1. A century of rising incomes

Since the Industrial Revolution the people of OECD countries have enjoyed continuing improvements in their living standards. The average person today has more living space, more domestic machines, more leisure time and travels more widely than ever before. This has been made possible by a sustained rise in income in real terms of 2 to 3 per cent a year on average (Figure 2.1). This increase in prosperity is largely due to gains in productivity and an expansion of the labour force, as more and more women have taken up paid employment. In the USA, for example, while the population grew by 50 per cent in the three decades up to 1980, jobs grew by 65 per cent. The proportion of women (aged 16 or over) in European Union (EU) countries in 1990 who were in full or part-time employment varied from 33 per cent in Spain to over 60 per cent in Denmark.

Even households with only one salary-earner enjoyed substantial increases in purchasing power in the two decades to 1992. In the UK, for instance, it took eight minutes for someone to earn the money to buy a litre of petrol in 1971, but only five minutes in 1992. The time taken to pay for a car licence fell equally dramatically (Table 2.1).

Many countries are, however, now facing recession rather than growth, and most Western economies are afflicted by debt and lack of confidence. In Central and Eastern Europe, there are problems from the disintegration of the former Soviet Union, the reconstruction of Central Europe and other macroeconomic changes. While some of the various problems may persist, few expect growth to remain static (or negative) for long. When it does resume, the pace of urban development can be expected to accelerate, ownership of cars to spread more widely and travel to increase.

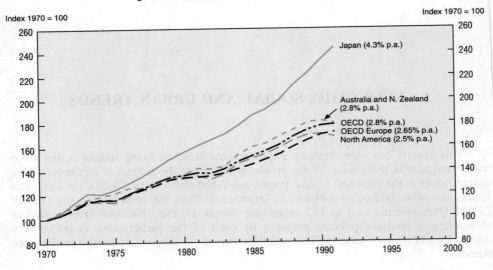

Figure 2.1. **Trends in GDP in OECD countries**

Index 1970 = 100

Source: OECD, 1993*a*.

Table 2.1. **Changes in purchasing power in the United Kingdom, 1971-1992**
Time taken to earn particular commodities[a]

	1971	1981	1986	1992
Large loaf of bread	9 mins	8 mins	6 mins	5 mins
Car licence	40 hrs 52 mins	27 hrs 3 mins	25 hrs 39 mins	16 hrs 43 mins
1 litre of petrol	8 mins	8 mins	6 mins	5 mins

a) For a household of a married man and wife (not working).
Source: UK CSO, 1993.

2. Car ownership

Not only has purchasing power been increasing consistently over the years, but the cost of buying and running a car has been falling in real terms. By contrast, public transport costs (and therefore fares, unless offset by greater productivity or subsidies) have been increasing in real terms in most OECD countries.

National trends

Car ownership is increasing everywhere and follows a similar trend in almost all countries (Figure 2.2). Even in the USA, where 58 per cent of households own two or more cars and 20 per cent have three or more, there is little sign, as was once expected, of saturation. The average rate of growth over the last 20 years in the number of cars owned has been 3.5 per cent p.a. in OECD countries and 4.2 per cent p.a. in the European Union. In the EU, the stock of private cars is expected to increase by 45 per cent from 115 million in 1987 to 167 million by 2010, leading to a car ownership of 503 cars per 1 000 inhabitants (EU Green Paper, 1992). Car ownership per capita has been increasing at 2.7 per cent p.a. in OECD countries since 1970: this is less than the growth in the number of cars because population has been increasing.

Urban trends

Car ownership is typically higher in rural areas and small towns than in cities. In Swiss communes with fewer than 1 000 inhabitants, for instance, 80 per cent of households own cars and half the journeys are made by car, whereas in cities with populations of 100 000 or more and well-developed transit systems, about half of households own a car and only a quarter of journeys are made by car (Swiss National Overview). More

Figure 2.2. **Car ownership trends in a selection of countries**

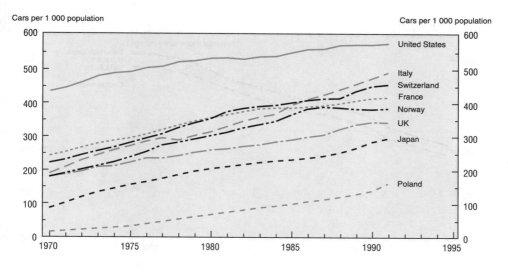

Source: OECD, 1993*a*.

detailed figures from the former west Germany show that car ownership is least in the cores of cities and even higher in their suburbs and rural surroundings than in more remote rural districts (Figure 2.3). In Poland, by contrast, where agricultural wages are low and well-to-do people have yet to adopt suburban or ex-urban lifestyles, incomes, and therefore car ownership levels, are higher in the cities than elsewhere.

Responses to the OECD/ECMT questionnaire (Annex 1) show that car ownership grew faster in the 1970s than in the 1980s (Figure 2.4). In 1970, fewer than 10 per cent of towns had car ownership levels exceeding 400 cars per 1 000 residents: by 1990, almost 40 per cent of the sample had. The responses also indicated that this trend towards higher levels of urban car ownership is expected to continue. In the largest cities, however, difficulties with using and parking cars can be expected to influence the growth of ownership. Thus in Greater London, households with cars grew by only 3 per cent between 1981 and 1991 (LRC, 1993).

When a car is acquired, it seems that householders travel more than before and to new destinations. Figure 2.5 shows that a London household without a car, but living in a district well served by public transport, makes about three mechanised journeys per day. With a car, it would make over five such trips, two of them entirely new or replacing former walk/cycle trips. Public transport trip-making would be halved (Wootton, 1993).

Figure 2.3. **Car ownership in different parts of German cities**

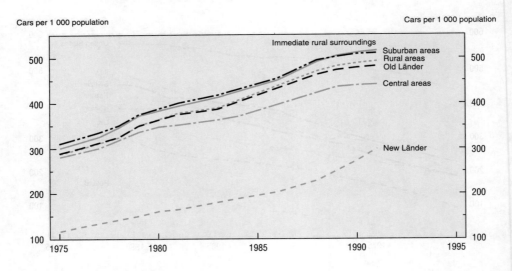

Source: German National Overview.

36

Figure 2.4. **Car ownership trends in towns and cities**
(sample of 59 cities)

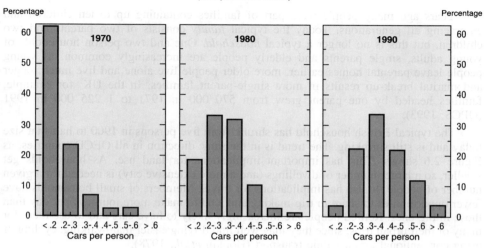

Source: Dasgupta, 1993.

Figure 2.5. **Travel in different car-owning households**

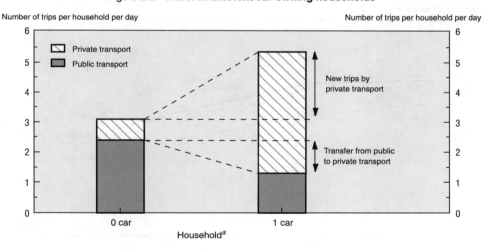

a) Households in London with one working member and average income in a medium bus accessibility area.
Source: Wootton, 1993.

37

3. Changing households

Years ago many people were part of families containing up to ten children and embracing all generations. Today the typical *family* consists of two parents and two children, but this is no longer a typical *household.* One and two person households of young adults, single parents and elderly people are increasingly common, as young people leave parental homes earlier, more older people live alone and live much longer and marital break-up results in more single-parent families. In the UK, for example, families headed by one parent grew from 570 000 in 1971 to 1 225 000 in 1991 (OPCS, 1993).

The typical British household has shrunk from five persons in 1900 to half that size today and is still shrinking. The trend is in the same direction in all OECD countries, as Figure 2.6 shows. This has important implications for land use. As households get smaller, so a larger number of dwellings (and a more extensive city) is needed for a given number of people. It also has implications for travel. Members of small households have fewer opportunities to share in trip-making and tend to make more journeys per day than those in big ones. Retired people are increasingly likely to have cars and to use them for many of their urban trips, since they may well find driving easier than walking, cycling or using conventional urban public transport (Hopkin *et al.*, 1978).

Figure 2.6. **Changes in household size**

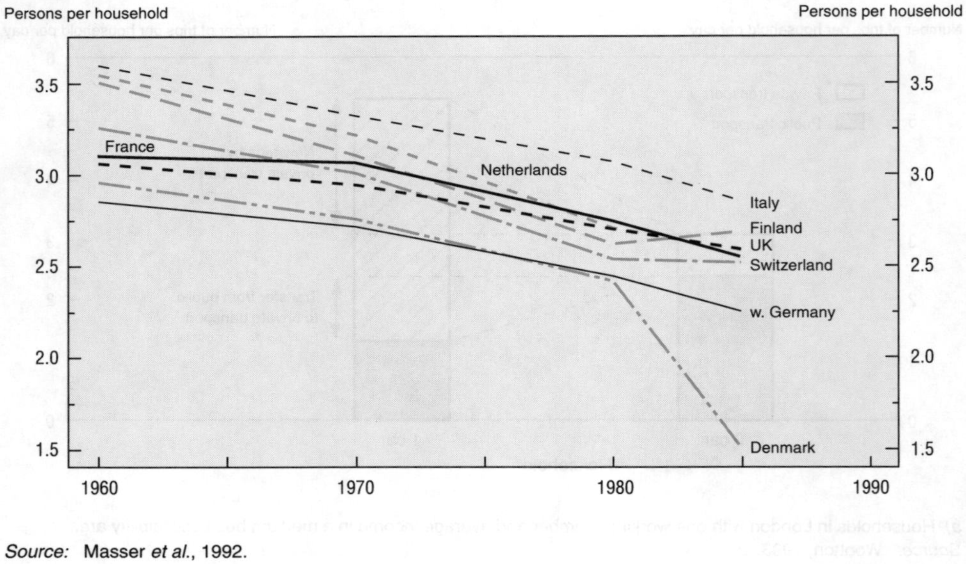

Source: Masser *et al.*, 1992.

Figure 2.7. Dominance of leisure trips over other vehicle uses in Germany

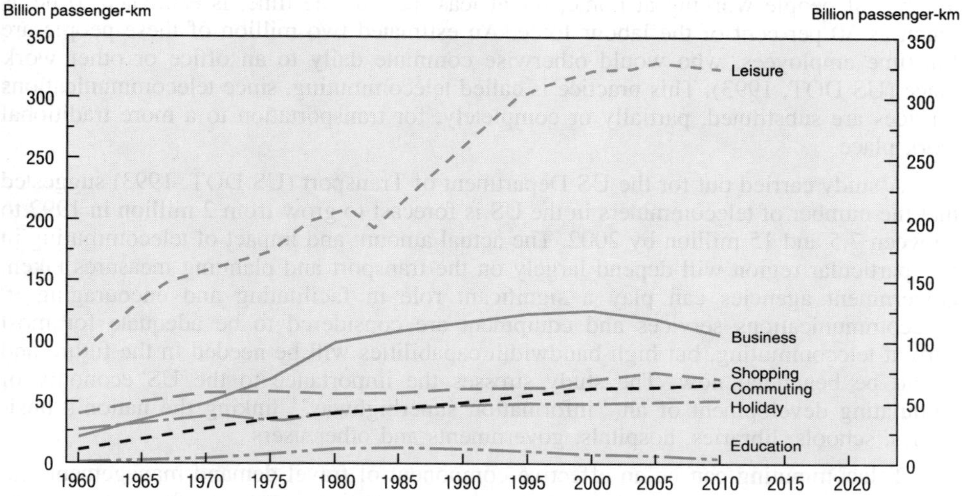

Billion passenger-km

Source: ERTI, 1992.

4. Changing lifestyles

In the 17th century Hobbes characterised life as "nasty, brutish and short". Parisians used to epitomise it as "Métro, boulot, dodo" (travel, work, sleep). A combination of rising incomes, car ownership and shorter working hours has for many replaced lives of unremitting labour by lifestyles enriched by leisure.

Many men and women today enjoy three, four or five weeks of paid holidays and five-day working weeks. They play games, go to gymnasiums, eat in restaurants, go to concerts, visit art galleries and indulge in a thousand and one activities hardly known to their parents. Elderly people are now more active and mobile than ever before and with a great deal of free time. The travel implications are enormous. Where once trips to and from work were the main load on urban transport systems, now travel is increasingly dominated by journeys for other purposes. These trips, often by car, by night as well as by day, already outnumber trips for work and are growing much faster (Figure 2.7).

5. Advances in telecommunications

Advances in computer and telecommunications in recent years, particularly in computer networks and data systems, Fax machines and electronic mail, have dramatically widened the choice of work place for many workers, allowing them to work wherever these tools are available, including the home. In the United States, for example, the number of people working at home, for at least part of the time, is estimated to be as much as 30 per cent of the labour force. An estimated two million of these people are full-time employees, who would otherwise commute daily to an office or other work place (US DOT, 1993). This practice is called telecommuting, since telecommunications services are substituted, partially or completely, for transportation to a more traditional work place.

A study carried out for the US Department of Transport (US DOT, 1993) suggested that the number of telecommuters in the US is forecast to grow from 2 million in 1992 to between 7.5 and 15 million by 2002. The actual amount and impact of telecommuting in any particular region will depend largely on the transport and planning measures taken. Government agencies can play a significant role in facilitating and encouraging it. Telecommunications services and equipment are considered to be adequate for most current telecommuting, but high bandwidth capabilities will be needed in the future and would be beneficial now. The study stresses the importance to the US economy of stimulating development of an "information superhighway" linking the nation's businesses, schools, libraries, hospitals, governments and other users.

Telecommuting can be an effective component of travel demand management and can contribute to reducing traffic congestion, air pollution, road casualties and energy consumption. However, because of the suppressed demand for car travel in most cities, the benefits could be largely eroded if newly-generated traffic is not restrained. Telecommuting will certainly bring about changes in travel patterns. Whether total travel will decrease or not is not clear at this stage, but there will be considerable redistribution of travel in time and space. Telecommuting might stimulate urban sprawl and have other adverse effects on land use and public transport use, if suitable counter measures are not taken.

Advances in telecommunications will ultimately have a substantial impact on shopping, leisure, conferencing and educational activities also, with important implications for travel. Such advances are also at the heart of the revolution which is taking place in information technology, in traffic management and public transport systems. Major research projects are on-going in Japan, the United States and Europe (see Chapter 6).

6. Urban structure

The form and spaciousness of cities are determined by intangibles such as history, cultural traditions and land values. Developments in transport, themselves the product of human aspirations, are enabling mechanisms. Rome and Milan reflect the more condensed, Mediterranean, apartment-house tradition in city building. Randstad Holland shows a cluster of rail- and road-linked compact cities operating as a single labour market, but kept apart by development controls. Sydney and Melbourne, with their very low densities, reflect both low land costs and the extensive, Anglo-Saxon house-and-garden urban tradition.

Urban densities

Densities of development vary considerably from one city to another, even within the same country. This has important implications for travel. Table 2.2 shows the modes of travel used for the journey to work in cities of different densities. Car travel ranges from 3 per cent of all work trips in Hong Kong, which has exceptionally high densities of development, to 93 per cent in Phoenix, with very low densities. Except in Amsterdam, where cycle/walk trips outnumber public transport trips by a factor of two, public transport is used between two and three times as much as the cycle/walk mode for work journeys.

In the early 20th century, trams and suburban railways made it possible for cities that were already congested to increase in population and for their residents to live more spaciously. Road transport took the process further and enabled cities to spread out even more widely and loosely, often taking in former free-standing small towns and villages.

The combined effects of these two trends (urbanisation and dispersion) can be seen in the Tokyo Metropolitan Region. The total number of residents grew from 21 to 31 million in the twenty-five years up to 1990, while those in the central wards fell from 8.9 to 8.2 million (Tokyo Case Study). The changes were even more dramatic in Seoul, which almost doubled its population over the same period. Greater London, which is ringed by a green belt, has, by contrast, experienced a fall in population, as have all the major British cities. The UK has long since passed through the urbanisation phase and population is being redistributed to small and medium-sized towns beyond the green belts of the major cities.

Table 2.2. **Travel modes for the journey to work in cities of different densities, 1980**

	Degree of land utilisation	Choice of transport type for travelling to work		
	(Housing and places of work per hectare)	Private automobile	Public transport	Foot and bicycle
Phoenix	13	93	3	3
Perth	15	84	12	4
Washington	21	81	14	5
Sydney	25	65	30	5
Toronto	59	63	31	6
Hamburg	66	44	42	15
Amsterdam	74	58	14	28
Stockholm	85	34	46	20
Munich	91	38	42	20
Vienna	111	40	45	15
Tokyo	171	16	59	25
Hong Kong	403	3	62	35

Source: Kenworthy and Newman, 1989.

Almost all cities are experiencing decentralisation of population, whether they are growing or not. Figure 2.8 shows that the proportion of the population living in inner areas has been falling consistently over the decades.

Decentralisation of employment

Decentralisation of employment is also taking place in most cities. In the UK, for example, districts adjacent to the M25, the London orbital motorway, attracted sufficient office space (2.4 million square metres) for 160 000 workers between 1989 and 1991.

The tendency for jobs to increase faster in the suburbs and on the urban fringes than in the centres and inner districts of metropolitan areas is characteristic of all developed countries. It is what happens when motor-age cities are shaped by market forces. Nowhere is this more true than in the USA, where in 1986 the suburbs of the 60 largest metropolitan areas contained 67 per cent of the jobs in those areas (US DOT, 1992a).

Cars may not be the *sole* cause of this phenomenon, but they do enable it to happen. Thus, a large insurance company which moved its office from near Copenhagen's central station to a suburban site far from a station, saw car commuters increase from 26 to 54 per cent – although the average home-to-work distance remained at about 20 km. Other Danish studies show that, as a rule, cars are used to access between 20 and 25 per cent of city-centre jobs, but up to 60 per cent of those in the suburbs, mainly because of free parking and the absence of satisfactory public transport services (Jorgensen, 1993).

A similar Norwegian study (Norwegian Overview) showed that the share of employees driving their own cars to work increased from 17 to 35 per cent when a firm moved from a city-centre location to 6 km outside the central business district (CBD), even though the new location had good accessibility both by train and bus. The number of persons travelling as car passengers was unchanged by the relocation. The average time spent on the home-to-work journey was almost the same, but the distance travelled by car commuters increased considerably.

Decentralisation of commercial activities

The latest stage in the process of urban change is taking place, as might be expected, in the USA – although it has parallels that have attracted less attention in Europe. Originally the suburbs were without large-scale concentrations of commercial activity. However, the 1980s saw the emergence of "edge" cities, clusters of shopping centres, drive-in office buildings, hotels and associated services built on cheap land at peripheral highway intersections. The US Department of Transportation, noting the growth of this phenomenon, concluded: "Like it or not, edge cities establish the context for much future transportation investment" (US DOT, 1992a).

In Europe, the tendency has been for hypermarkets, superstores, DIY ("Do-It-Yourself") stores and occasionally branches of department stores to be set up outside city centres, sometimes on green field sites. These developments, which usually offer free parking and occasionally other facilities, such as child minding, have encouraged shopping travel by car.

Figure 2.8. **Changes in the proportion of people living in the inner areas of cities**

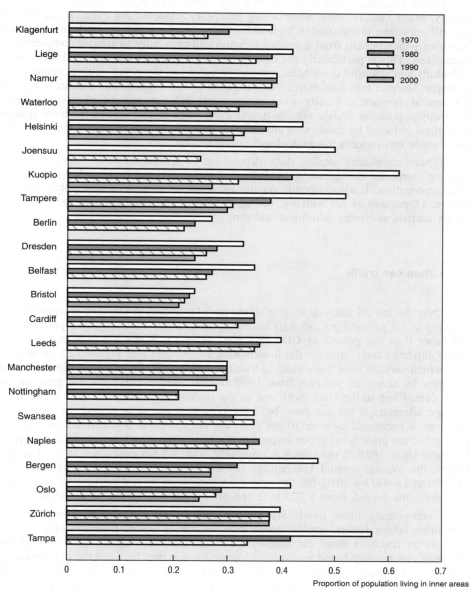

Proportion of population living in inner areas

Source: OECD/ECMT Questionnaire.

City centres

Urban decentralisation does not, however, have to be at the expense of city-centre vitality. Many OECD cities, while losing inner-city residents and even city-centre jobs, are still attracting investment in high-tech offices, hotels, shopping malls and museums, activities which benefit from a central location and proximity to similar complementary institutions. This is particularly the case in Europe where city centres, with their ancient cathedrals and splendid town halls, are highly valued as civic and cultural symbols. Yet in North America too, Baltimore, Boston, Toronto, San Francisco and other cities show that central commercial vitality is not incompatible with growing suburbanisation. Indeed inner-city population decline may be necessary in some cases to create the more spacious conditions required by those who are obliged, or wish, to live in inner cities, though in many cities this process has undoubtedly gone too far.

What central-area vitality does depend on is specialisation in services such as banking, corporate management, marketing, communications, high-quality retailing and higher education. It also depends on the existence of a high-quality public transport system. Opportunities for walking, eating, exploring and entertainment are vital: these attract tourists and bring additional spending.

7. Urban car traffic

Over the last 20 years or so, overall car travel (car-km) in OECD countries has been growing at 3.3 per cent p.a., slightly under the rate for car ownership (3.5 per cent p.a.), but faster than the growth in GDP (2.8 per cent p.a.). While the growth rates in car ownership have been fairly similar in most OECD countries (see Figure 2.2), the intensity with which cars are used has varied. In Sweden and the UK, for example, kilometrage per car grew by nearly 20 per cent from 1970 to 1991, whereas in France it grew by only 2 per cent. Even in the USA, with one of the highest car ownership rates in the world, average kilometrage per car grew by 7 per cent over the same period. In Switzerland, however, it decreased by over 10 per cent. Car occupancy in Switzerland has also been falling and the growth in car passenger-km has been almost half the rate of that by public transport since 1985 (2 per cent p.a. compared with 3.5 per cent p.a.). In the European Union, the average annual kilometrage per car is expected to decrease from 14 400 in 1990 to 13 400 by 2010, but the total car kilometrage should increase by 25 per cent, over the same period, from 1 727 to 2 166 billion km (EU Green paper, 1992).

Underpinning these trends are all the changes set out above. Rising incomes, expanding labour forces, smaller households, increased leisure time and other lifestyle changes all result in more car journeys. Suburbanisation, "edge" cities, out-of-town shopping and country-based recreation increase the distance between the beginnings and ends of such journeys, for many of which, there is no viable alternative to the use of the car. Car traffic has, as a result, grown substantially in practically all towns, as Figure 2.9 shows. A similar trend is predicted for the 1990s.

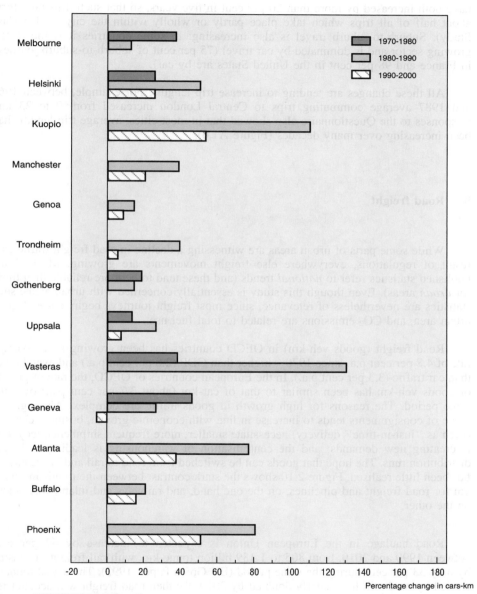

Figure 2.9. **Percentage change in traffic levels:**
trends and forecasts

Melbourne

Helsinki

Kuopio

Manchester

Genoa

Trondheim

Gothenberg

Uppsala

Vasteras

Geneva

Atlanta

Buffalo

Phoenix

1970-1980
1980-1990
1990-2000

-20   0   20   40   60   80   100   120   140   160   180

Percentage change in cars-km

Source: OECD/ECMT Questionnaire.

The pattern of journeys has been changing too. Journeys from surrounding rural areas to city centres have been increasing and now exceed the number of journeys from the suburbs to the centres in some cities. In Milan, for instance, in- and out-commuting have both increased by more than 20 per cent in five years, so that such trips now form about half of all trips which take place partly or wholly within the city (Milan Case Study). Suburb-to-suburb travel is also increasing: in some countries it is the fastest growing sector and is dominated by car travel (75 per cent of suburb-to-suburb journeys in France and 98 per cent in the United States are by car).

All these changes are tending to increase trip lengths. For example, between 1962 and 1987 average commuting trips to Central London increased from 9 to 23 km. Responses to the Questionnaire also showed that in most cities, average trip lengths had been increasing over many decades (Figure A1.6).

8. Road freight

While some parts of urban areas are witnessing a decline in road freight traffic as a result of regulations, everywhere else freight movements are growing. Most of the published statistics refer to *national* trends (and these tend to be more reliable than those for *urban* areas). Even though this study is essentially concerned with urban areas, such statistics are nevertheless of relevance, since most freight journeys begin and end in an urban area, and CO_2 emissions are related to total fuel use.

Road freight (goods veh-km) in OECD countries has been growing at an average rate of 4.8 per cent p.a. since 1970 – higher than GDP (2.8 per cent p.a.) and even higher than car traffic (3.3 per cent p.a.). In the European countries of OECD, the rate of growth of goods veh-km has been similar to that of car-km (about 3.7 per cent p.a.) over the same period. The reasons for high growth in goods traffic are complex. Although the value of consignments tends to increase in line with economic growth, business changes (such as ''just-in-time'' delivery) necessitate smaller, more frequent shipments; recycling is creating new demands; and the centralisation of warehousing is leading to longer distribution runs. The hope that goods can be switched from road to rail and barge has, so far, been little realised. Figure 2.10 shows the stark contrast between the trends in tonne-km for road freight and pipelines, on the one hand, and railways and inland waterways, on the other.

Road haulage in the European Union is expected to increase by 42 per cent between 1990 and 2010, from 805 to 1 139 billion tonne-km, with rail freight increasing by only 33 per cent during the same period (EU Green Paper, 1992). The actual tonnage carried by road will have nearly doubled by 2010. By then road freight will account for 16.5 billion tonnes a year, much of which will begin and end its journey in cities.

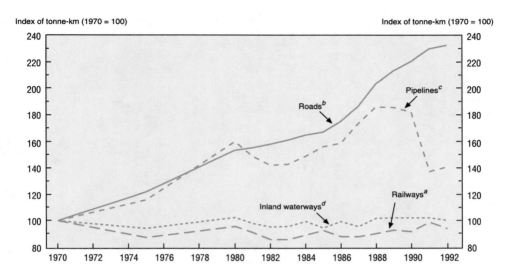

Figure 2.10. **Freight traffic trends in ECMT countries**

Index of tonne-km (1970 = 100)

a) All ECMT countries.
b) 15 countries: A, B, DK, SF, F, D, I, L, NL, N, E, S, CH, TR, UK.
c) 12 countries: A, B, CH, D, E, F, I, NL, N, E, TR, UK.
d) 10 countries: A, B, CH, D, F, FIN, I, NL, L, UK.
See "Definitions and Abbreviations" for names of the countries.
Source: ECMT, 1994.

9. Concluding remarks

Increasing wealth, brought about by higher productivity and expanding labour forces, has resulted in car travel soaring in all Western industrialised nations. Changing work patterns and lifestyles have led to greater demands for personal mobility, more time to travel and more dispersed patterns of travel.

The same increase in spending power has allowed people to live in more spacious surroundings, which necessitate the use of cars. Industry and commerce have not been slow to exploit the increased personal mobility of car owners by siting shopping, leisure and industrial complexes on cheap land on the outskirts of cities. Goods transport too, has increased as a result of greater consumption; and changes in manufacturing practices, together with changes in the patterns of distribution, have favoured the growth of road-based haulage.

All these trends have been responsible, individually or collectively, for the problems which will be discussed in the next chapter.

3. PROBLEMS EXPERIENCED

The previous chapter has shown how economic, demographic and social trends have led to increases in car use and to a dispersal of population and employment. This chapter, which draws heavily from the National Overviews, Case Studies and responses to the Questionnaire, considers the consequences of these changes.

1. Congestion

Severity of congestion

Congestion in cities was acknowledged to be a problem by all the countries participating in this study. It was a problem in countries with generous road systems and low residential densities, like the United States, and in countries, like Turkey and Poland, with relatively low levels of car ownership, but poor road infrastructure. No large city seems to have escaped peak-period congestion. Table A3.2 of Annex 3 shows that all the very large cities included in the Case Studies regarded their congestion levels as serious.

The questionnaire analysis, reported in Annex 1, refers to a wide range of city sizes, but mostly with populations smaller than the ones in the Case Studies. The analysis shows that only about 5 per cent of the cities reported no congestion problems, while roughly 7 per cent described their problems as very severe (Figure 3.1). Almost three-quarters of them felt that congestion was getting worse, though more than half perceived the problem to be fairly localised. As expected, the degree of severity rose with size of city, as indicated in Table 3.1. In many of the larger conurbations, congestion has also spread to the inter-peak period, and in some cities, particularly in the United States, it extends as far as the suburbs.

Of those towns and cities which were able to provide information on travel speeds, the ones with the highest congestion index (score of 5) had mean speeds over the whole built-up area of 27 km/h, and in the CBD of 17 km/h during the morning peak period. Speeds rose progressively to 41 and 23 km/h respectively, for towns with a lower level of congestion (those with a score of 2), as can be seen in Table A1.5 of Annex 1 (of the towns able to provide speed information, there was only one in the sample with a score of 1). On the whole, speeds are continuing to fall, as indicated in Figure 3.2.

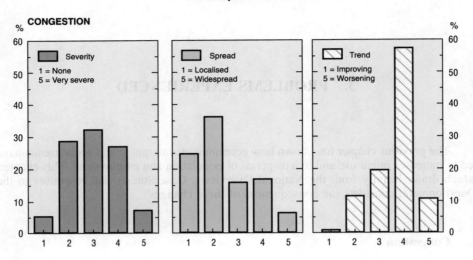

Figure 3.1. **Perceived concerns over congestion
in a sample of cities**

Source: OECD/ECMT Questionnaire.

Table 3.1. **City size and severity of congestion**

City size (population)	Average score[a] for severity of congestion
25 000-100 000	2.5
100 000-500 000	3.1
500 000-1 million	3.2
1-3 million	3.2
Over 3 million	4.0

a) Score 1 to 5 (1 = no problem, 5 = very severe congestion).
Source: Annex 1.

Costs of congestion

It is difficult to estimate the true costs of congestion because it depends very much on the definition chosen, but on almost any definition, the costs are extremely high. The total cost of the time spent travelling in OECD countries is equivalent to roughly 7 per cent of GDP. Using the definition of "additional time spent travelling compared with free-flowing travel", congestion is estimated to cost the equivalent of about 2 per cent of GDP (Quinet, 1994).

50

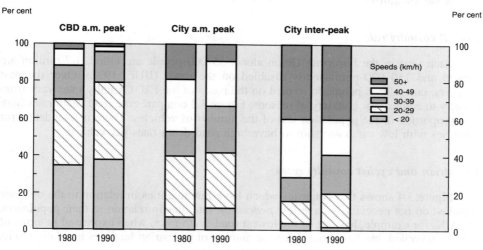

Figure 3.2. **Changes in speed over time**

Figures from the National Overviews for individual countries confirm this estimate, though there are one or two exceptions. It should be noted, however, that individual estimates are not necessarily based on the same assumptions, so might not be strictly comparable. In the UK, estimates range from about £5 billion (ECU 6.3 billion) per year to the Confederation of British Industry's value of £15 billion (ECU 19 billion) per year, approximately 3 per cent of GDP, while in the United States the figure is put at US$ 100 billion (ECU 82 billion) per year, equivalent to about 2 per cent of GDP. In the Netherlands, however, the figure of Gld 1 billion (ECU 0.5 billion) works out at only 0.2 per cent of GDP.

A high proportion of congestion naturally occurs in cities: in Amsterdam alone, the cost in 1989 was estimated to be Gld 300 million (ECU 140 million), a third of the country's total congestion costs, while in the 39 largest urban areas in the USA, congestion was costed in 1989 at US$ 39 billion (ECU 32 billion), nearly 40 per cent of the total cost. In these cities, over 40 per cent of major urban arteries were highly congested at some period of the day. In the UK, it is estimated that about two-thirds of the costs of congestion is attributable to urban areas. This is probably typical also of other European countries.

As roads approach saturation levels, even small changes in traffic (increases or decreases) have disproportionate impacts on congestion. Australian calculations suggest that, at 1982 prices, one extra peak veh-km in Sydney imposes 59c (ECU 0.38) of extra costs on other vehicles – very much more than its own costs.

2. Road casualties

Overall casualty rates

Each year in the European Union alone, 55 000 people are killed, 1.7 million are injured and 150 000 permanently disabled on the roads (IIUE, 1992). Over the past 20 years, one million people have died on the roads of the EU. Casualty rates vary from country to country for a variety of reasons: Figure 3.3 compares the road death rates both as a proportion of the population and of the number of vehicles. There is a tendency for countries with low car ownership to have high road death rates per vehicle.

Pedestrian and cyclist casualty rates

Figure 3.4 shows that countries which have few fatalities in relation to the distance travelled do not necessarily have few *pedestrian* fatalities in relation to their population. The UK, for example, has one of the lowest road death rates, when expressed in terms of veh-km travelled, but has about twice the number of pedestrian fatalities in relation to its population than countries like the Netherlands and Sweden.

Figure 3.3. **Road death rate in the European Union,** 1990

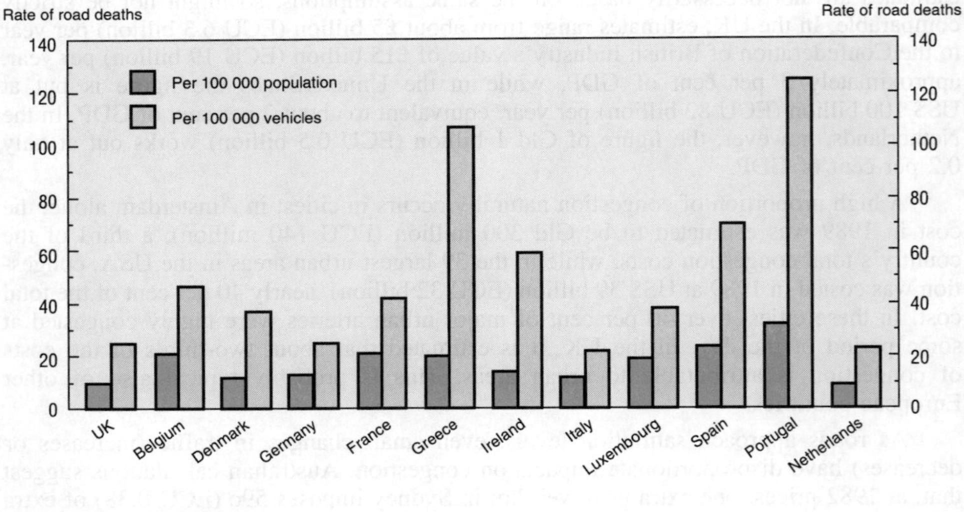

Rate of road deaths

Rate of road deaths

- Per 100 000 population
- Per 100 000 vehicles

Source : UK DOT, 1991*a*.

52

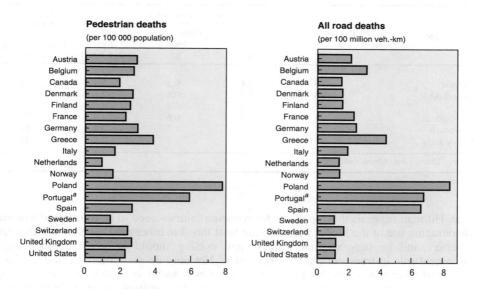

Figure 3.4. **Road traffic mortality,** 1991

a) Data for Portugal refer to 1990.
Source: UN, 1993.

Calculations indicate that the fatality rate per km for walking and cycling in the UK is 15 and 12 times, respectively, the rate for car travel (UK DOT, 1991b). In a study by Hillman and Adams (1992), it was found that the proportion of seven and eight year olds being allowed to take themselves to school has fallen from 80 per cent in 1970 to just 9 per cent in 1990, largely because of the fear of accidents. This corresponds with 70 per cent who walked to school in the former west Germany (see also Hillman, 1991).

The corresponding fatality rates for walking and cycling, compared with bus passengers, are even more extreme at 66 and 55 times, respectively. The fact that walking and cycling are much less "safe" forms of travel than car and bus, might encourage authorities to try to shift travellers from these "unsafe" modes on to mechanised modes in order to reduce road casualties. If, however, the *overall* fatality rate associated with each km of travel by different road users is considered, a different picture emerges, as indicated in Table 3.2.

This table shows that users of the heaviest and sturdiest vehicles naturally run a very low risk of being killed in a road accident, but there is a very much greater risk that other road users will be killed, especially the more vulnerable ones. It shows, for example, that per-km travelled, a cyclist is 24 times more likely to die than a heavy lorry driver, but the latter is 12 times more likely than a cyclist to be associated with the death of another road

53

Table 3.2. **Fatality rates by vehicle user, United Kingdom**

Vehicle type	Fatalities per 100 million veh-km to:				Other fatalities as a percentage of all $\dfrac{100\,(b + c)}{a + b + c}$ %
	The vehicle users themselves (a)	Pedestrians (b)	Other vehicle users (c)	All road users (a + b + c)	
Bicycle	4.9	0.1	0.1	5.1	4
Motorbike	10.3	1.7	0.6	12.6	18
Car	0.7	0.4	0.4	1.5	53
Light goods	0.4	0.4	0.6	1.4	71
Bus/coach	0.4	1.8	1.7	3.9	90
Heavy lorry	0.2	0.5	1.9	2.6	93

Source: Hillman and Adams, 1992.

user. Hillman suggests that ''policies for reducing injuries need to be re-oriented towards encouraging use of the modes incurring the least threat to other road users, rather than the reverse'' and he suggests that walking and cycling should be given a much more prominent role in transport policy formulation. Not only do these modes cause the least danger to other road users, but they incur much lower social, economic and environmental costs than motorised modes (Hillman, 1992). The situation is more favourable to cyclists in countries like Denmark and the Netherlands, which make better provision for them.

Costs of road casualties and collisions

Apart from the human suffering caused by road casualties, the economic and social costs associated with them are high in all countries. Overall costs of road casualties and collisions in OECD countries are estimated to be equivalent to roughly 2 per cent of GDP – comparable to the costs of congestion – though this estimate is based on a number of calculations using different assumptions, judgements and methodologies (Quinet, 1994). Some of the calculations are based on willingness to pay and some on gross production costs and losses (including medical care and the cost of damage). Some include an allowance for pain and suffering and loss of quality of life, but these aspects are not treated in a uniform manner.

Figures from the National Overviews suggest a wide range of costs. In the UK, road accident costs, at about £10 billion (ECU 13 billion) per year (approximately 2 per cent of GDP), are about the same as the mid-range estimate of the costs of congestion. Urban accidents account for about 60 per cent of this cost. In Australia, metropolitan area road accidents alone are thought to cost about A$ 4 billion (ECU 2.5 billion) per year – just over 1 per cent of GDP: this is about the same as the total congestion cost in cities (including the costs of pollution). The costs of road casualties and collisions in Switzerland (SF 570 million in 1988 – ECU 360 million), however, is put at between two and five times the estimated costs of congestion.

54

In the Netherlands, the equivalent costs are estimated to be Gld 6 billion (ECU 2.8 billion) per year, about six times the estimated costs of congestion and equivalent to 1.4 per cent of GDP. The largest of all the estimates of accident costs, however, is the United States' figure of US$ 358 billion (ECU 293 billion) per year, equivalent to about 8 per cent of GDP. Nearly two-thirds of this represents the cost of pain, suffering and loss of quality of living (MacKenzie *et al.*, 1992), which is not included to the same extent in the other estimates.

Trends in road casualties

While road death rates are unacceptably high, particularly for pedestrians and cyclists in urban areas, they are declining in most Western industrialised countries. Figure 3.5 shows that the number of road deaths has fallen by between 10 and 30 per cent in most of these countries during the 1980s, though it has risen by as much as 50 per cent in some, mainly those which initially had low car-ownership levels. When injuries are included, Figure 3.6 shows that the total number of accidents in ECMT countries as a whole reached a minimum in 1985 and then rose, though it might now be falling again. In some of the countries of Central and Eastern Europe, accident rates are very high and since 1987 have been increasing sharply, though there is some evidence of a levelling off (Figure 3.7).

Figure 3.5. **Trends in road deaths in a number of countries,**[a] 1980-1991

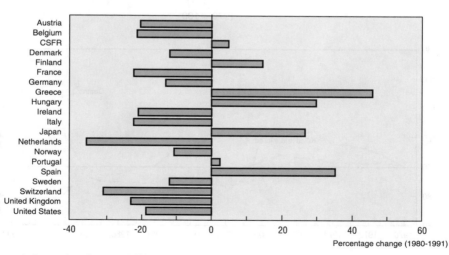

a) Changes in the number of persons killed in road traffic accidents in 1991 compared to 1980.
Source: UN, 1993.

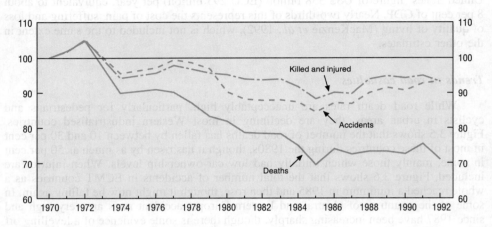

Figure 3.6. **Overall trends in road accidents in ECMT countries**[a]
(number)
1970 = 100

a) 18 countries: A, B, CH, D, DK, E, F, FIN, GR, I, IRL, L, N, NL, P, S, TR, UK.
See "Definitions and Abbreviations" for names of the countries.
Source: ECMT, 1994.

Figure 3.7. **Overall trends in road accidents in Central and Eastern Europe**[a]
(number)
1970 = 100

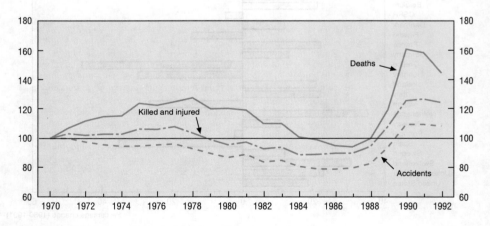

a) 7 countries: CSFR, Estonia, Hungary, Lithuania, Poland, Romania, Slovenia.
Source: ECMT, 1994.

3. Inaccessibility and car dependence

Problems due to new patterns of urban development

With more and more offices, leisure and shopping facilities located on green field sites in peripheral areas, access by people without a car is becoming ever more difficult. The scale of these enterprises, with their vast car parks, roads and sprawling single-storey buildings, makes them unsuitable for pedestrian access. While it is possible to plan such developments to be served by public transport (Euro-Disney near Paris is on both the Regional Express Metro and the TGV), they are more often situated in or close to low-density residential areas, which are themselves not conducive to the provision of satisfactory public transport. The costs of providing local public transport under these conditions is, in general, extremely high.

That these developments suit the car user particularly well might be sufficient justification for their existence, if alternative local facilities (or transport) were available for those without cars. But the effect of concentrating development, such as shopping, at locations which provide economies of scale and low development costs is that local facilities (with relatively higher costs and a shrinking clientele) cannot remain in business for long. The people who depend on the latter become increasingly isolated from the services they require.

Problems due to changing lifestyles

Many OECD/ECMT governments are considering whether accessibility can be increased by raising densities and mixing development in order to bring jobs, services and other facilities nearer to people's homes (see Chapter 5). It does not follow, however, that people will take advantage of such arrangements, if by travelling further they can significantly improve their choice of destination.

Research into work journeys in six densely-populated, mixed land-use districts in inner Copenhagen, while confirming that local accessibility generates local trips, throws light too on why the length of home-to-work journeys in Denmark increased by 30 per cent between 1975 and 1986. The study found that, notwithstanding the presence of nearby jobs, only 7 per cent of wage-earners worked locally, and only 18 per cent worked in an adjacent district or within about 5 km of where they lived. Women were more likely than men to work locally, but even in the densest and most mixed parts of Copenhagen, only one in four of employed persons worked within a short bicycle ride of home.

Education levels and work journey distances were found to be linked. The shorter a person's education, the less the specialisation and the greater the likelihood of working near home. Over one third of unskilled women therefore worked in their own or a neighbouring district. Graduates of both sexes, by contrast, were much less likely to. With education levels rising, job specialisation increasing and two-career families becoming more common in all OECD countries, it is clear that, even where jobs are available close to homes, powerful forces will be pulling people to more attractive jobs further away (Jorgensen, 1993).

Problems due to deteriorating transit service

Urban public transport users not only suffer the effects of congestion and pollution, but in some countries, steadily deteriorating levels of service, as more and more passengers forsake public transport for cars. This is by no means a universal phenomenon: in many countries public transport use is increasing for a variety of reasons, *e.g.,* increasing population, urbanisation, transfer of passengers from cycling and walking and investment to improve the service and keep fares low.

Where patronage is in decline, however, the operating costs have to be met by higher fares, a cut back in service levels or by increases in subsidy. The first two cause hardship to the users and precipitate a downward spiral of poorer service, higher fares and still lower patronage levels, while the third causes problems for the subsidising authorities.

Let us look at what has been happening. For nearly 20 years prior to 1982, ECMT countries were roughly equally divided between those with increasing and those with decreasing urban patronage levels (Webster *et al.,* 1985). Even in some of the countries where patronage was buoyant, transit's *share* of travel was falling. Thus, in the Netherlands, despite low fares, the *share* (in passenger-km) of travel by train, bus, tram and metro fell from 14.6 per cent in 1970 to 9.2 per cent in 1990. The replies to the Questionnaire showed that the modal share to public transport fell in most towns and cities between 1970 and 1990, as car ownership grew (Figure A1.3 of Annex 1). Even in countries like Sweden, with a strong commitment to communal services, the car has been eclipsing public transport. In Stockholm between 1980 and 1987 car travel increased by 17 per cent, while the number of public transport passengers declined by 7 to 8 per cent, and similar trends were observed in other Swedish cities too (MENR, 1992).

In Central Europe, recent political changes have had unexpected effects on public transport. With a rapid increase in car traffic and increasing fares, travel by public transport has fallen dramatically. In Warsaw, for instance, public transport's share decreased from 93 per cent of non-walk trips in 1970, to 79 per cent in 1987 and 68 per cent in 1993. A declining trend is observed in Norwegian cities also. Figure 3.8 compares the average patronage trend of the ten largest cities in Norway over the 1980s with those of three Swiss cities, where improvements to public transport and to the environment in which it operates, have resulted in an increased share of the travel market. Transit's share of passenger-km in Switzerland was nation-wide lowest in the mid-1980s (18.5 per cent) and has since risen to 20 per cent.

With regard to the future, the main trends which support transit use, *i.e.* urbanisation, increasing population, transfer of passengers from cycle and walk and increasing subsidies, are bound to level off ultimately, so that even those cities with buoyant patronage levels at present are likely to follow the same trend as the others, *unless landuse patterns are changed to favour transit use, and more severe restraint mechanisms are applied to cars.*

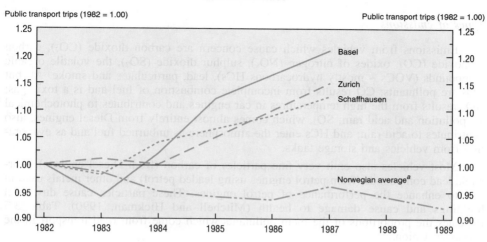

Figure 3.8. **Public transport use in Norwegian and Swiss cities**

Public transport trips (1982 = 1.00)

Public transport trips (1982 = 1.00)

Basel

Zurich

Schaffhausen

Norwegian average[a]

a) Average for 10 largest Norwegian cities.
Source: Norwegian Overview.

Public transport subsidies (as a proportion of total operating costs) rose rapidly during the 1970s in most countries (Webster *et al.,* 1985). They have levelled off in more recent years and in some cases might actually have fallen, though in absolute terms they are still high in most countries. In Italy, the Netherlands and Belgium, for example, less than half the operating costs are recovered from the fare box.

As far as individual cities are concerned, there is a wide variation in the level of cost recovery. Patronage on the new light rail system in Manchester, for example, has exceeded expectations and the system is breaking even, excluding the capital costs of construction. By contrast, the new Blue Line LRT in Los Angeles recovers only 11 per cent of its operating costs. This amounts to a subsidy of US$ 12 per trip compared to the US$ 1.50 taxpayer contribution to the cost of every bus trip in Los Angeles (Wachs, 1993). The Los Angeles Metrolink, a new commuter railway, has even lower cost recovery than the Blue Line. Each time a traveller pays US$ 4.50 for a one-way trip, the taxpayers contribute an additional US$ 26.5. Furthermore, those riding on Metrolink are amongst the wealthiest citizens in the region, with a median income of US$ 63 000 per year (Wachs, 1993).

4. Air pollution

Types of emissions

Emissions from vehicles which cause concern are carbon dioxide (CO_2), carbon monoxide (CO), oxides of nitrogen (NO_x), sulphur dioxide (SO_2), the volatile organic compounds (VOCs – mostly hydrocarbons HCs), lead, particulates and smoke. All but CO_2 are pollutants: CO results from incomplete combustion of fuel and is a toxic gas; NO_x results from the high temperatures in car engines and contributes to photochemical air pollution and acid rain; SO_2, which comes almost entirely from Diesel engines, also contributes to acid rain; and HCs enter the atmosphere as unburned fuel and as evaporation from vehicles and storage tanks.

Most vehicles also emit very fine particles of carbon (from Diesel engines), inorganic lead compounds (from petrol engines using leaded petrol) and other metals used in oils to enhance the performance of petrol engines. These particles cause dust, soil buildings and cause damage to health (Mitchell and Hickman, 1990). Table 3.3 indicates the proportions of the main pollutants which come from road transport in the European Union.

According to Swedish studies, urban air pollution causes between 300 and 2 000 new cases of cancer annually. Traffic accounts for 70 per cent of the emissions of carcinogenic substances and substances that may affect the genes of people living in urban areas. Most of the problems arise from hydrocarbon emissions (MENR, 1992). A recent study carried out for the British Government (Brown, 1994) suggested that up to 10 000 people each year are killed by exhaust fumes in England and Wales. The study found new evidence of a link between emission particle levels and cardio-vascular

Table 3.3. **Proportion of pollutants from road traffic in the European Union in 1985**

Pollutant	% of total emissions from road transport (range in brackets)[a]	% of transport emissions from:		
		Private cars and vans	Urban roads	
			Cars only[b]	All vehs[c]
NO_x	54 (26-84)	56	22	26
VOC	27 (16-61)	67	60	61
SO_2	3 (1-13)	50	36	41
CO	74 (66-100)	> 80[b, c]	44	54
Particulates	(2-20)	30[c]	34	58
Lead	87[c]	94[c]	..	..

a) Range refers to 1980 figures.
b) Figures from Germany.
c) Figures from the Netherlands. All other figures relate to the EU.
Source: EU Green Paper, 1992 and OECD, 1988a.

disease. Another British study has demonstrated a clear and quantifiable link between incidents of reported illness (particularly asthma and sore throats) and the level of local traffic (Whitelegg *et al.*, 1993).

Photo-chemical smog is caused when the sun shines on air containing traces of nitric oxide and hydrocarbons: the photo-chemical reactions create ozone close to the earth's surface, which becomes tinted brown by NO_2. Ozone near the earth's surface is called tropospheric ozone, not to be confused with the ozone layer. The latter is a band of ozone at a very high altitude (in the stratosphere) and is beneficial in absorbing much of the ultra-violet radiation from the sun. Tropospheric ozone is a strong oxidiser and can damage the linings of people's lungs. It can also damage vegetation.

Spread and severity of pollution levels

Tropospheric ozone (smog) is a problem in Australia and the United States, where acceptable levels have been breached on many occasions in the largest cities and is becoming a problem in many European cities also, *e.g.*, Athens and London. In the USA, 98 urban areas in 1991 failed to meet the National Ambient Air Quality Standard (NAAQS) for ozone with the result that half the urban population was living in non-attainment areas.

In Switzerland, concentrations of NO_x regularly exceed the standards for cities laid down in the 1985 Order for the Protection of Air, which fixes emissions standards in accordance with the principles of the 1983 Federal Law for the Protection of the Environment (Federal Council of Switzerland, 1986).

Lead compounds in the atmosphere are still a concern in some countries, though they have been greatly reduced over the past decade or so. In Australia, the levels of lead are still higher than the World Health Organisation (WHO) standards, but are decreasing. At present 30 per cent of the car fleet in Australia is unleaded. In the USA, lead used in petrol decreased by 99 per cent between 1975 and 1988, and in the Netherlands, emissions of lead by road traffic are now only about 1.5 per cent of the 1970 level. Figure 3.9 shows how the problem of lead in the atmosphere has all but disappeared in the UK, but other pollutants are still increasing.

Figure 3.10 shows that only about 6 per cent of towns and cities which responded to the Questionnaire felt that they had no pollution problems. Most felt the problem to be localised, but at least a third thought that the problem was getting worse. Table A3.2 of Annex 3, however, shows that pollution was rated extremely seriously by the cities in the Case Studies (these were much larger cities, on the whole, than those covered by the Questionnaire).

Costs of air pollution

The costs of air pollution are difficult to estimate and all figures should be treated with caution. Researchers at the University of California, Davis, estimated the costs of transport-related air pollution in the United States at between US$ 10 and 200 billion

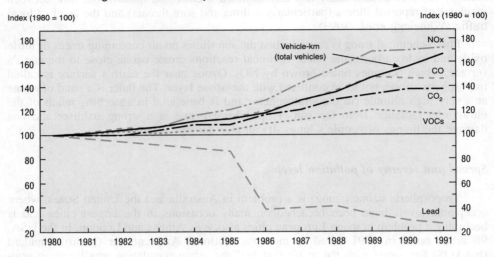

Figure 3.9. **Trends in pollution levels in the United Kingdom**[a]

a) Atmospheric pollution from road transport only.
Source: UK, Department of the Environment.

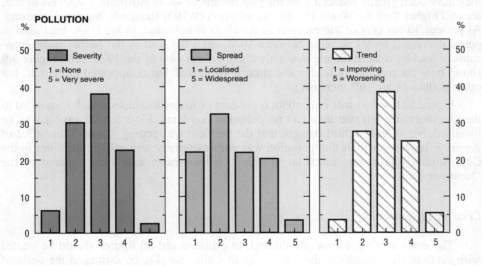

Figure 3.10. **Perceived severity of air pollution problems in cities**

Source: OECD/ECMT Questionnaire.

(ECU 8-165 billion) per year, *i.e.* at the very least 0.2 per cent of GDP and possibly very much more (MacKenzie *et al.,* 1992). In Switzerland, the cost, in terms of damage caused to buildings, was about SF 400 million (ECU 250 million) in 1988. Impacts on health were estimated at SF 300-800 million (ECU 190-500 million). Negative effects on the biosphere were not included in these figures. In total these costs are equivalent to between 0.25 and 0.4 per cent of GDP. The costs of local air pollution in OECD countries have been estimated at about 0.3 per cent of GDP (Quinet, 1994): for the European Union, a figure of 0.3 per cent to 0.4 per cent of GDP, with 90 per cent of the costs attributed to road transport, is quoted in the EU Green Paper (1992).

5.   Water pollution

Urban rainwater run-off can be contaminated by pollutants from the road surface, such as lead, cadmium from tyres and other chemicals from oil spills, and this affects the water quality in the area concerned. Airborne dispersal of material from the road surface by vehicle-generated turbulence and spray can also affect water quality in the immediate vicinity of roads. Salt, used for de-icing the road surface, is the most concentrated contaminant in run-off during winter.

Direct pollution of the surface water by road traffic in 1990 in the Netherlands is given in Table 3.4 and for a heavily trafficked rural motorway in the UK, the total annual yields of suspended solids (salts), lead, oil and polynuclear aromatic hydrocarbons per km of road have been estimated (Colwill *et al.,* 1984) to be 1 500 kg, 4 kg, 125 kg and 18 g respectively.

Table 3.4.   **Contamination of surface water, Netherlands**

	Cadmium	Chromium	Copper	Nickel	Zinc	Lead	Oil	Salt
Emissions (tonne/year)	0.07	0.22	2.4	0.22	13.0	2.2	406	..
% of total burden	1.8	1	3	1	10	1.7	5.5	76

Source: Netherlands Overview.

6.   Noise and vibration

Severity and spread of noise pollution

Surveys carried out in the 1970s by Morton-Williams *et al.* (1978) showed that road traffic was the most common cause of unwanted noise in people's homes (Figure 3.11), with heavy goods vehicles and motorcycles being the main culprits. Psycho-sociological

Figure 3.11. **Noise nuisance to people in their homes**

Figure 3.11. **Noise nuisance to people in their homes**

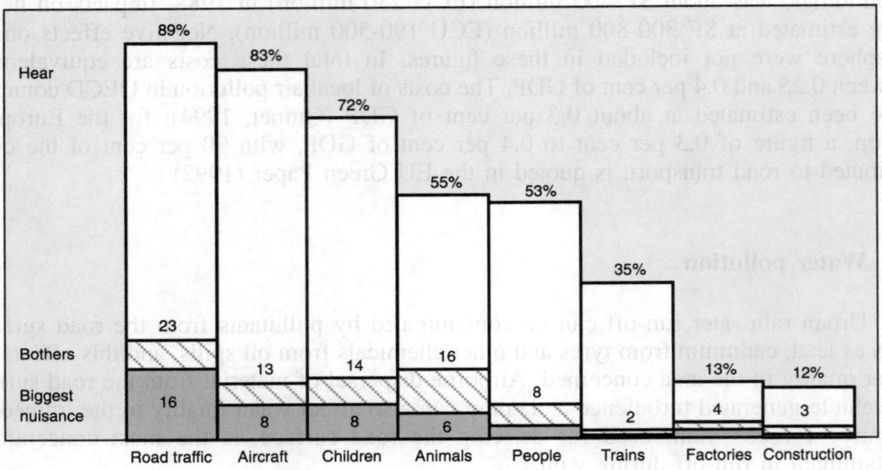

Source : Morton-Williams *et al.,* 1978.

studies have shown that the noise of a single lorry is equivalent to that of six passenger cars in terms of perceived annoyance, but can be as high as 15 on roads with intermittent traffic (Delsey, 1991). The OECD describe noise levels greater than 65 dB(A) (decibels "A", weighted corresponding to the response of human beings) as unacceptable and between 55 and 65 dB(A) as undesirable (OECD, 1986).

On this basis almost half of the urban population in EU countries is adversely affected by road traffic noise, ranging from 34 per cent in Denmark to 74 per cent in Spain. As much as 17 per cent of the population in these countries is exposed to levels of noise above 65 dB(A), ranging from 4 per cent in the Netherlands to 23 per cent in Spain (EU Green Paper, 1992). Only 7 per cent of the population in the United States is exposed to noise levels above the higher threshold [65 dB(A)], whereas 30 per cent in Japan are (Orfeuil, 1992). The proportion of the population exposed to railway noise above the higher threshold varies from 0.3 per cent in the UK to 1.7 per cent in Germany.

The percentage of city residents living with unacceptable noise levels varies with the type of city. Table 3.5 gives a few examples: a possible reason for the relatively low level of noise pollution in Sydney is its low residential density. In Warsaw, noise levels are increasing with the growth of both car and road freight, so that now 87 per cent of analysed main-road links have noise levels > 65 dB(A) during the busiest period of the day. This is partly because of the absence of by-passes to avoid through traffic in the city centre and partly because of ageing vehicles (Polish Overview). In Gothenburg, 25 000 people live along streets with noise levels > 65 dB(A) and 80 000 with noise levels > 55 dB(A) out of a population of about half a million.

Table 3.5. **Percentage of population living with noise levels > 65 dB (A)**

Amsterdam	Detroit	Paris	Sydney
19	60	50	10

Source: National Overviews.

Responses to the Questionnaire (Figure 3.12) suggested that traffic noise was regarded as a serious problem in about a quarter of the towns and cities surveyed and very severe in about 5 per cent of cases. It was fairly localised in most towns, but widespread in about a quarter of them. About half the towns reported that urban traffic noise was getting worse.

While manufacturers have made great strides to reduce engine and transmission noise and make cars and lorries quiet on the inside, traffic noise has not been reduced to anything like the same extent, and may in some cases, have increased over the years as acceleration and speed (on uncongested roads) have risen. There is a limit to the amount of improvement possible as far as private cars are concerned because, even at moderate speeds, a considerable proportion of the noise produced is from the road surface.

Figure 3.12. **Perceived noise problems in cities**

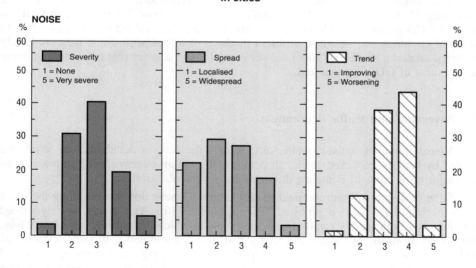

Source: OECD/ECMT Questionnaire.

65

In Austria, the proportion of households seriously affected by traffic noise is reported to have fallen nationwide (from 21 per cent in 1973 to 13 per cent in 1985), though the number affected to a less serious extent might well have risen (Lang, 1987). Surveys of noise in France also suggested an improvement, but not for the inner areas of Paris, where noise levels have increased: in the rest of the country there was an average fall of 5 dB(A) between 1976 and 1986 (Maurin *et al.,* 1988). With increasing levels of road traffic, however, and higher speeds on uncongested roads, noise levels might well increase in the future.

Costs of noise pollution

In the United States, it has been estimated that for every extra decibel of road traffic noise, property prices fall by between US$ 6 and US$ 182 (between ECU 5 and 150), depending on the type of property (Allen, 1981). Another estimate puts the cost of noise at US$ 21 (ECU 17), at 1981 prices, per housing unit per year for each extra decibel of road traffic noise (quoted in MacKenzie *et al.,* 1992). For the USA as a whole, noise pollution is estimated to cost US$ 9 billion (ECU 7 billion) per year, with goods vehicles responsible for between 65 and 85 per cent of the total (MacKenzie *et al.,* 1992). This is equivalent to 0.2 per cent of GDP. Damage to buildings from vibrations is put at about US$ 7 billion (ECU 6 billion) at 1989 values (Ketcham, 1991).

Estimates of the total social cost of noise from inland transport, based on loss of productivity, health care, effects on property values and loss of psychological well-being are said to hover around 0.1 per cent of GDP, according to the EU Green Paper (1992). Two-thirds of this cost is attributable to road traffic, a quarter to aviation and 10 per cent to rail. An estimate of the cost of traffic noise in Switzerland in 1988 suggested a value exceeding SF 800 million (ECU 500 million), which is about 0.3 per cent of GDP. A recent OECD publication (Quinet, 1994) gives a range of evaluations corresponding to different countries and based on different methods of assessment. These data are highly scattered around a *median* of about 0.2 per cent of GDP: a *mean* cost equivalent to about 0.3 per cent of GDP is suggested.

7.   Severance and traffic domination

Visual intrusion, noise, smells, dirt, fumes, the fear of accidents and severance caused by heavily-trafficked roads, all combine to give an overwhelming impression in the majority of cities of complete domination by vehicular traffic.

Such problems are not confined to city centres. Traffic domination along the main roads in suburbs is also a problem. The combination of wide roads, widely-spaced junctions and high speeds greatly limits the points at which pedestrians can cross safely. Even away from the major arteries, heavy fast traffic, combined with large numbers of parked vehicles at particularly vulnerable places (like shopping parades and schools), add to the danger. And in all these areas, noise and fumes make the experience even less pleasant.

The problems for pedestrians and cyclists are not nearly as bad in cities which are well provided with special footpaths and cycleways. But such facilities tend to be confined to a few selected cities, like Cambridge in the UK, and to countries with a strong cycling tradition, like Denmark and the Netherlands. These countries have done much more to "humanise" their towns and villages than most.

8. Energy consumption and global warming

Energy consumption and CO_2 emission contributing to global warming were not even thought to be problems a short while ago and some countries even now do not seem to be taking such matters seriously. It is only when fuel supplies are threatened or there is a shortage that there is considered to be a problem in many countries.

Energy consumption

The largest consumer of energy anywhere in the world is the USA: there transportation consumes more than a quarter of all the energy used and more than 60 per cent of all petroleum, with road vehicles consuming nearly 80 per cent of the total energy used in the transport sector. Total energy consumption in OECD countries increased by 26 per cent between 1970 and 1991, with the transport share increasing from 24 per cent of all energy used in 1970 to 31 per cent in 1991 (OECD, 1993a). Energy solely for road transport increased by 65 per cent over approximately the same period (a rate of 2.6 per cent p.a.) and in the European Union, by over 100 per cent (a rate of 3.8 per cent p.a.). Between 1981 and 1987, petrol consumption in the EU increased by 9 per cent and Diesel fuel by 38 per cent. While annual consumption of Diesel fuel was half that of petrol in 1981, it now amounts to two thirds. Petrol consumption is rising by 1.5 per cent and Diesel by 6 per cent annually. Road haulage is responsible for most of the increase in Diesel consumption, although the share of Diesel-driven cars is also on the increase – 3.5 per cent in 1980, 11 per cent in 1990 (Taschner, 1992).

A recent study "Energy for Tomorrow's World" (World Energy Council, 1993) concluded that there is probably about 40 years' supply of oil, 65 years of natural gas and 250 years of coal at current consumption rates. These estimates allow for between two and five times the present fossil fuel reserves being discovered.

CO_2 emissions

When any fossil fuel is burned, CO_2 is produced which contributes to global warming through the greenhouse effect. The atmosphere surrounding the Earth acts like a greenhouse in allowing energy from the sun to reach the Earth's surface relatively unhindered, but reducing the amount of heat radiating from the Earth into space. Because of the natural greenhouse effect caused mainly by water vapour, the surface of the earth is about 30°C higher than it would otherwise be (Mitchell, 1991, Waters, 1990).

The concentration of CO_2 in the atmosphere (the main greenhouse gas which is affected by human activity) has been increasing steadily since the Industrial Revolution, from a natural background level of 270 parts/million to a current estimated level of 350 parts/million. Over the same period, the concentration of methane (another greenhouse gas which comes mainly from cattle and insects, rice paddies, swamps and gas leaks) has doubled. This is a more potent greenhouse gas than CO_2, but its concentration in the atmosphere is much lower. Chloro fluoro carbons (CFCs) are about 10 000 times more potent than CO_2, but they are present in only minute concentrations. Other greenhouse gases are tropospheric ozone, water vapour and NO_2.

The proportion of all CO_2 emissions which comes from the transport sector varies between about 15 per cent and 25 per cent for different countries (in Sweden, it is as high as 40 per cent because much of the energy produced for non-transport uses is nuclear-powered electricity). In 1986, CO_2 emissions reached 577 million tonnes or 22.5 per cent of the total for the European Union as a whole, 80 per cent of which was from road-based transport (55 per cent cars, 23 per cent goods vehicles and 2 per cent buses) (EU Green Paper, 1992). While CO_2 is by far the largest greenhouse gas, as Table 3.6 shows, other gases indirectly give rise to global warming: CO prolongs the effect of methane and NO_x and HC produce tropospheric ozone. The main CFC contribution from road traffic is through the escape of CFCs from vehicles fitted with air conditioners and from the manufacturing process of electronic equipment, plastic components and foam plastic for seat cushions. When the effect of other greenhouse gases are taken into account, it appears that road traffic is causing only about 10-15 per cent of Britain's contribution to the global greenhouse effect, but it is growing (Waters, 1990).

The Intergovernmental Panel on Climate Change (IPCC, 1990) has stated that the nations of the world will have to cut CO_2 emissions by fully 60 to 80 per cent to stabilise atmospheric CO_2concentrations. The "Energy for Tomorrow's World" study (World

Table 3.6.   **Effects of various emissions on global warming, United Kingdom**

| | Percentage of all "greenhouse gases" from: | | Percentage contribution from transport |
	Road transport	Other sources	
CO_2	8	44	19
CO	2.5	0.5	88
NO_x	2.5	3	48
HC	1	3	37
Methane	0	16.5	0
Ozone	0	5	0
CFCs	0	14	0
Total	14	86	
	100		

Source: Based on figures given in Waters, 1990.

Energy Council, 1993) concluded that the developing world's rising demand for fossil fuels means that, even with a doubling of present energy efficiency, nothing can be done to reduce possible global warming from the greenhouse effect until after 2070!

9. Imbalance of economic activity

In almost all countries, there is, or has been, a tendency for the largest cities to take the lion's share of the nation's economic growth. This has happened in London and Paris in the past and is presently happening in some of the very large metropolises like Tokyo and Seoul, as the Case Study reports illustrate (see Annex 3). Too much growth results in too much traffic, undue congestion, overcrowding of the public transport system, longer trip lengths, spreading out of the urban area giving limited access to open countryside and high land and property prices. At the same time, other cities may be starved of growth and not able to develop to their full potential, with poor job prospects for the inhabitants and fewer resources to pay for the infrastructure and other facilities which a thriving city needs.

A similar situation can sometimes occur within large metropolitan regions when the central area of the major city of the region takes the bulk of the growth in new employment at the expense of other centres: the area which attracts the high growth frequently suffers from congestion and many other problems as a result. This has happened in Tokyo, Seoul and Hiroshima, as described in the Case Study reports summarised in Annex 3.

10. High land and property prices

Undue pressure to locate in a city can cause land and property prices to soar. Tokyo is again a prime example of this. House prices have risen so much that few people can afford to live in the inner areas. The average house price within 10 km of the centre is 17 times the average salary of the workforce. Even 50 km away from the centre, the average price is equivalent to 7 times the average salary, with the result that many commuters are spending upwards of 2 hours on their journey to work and the same again in the evening. The situation is similar (though not as serious) in Hiroshima, where demand is high and land is scarce (see Annex 3). Japan is unusual in this respect because of the high proportion of its land which is mountainous and unsuitable for urban living.

On the other hand, high land and property prices (within reason) are a sign of a healthy economy: if people and firms are willing to pay such high prices, it must be because it is worth it to them. But this does not mean that the situation is optimal: other areas of the country are deprived of growth and residents and workers suffer the problems of high prices or inordinately long journeys, or both. Appropriate planning measures should be able to achieve a more efficient balance.

11. Decaying urban fabric

There are decaying areas in almost every city. These are usually in the ring immediately outside the central area, but in some cities, particularly in the United States, downtown areas have been allowed to fall into neglect, as more and more people (especially the middle classes) have forsaken city-centre activities in favour of out-of-town shopping malls and business parks. This was the case in Portland, Oregon until recently, when a combination of transport and land-use measures were taken to regenerate the central area with surprising results. It now has a clean, attractive, vibrant city centre with more jobs, better shops, a wider range of activities and a more pleasant environment: it is in stark contrast to neighbouring towns where little has been done to revitalise them (see Chapter 5 and Case Study summaries in Annex 3).

12. Urban sprawl and peripheral development

Urban sprawl is caused when development is allowed at very low density. It is encouraged by "edge city" developments, which exacerbate the problems of inaccessibility for those without cars, as discussed in Section 3 of this chapter. Low densities and peripheral development tend to weaken the city centre, enabling decay to set in and, quite often, increasing vandalism and violence. Very low densities lengthen journeys and make it harder for public transport to operate effectively and they encourage more car use with all the attendant problems of this. On the other hand, many of the car owners living in spacious and not unattractive suburbs would not wish to change the status quo. As with many problems of this sort, planners are having to tread a tight-rope to arrive at a satisfactory compromise which maximises benefits while minimising hardship.

13. Concluding remarks

Increasing car travel is causing congestion, noise, pollution and accidents in almost all cities large and small. People are becoming more dependent on cars and this has adverse effects on everyone, but especially on those without a car, who are becoming more and more isolated. The associated social and economic costs run into billions of ECUs and in most OECD countries the costs of congestion and accidents separately are equivalent to about two per cent of GDP, with noise and local air pollution amounting to a further 0.5 to 1 per cent of GDP. Estimates of the long-term cost of CO_2 emissions to global warming vary between one and 10 per cent of GDP.

At the present time, most of the world's car fleet, and most of the local and global environmental problems created by cars in cities, are found in developed countries (Figure 3.13). The transfer to cities in the developing countries of South America and South East Asia of the resource-hungry characteristics of Western urbanisation is an additional risk. Governments in all OECD countries need to raise consciousness about the dangers of such a future and to take action to prevent its coming about.

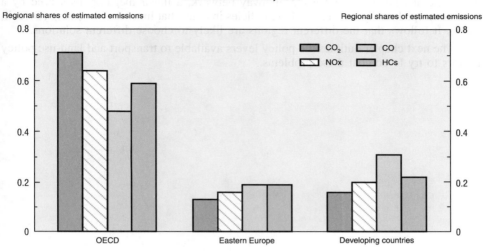

Figure 3.13. **Regional shares of motor vehicle emissions,** 1990

Regional shares of estimated emissions

Regional shares of estimated emissions

CO$_2$ CO
NOx HCs

OECD Eastern Europe Developing countries

Source: OECD.

A comparison of the three OECD sub-regions of Europe, the United States and Japan, makes clear that they face different basic problems (Table 3.7). In the United States, total vehicular travel per head and per year is twice the level in European countries, while transport energy demand is three times higher. This difference seems to be explained by America's great size, its low density cities and the absence of alternatives to cars for urban travel. In Japan, vehicular travel per head is lower than in Europe

Table 3.7. **Car-km and energy use in different OECD regions in 1990**

OECD region	Population (millions)	Car-km (billions)	Energy used in road transport (millions of TOE)[a]	Car-km p.a. per person	Energy p.a. per person (TOE)[a]
USA	252	2 438	392	9 675	1.55
Japan	124	354	61	2 855	0.49
OECD (Europe)	417	1 804	227	4 326	0.54

a) TOE: Ton of oil equivalent.
Source: OECD,1993a.

despite greater output per head. This appears to relate to the high density of Japanese cities, the absence of an extensive highway network, a linear megalopolis served by a well-developed rail system and parking policies in cities that limit car ownership (Orfeuil, 1992). It follows that the different regions are likely to choose different solutions.

The next chapter outlines the policy levers available to transport and land-use policy makers to try to combat these problems.

Part 2

POLICY ANALYSIS

4. POLICY LEVERS AVAILABLE

A wide variety of policies and measures is available to governments at all levels to tackle the problems reported in the previous chapter. Some policies are concerned solely with land-use planning, others with transport. If congestion, rising fuel consumption, casualties and environmental damage are to be dealt with effectively, it will not be enough to design and implement transport and planning policies independently. A combination of carefully-selected policies that reinforce each other and avoid adverse side-effects will be required. This chapter discusses the policy levers which are available at different levels of government, the types of interactions which might occur when policies are combined, and the social implications of different types of policies.

1. Policies and measures in current use

In addition to the implementation of clearly-defined land-use and transport measures, governments often set *targets* for achieving reductions in some of the unwanted side-effects of travel and urban living. They may also set targets to boost particular impacts of policies, which are considered to be beneficial and set standards which vehicle manufacturers and local authorities are required to meet. Table 4.1 lists the more common types of measures and the sort of targets and standards used (but it is by no means exhaustive).

Policy making at different levels of government

While all countries tend to have different practices in the implementation of urban policies, there is a good deal of similarity in the types of functions for which the various levels of government (national, regional and city) take responsibility. National governments, for example, tend to set standards, make regulations and recommendations, provide policy guidance to local planning authorities, encourage or discourage particular measures by offering or withholding financial inducements, etc., while local authorities implement measures within the accepted framework which are more directly concerned with improving the city and overcoming their particular problems. It is not surprising therefore that global warming and other problems which are on a regional or global scale might not be high on the list of objectives for a city authority. As well as differing in

75

Table 4.1. **Policies and measures in current use**

Planning measures

- Strategic policy for land-use and transport planning
- Regional policy affecting economic development in different areas of the country
- Restraint on economic growth of principal city centres
- Designated cities or areas for growth/control over the pattern of development
- Relocation of particular employment groups/sectors
- Use of preferred locations for travel-generating activities (*e.g.* town centres)
- Fiscal inducements to relocate in designated areas
- Zoning regulations (single use, mixed use, densities, etc.)
- Green belts
- Regeneration of decaying areas (city centres, inner-city areas)
- Improvements to housing and neighbourhood quality/facilities
- Parking standards for new developments

Transport supply measures

- Road construction
- Rail investment/construction
- Improved public transport service, fares, ticketing and information
- Traffic management, driver information
- Park-and-ride
- Pedestrian areas, cycle and walk ways

Transport demand management

- Car restraint/road pricing
- Toll charges
- Parking controls
- Entry prohibitions
- Goods traffic restraint
- Pedestrian priority
- Cycle priority
- Bus/tram priority
- Traffic calming
- Car pooling/sharing

Targets and standards

- Targets for improved road safety, reduction of noise and air pollution levels
- Targets for reduced traffic levels, certain types of traffic (*e.g.* heavy goods vehicles) and car park supply
- Targets for reduced fuel consumption and CO_2 emissions
- Targets for increased car pooling, public transport use, cycling and walking
- Standards for vehicle noise, emission control and safety

emphasis, the aims of national governments are likely to be couched in rather more general terms than those of the city authorities. In general, local authorities make most of the planning decisions, but in Switzerland, the cantons have the main responsibility in planning and share it with the local level: the national level provides only the legal framework and guidelines.

The financial responsibilities for carrying out different types of policies are also different at the different levels of government. Road and rail construction, for example, is largely financed from central government (which undoubtedly encourages some local authorities to apply for new infrastructure whether they strictly need it or not), while parking measures and street improvements are generally financed more locally. Subsidies to public transport operators usually come from central government, but can also come from more local sources.

Standards and targets for emission controls are generally at the national, or even international, level, but some cities have set emission targets or designed their policies to achieve specific emission levels (*e.g.* Newcastle).

Annex 2 gives a brief description of the main national policies adopted by the various countries taking part in this project. A good example of a national policy which encompasses all types of policies and involves all levels of government is Australia's "Building Better Cities programme". This is part of a long-term strategy to create more efficient, equitable, ecologically-sustainable and liveable cities, through better-integrated urban development, urban consolidation and urban renewal. The programme is based on a partnership with the federal, state and local governments.

Popularity of different policies in practice

In the twelve cities covered by the Case Studies, the popularity of the various types of measures adopted is indicated in Table 4.2 (see Annex 3 for a fuller description). The cities are grouped into three categories based on population.

Strategic land-use/transport planning in the Case-Study cities, consisted mainly of linking major new developments to the provision of good public transport facilities. This was a strong feature in most of the cities studied, whatever their size. Regional policy, concerning policy packages which encouraged a shift of development from one part of the country to another, was an important issue in the large metropolitan regions only. It was usually accompanied by restraint measures on the growth of the principle city centre and complementary measures designed to encourage relocation. Policies to encourage a multi-centric structure within the metropolitan region were particularly popular in all the metropolitan areas and very large cities, *e.g.,* Tokyo and Paris. These policies were also accompanied by measures to restrain growth of the central city, the setting up of new towns and specially-designated growth areas, and included the use of financial and other types of inducements (Table 4.2).

On the transport side, rail construction was one of the most popular measures taken, particularly in the metropolitan areas and very large cities, while improving public transport by other means (including bus priority) became the more dominant policy in the smaller cities. In the middle range of cities, both new construction and improvements by

Table 4.2. **Popularity of measures in Case Studies**

Policy/measure	Metropolises (10 to 30 m)	Large cities (1.5-5 m)	Medium cities (0.5-1.5 m)
Planning			
Strategic land-use/transport planning[a]	**	***	**
Regional policy[b]	**	*	
Restraint on central city growth	**	*	
Designated growth areas & new towns	***	**	*
Regeneration of city centre/inner areas			*
Relocation of employment groups	*		
Fiscal inducements to locate	**		
Zoning regulations	*		
Green belts	*		
Transport			
Road construction	*	*	*
Rail construction	***	**	**
Improved service/lower fares	*	**	***
Traffic management	**	**	**
Bus/tram priority	*	**	**
Toll charges/road pricing			
Parking controls	**	**	**
Park and ride	*	*	*
Car restraint	*		
Cycle priority		*	*
Pedestrian priority		*	*
Traffic calming		*	*
Car pooling			
Standards for noise/air pollution		*	

Note: * to *** denotes degree of popularity of measures tried.
a) e.g. new developments linked to provision of public transport.
b) e.g. employment encouraged to move to other parts of the country.

other means, were equally popular. Road construction does not feature strongly in any of the cities, with one or two exceptions: Tokyo and Hiroshima (to increase road capacity) and Stockholm (mainly for environmental reasons). Parking controls were the most common type of restraint used in all the cities studied. Pedestrian priority, traffic calming and the provision of cycleways featured very little in the policies of the large metropolises, and with one or two exceptions, not a great deal in the other cities. More details of the various land-use and transport policies used are given in Chapters 5 and 6 and Annex 3.

In the smaller towns and cities analysed in the Questionnaire Survey, land-use policies were mentioned in only a small number of cases, as can be seen in Figure 4.1. They are even less prominent in the list of measures planned for the future than they have been in the past. This might reflect a tendency for the questionnaires to be completed

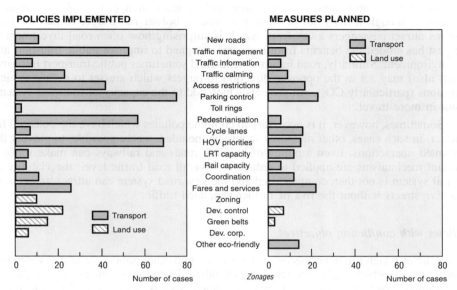

Figure 4.1. **Past and future policies in a selection of towns and cities**

POLICIES IMPLEMENTED   MEASURES PLANNED

Number of cases   Zonages   Number of cases

Source: Dasgupta, 1993.

more by transport authorities than by planning authorities. Reliance has tended to be placed on traffic management, access restrictions, parking controls, pedestrianisation and priorities to high-occupancy vehicles. Measures planned for the future are much more evenly spread amongst those available, but parking controls still appears to be the most popular measure, with changes to fares and public transport service levels, the next most popular. This survey tends to confirm the impression that most city authorities were not, at the time of the survey, planning for sustainable travel and urban development.

2.   Interactions between policies

There are interactions both between different policies and between the various impacts of the same policy. Some policies tend to negate other policies; some reinforce others. Some have impacts which satisfy particular objectives, though working against other equally desirable objectives. Others have (or appear to have) desirable impacts only, with apparently no adverse side effects. In general, conflicts can hardly be avoided, though they should be taken into account when assessing the merits of particular policies or combinations of policies. This section gives a number of examples to illustrate the type of interactions which occur in practice.

Policies which interfere with other policies

Investing in both new road and new rail systems in a city *could* be counter-productive, though it *need* not be: new rail systems bolster rail usage, while new road systems attract passengers away from rail. It is surprising how often road investment in the past has eroded the benefits from measures designed to improve public transport and the environment. Similarly, road improvements (and sometimes public transport improvements also) may act in the opposite direction to targets which are set to reduce vehicle emissions (particularly CO_2). All projects which add to the capacity of transport systems result in more travel.

Sometimes, however, it is necessary to combine policies which have the potential for conflict. In such cases, other measures should be included, where possible, to prevent the unwanted interactions. Even a policy of building roads and railways can make sense if restraint mechanisms are applied to reduce the overall road traffic level: the viability of the rail system is not then compromised and the new road system can attract traffic from sensitive streets without the risk of further generated traffic.

Policies with conflicting objectives

Policies which might not necessarily interfere with other policies, might nevertheless produce results which are in conflict with each other, depending on the objectives chosen. For example, road schemes which increase vehicle speeds, save travel time, but might increase the number and severity of accidents and generate more traffic. On-street parking controls might reduce congestion, but encourage through traffic. Goods vehicle bans might improve the urban environment, but increase the costs to traders. Even measures which divert traffic away from sensitive areas make the conditions worse for those who live, work and shop on the main roads which are affected by the measures.

On the planning side, higher densities make it easier for public transport to function and favour walk and cycle modes, but enable fewer people to have their own gardens and private space. Out-of-town shopping centres provide benefits of cheaper goods and easier parking, but lead to a decline in the viability and vitality of town centres, reduced access for those without cars and an increase in the overall level of car travel.

Policies which reinforce each other

Some policies blend naturally with other policies and enhance the results of each. The combination of restraint measures and improved public transport increase the effectiveness of the transit improvements and make the impact on car drivers more palatable. Similarly, policies which increase the cost of car travel, when coupled to land-use policies which bring homes, jobs and other activities closer together, accelerate the take-up rate of local facilities and make it easier for those displaced from their cars to find acceptable alternative modes. Land-use policies which encourage the location of travel-generating uses in areas well-served by public transport, enable access by means other than the car and allow people to make multi-purpose trips. Combining policies which reinforce the desirable impacts in this way and reduce or eliminate adverse effects, should be a prime consideration in the selection of policy packages. Unfortunately, all too often, individual policies are introduced without reference to other policies which are currently in operation.

3. Adaptability of people and firms

The way people and firms adapt to the situation in which they find themselves is almost invariably given insufficient recognition in policy formulation. There has been a failure in most countries in the past to fully realise that people and firms will, in general, do only what is in their own best interests and not necessarily what is in the nation's or city's best interests. It is not just a question of whether people are selfish, though they may be; they know that *their* action alone is not likely to produce the result which the nation or city is looking for – it requires *collective* action to do this.

A simple example is a traffic diversion around an historic town centre. It is in everyone's interest (collectively) for through traffic to avoid the centre, but it may well be in an individual motorist's interest to ignore the routing advice and go straight through the centre. The application of parking controls in a city centre is another case in which the ultimate result might not be the desired one. If the controls are too strict, workers and visitors may "vote with their wheels" and go elsewhere, especially if the city is not particularly attractive. Firms will soon follow and then the city centre becomes even less attractive. Measures to make the city centre more attractive should be introduced at the same time as the parking controls; and policies incorporating maximum parking standards should be applied uniformly over a wide area.

While adaptability often leads to unwanted side-effects, as in the above examples, it can have beneficial effects also and can even overcome some of the shortcomings of ill-judged policies. For example, failure to invest in an adequate transport system does not lead to a city grinding to a halt: some firms move out and commuters and visitors readjust both their times and modes of travel to suit the facilities available. Cities will carry on functioning almost regardless of the transport and land-use policies which are implemented. This does not mean that it does not matter what is done: there is a difference between an optimal situation (which can only come about with the right mix of planning and transportation policies) and one in which people are left to optimise their own situations without regard to the overall good. The latter is bound to lead to a sub-optimal solution and the difference between this and the optimal one could be large.

4. Social implications of policies

In any solution, optimal or otherwise, there are bound to be winners and losers. New roads through inner-city areas provide quicker travel for suburban dwellers (generally the better-off) and a poorer environment (more noise, pollution and a barrier to movement) for inner city dwellers (generally the poorer section of the community). The acquisition of a car provides the new owner with the freedom to travel when and where he likes, but leaves those travelling by public transport with a poorer and/or a dearer service. Even under almost saturated vehicle ownership, there will still be probably about a third of the population without a car available at the particular times that they would like to make their journeys. For most of these people, public transport, walking or cycling are the only options. For social justice, these modes must be satisfactorily catered for.

There has been much discussion over the years on the merits of fiscal restraint systems versus those which rely on queuing or, in the case of parking, searching for a free space. Using *time* as a means of rationing is wasteful of valuable resources, but using *money* is more efficient, because the money paid is effectively a transfer payment (less the costs of administration) and can be used for other purposes (*e.g.,* for public transport or environmental improvements, as in the City of Westminster, London). The argument often advanced is that everyone has the same 24 hours in the day, whereas people have vastly different amounts of money, so using time to ration scarce resources is more equitable. While there is some merit in this argument from a social point of view, wastefulness on this scale cannot be excused. In any case, paying for a scarce commodity in this way is no different from many other purchases which are made. If the implementing authority feels strongly about the equity aspect, it would still be preferable to use a fiscal method and use the money to help the people who are disadvantaged by the measures taken, *i.e.* through public transport improvements or the provision of cycle or walk ways (though this would be less cost-efficient than allowing the revenue to be used in whatever way produced the best return).

In the end, policies have got to be acceptable to public and politicians alike. It should also be realised that the repercussions of policies (even the simplest of policies) take years, even decades, to work through the system, because of the adaptability of people and firms to the changes brought about. By making it known well in advance what changes are planned, and avoiding anything sudden and dramatic, hardship can be minimised, because people and firms can take into account future changes in fiscal, transport and land-use policy when they are deciding where and when to relocate.

Harsh, but necessary, policies (from the overall environmental point of view) may put particular parts of cities, the cities themselves or even the countries themselves at a disadvantage compared with their rivals when trying to attract industry or commerce. Creating a "level playing field" between different areas of a country and between different countries is necessary to ensure fairness and the furtherance of policies which are essential for the well-being of everybody. National and international agreements, co-operation and pressure can help in this respect.

Having said this, however, many countries and cities that have been more progressive than most in adopting green policies, far from putting themselves at a disadvantage, have prospered the more. Examples are Sweden, Switzerland and Austria and the cities of Zurich, Vienna and Munster.

5. Policy mix – participation and acceptance

Urban land use and transport comprise a very complex sub-system. Management of them demands a complex response.

Catering for the needs of different types of travellers, different modes of travel, different types of people and households, different sectors of employment and different types of activity can only be accomplished by a carefully chosen mix of policies and related instruments. This is necessary if the disparate views of the various pressure and interest groups are to be taken into account and if a better balance of distributional effects of policies is to be achieved. Participation by the various interest groups in the formulation of policy, and their acceptance of the decisions made, are essential parts of the policy process.

6. Concluding remarks

Urban travel, the urban environment, the viability of the city and the quality of life in the city are affected by policies at all levels of government – national, regional and city (even international). The actions taken are a combination of land-use, transport, economic and social measures; they are sometimes used individually, but mostly in combination. They interact with each other producing both good (intended) and bad (unintended) results. Adaptability by people and firms plays a crucial role in the final result – in avoiding catastrophe, but in missing the best solution. There are losers and gainers, but if policies are to be implemented which are best for the city, the country and the planet, national and international pressure and agreement are essential ingredients in creating the conditions under which such action can take place.

The next two chapters describe in greater detail land-use policies (Chapter 5) and transport policies (Chapter 6), which have been found to be successful, either individually or in combination, as well as those which have been less successful in meeting their objectives.

5. LAND-USE PLANNING POLICIES

By affecting where people live and where activities take place, land-use policies influence the sort of journeys which are made, the distance travelled and the mode used, and all these have a bearing on the problems raised in Chapter 3. However, the relationship between the planning policies implemented and the problems of congestion, casualties, pollution, etc., is less direct than it is with transport policies, so that the resultant effect is not always what was intended. This chapter reviews the *existing role* of land-use planning policies and considers their *potential* for influencing urban travel and environmental nuisances.

Land-use policies are taken here to encompass the regulation of both the overall pattern of settlement and the locational and functional aspects of new development and redevelopment by plan making, development control or building permits. However, the division between the planning policies discussed here and the transport measures considered in Chapter 6 is not precise. For example, planning authorities typically impose maximum and/or minimum parking standards on new non-residential developments and – in the United States – often link building permissions to other aspects of transport demand management. Town planning is also concerned with the provision of facilities for walking and cycling in new developments, an aspect of transport infrastructure provision, which is also discussed in Chapter 6.

1. Established policies

If planning policies are to be effective in this area, they have to bring about a reduction in car travel and an increase in the use of the more environmentally-friendly modes. Annex 2 shows that few of the Case-Study cities emphasised land-use policy as an instrument for influencing the growth of car travel. However, all the cities studied are characterised by active land-use policies and it is useful to consider the travel implications of the policies pursued, even where this is not their primary objective. Examples of policy from outside the Case-Study cities will also be reviewed.

Using planning policies to reduce car travel

Land-use policies can seek to limit car travel through two main mechanisms:

- reducing the need to travel, either through ensuring reasonable proximity between places of residence, employment and other facilities, thereby minimising the length of trip necessary to access particular opportunities; or through creating mixes of facilities, which increase the scope for multipurpose trips; and
- increasing the scope for non-motorised travel, such as walking and cycling; or by forms of public transport, such as rail and bus, which are likely to be less environmentally-damaging than private cars.

In practice there are strong links between these mechanisms. Data from Germany suggests that in the hierarchy of travel modes, walking is dominant up to about 1.5 km, cycling between 1.5 and 3.3 km and cars for longer distances (Figure 5.1). However, whereas walking trips of over 4 km are rare, cycling still accounts for about 20 per cent of trips at 10 km. Furthermore, where cyclists are numerous they tend to ride further. In Copenhagen, for instance, about one quarter of all cycle trips exceed 9 km (Krag, 1993).

Minimising car travel has not traditionally been a significant policy objective in any of the countries considered. In many cases it appears scarcely to figure as an objective at all, although the Dutch "compact city" policy, which has been in effect for ten years, and green belts in the UK, both of them policies of urban containment, may be seen as precursors of today's concerns to achieve sustainable development. Established land-use policies which have the reduction of car travel as at least a partial objective, may be grouped into several broad categories.

Figure 5.1. **The share of travel by walking, cycling and car in the Federal Republic of Germany, 1989**

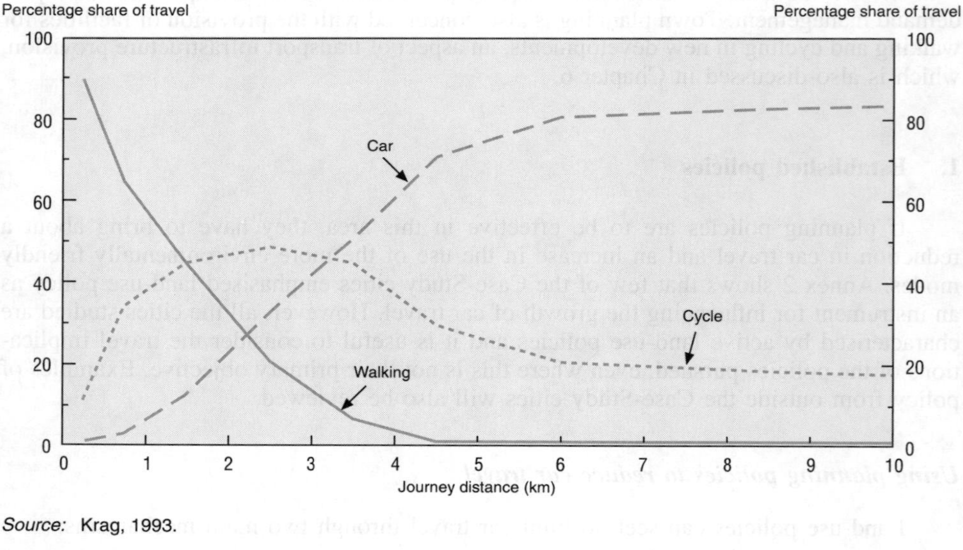

Source: Krag, 1993.

Residential densities and urban intensification

The European Union's 1990 Green Paper on the Urban Environment, and a range of academic studies, have advocated the benefits of high-density compact cities (EU Green Paper, 1990; McLaren, 1992). High residential densities within cities or individual districts have the potential to reduce car travel in a number of ways: they increase the scope to make contacts or pursue activities without resort to motorised transport; they increase the range of local shopping and other facilities which can be supported by local expenditure; and, by concentrating travel demand at the local level, they improve the viability of public transport, whilst making the ownership and use of private cars more difficult. They also have financial implications since, other things being equal, the value of property per square metre increases as the occupation of land becomes more intense.

In practice, policies to achieve high residential densities do not generally emerge as prominent features of land-use planning. This was clearly so in the Case-Study cities. Public policies in a number of countries, such as the UK, have in the past sought to *reduce* inner-city densities through dispersal – on environmental, social or public health grounds. Aspects of this type of policy perspective are still evident from the Case Studies for cities such as Tokyo. Additionally, there has clearly been a general market-led trend towards decentralisation of both population and employment in all the Case-Study cities and this has reduced average urban residential densities in most, if not all, cases. However, densities in new post-1945 suburbs in the UK are higher than those of the 1930s, expressly because of development control. Densities are now rising again.

The beginnings of a further shift in policy are evident in some countries. The $ 850 million Australian Better Cities Programme is concerned to demonstrate innovations in affordable high-density housing (Newman, 1992). The recommendations of the "Clouds of Change" report, adopted by the City of Vancouver (CMHC, 1993), include the encouragement of higher residential densities through multiple-unit residential developments. A number of countries, as discussed below, already favour high densities in central areas and other locations, where they can help support the role of public transport. Policies for increasing densities may, however, still prove controversial in practice and raise concerns about reconciling the goals of amenity and proximity. As recreation, both within and outside the house, becomes an ever more important part of life, so such reconciliation will become more challenging.

Inter-relationships with transport planning and public transport provision

The extent to which the planning of urban development, roads and public transport is integrated, differs widely. Integration is well established in the Netherlands and France and most of the Case-Study cities attached a good deal of importance to it, as Table A3.3 shows. But these cities are probably exceptional in this respect: in general, transport planning and urban development have tended to go their separate ways. Governmental efforts to combine land-use and transport planning are, however, increasing. In Norway, integration is being stepped up by new national guidelines based on the Planning and Building Act. In some other countries, as is indicated by the Helsinki Case Study, cities are evaluating the transport investment implications of different population-growth and land-use futures.

Examples of the ways in which planning policies are linked to public transport provision in practice include:

- *concentrating high-density residential development near stations along public transport corridors:* This has been done in Portland (Oregon), Stockholm, Toronto, Vienna and Copenhagen, where the so-called Finger Plan has played a significant role in post-war planning policies. The motivation underlying such strategies has not necessarily been solely or even mainly, the minimisation of car travel. In the case of Copenhagen, for example, the original planning objectives apparently related primarily to the preservation of open space and improvement of accessibility;
- creating or preserving a *high density of trip-attracting activities in central areas and other locations well served by public transport:* This has been an aspect of urban regeneration in Portland. It is also associated with policies for restricted parking in the centres of cities such as Amsterdam, Copenhagen and Vienna. In the UK, "preferred office locations" were established at main-line railway termini in the 1976 Greater London Development Plan; and in the 1992 plan for the London Borough of Hammersmith and Fulham, the same objective was pursued by discouraging commercial development where access by public transport was poor;
- *focusing of new residential development in areas well served by public transport:* This is nowadays relatively common in land-use policy and in Switzerland it is a requirement of a Federal Council Order covering the whole country. Its importance was stressed in the Zurich Case Study;
- *using developer contributions to finance new transport infrastructure:* In the UK, planning agreements are used to help finance road and rail improvements and in the United States, impact fees are levied on new development. However, in both cases, as elsewhere, it is clear that consideration of the transport impacts of new developments focuses on issues of local traffic generation to the exclusion of the wider effects of development on total travel demand; and
- *issuing guidelines which seek to ensure that new development is accessible to public transport:* Seattle, Oakland and Orange County in California are examples of areas which aggressively promote such ideas (Cervero, 1991). Similar initiatives have been undertaken by the Province of Ontario, Canada, and the UK.

Maintaining and developing the role of urban centres

The Case-Study cities exhibit very different population trends. Whilst Asian cities in general have to contend with the pressures of growth, UK and US cities suffer in many cases from problems of population decline. This latter trend is often linked to problems of economic decline in the inner cities, although in Continental Europe the fall in the population of the urban core is generally for other reasons, not least the demand for greater residential space associated with rising household incomes. Policies have been implemented to maintain the vitality of inner-area residential districts and to enhance the role of central and inner-area employment and other economic functions (as for example, in the UK's Urban Programme). These policies have typically been undertaken for a mix of economic, social and environmental, as well as political, reasons. Since a relatively high proportion of trips to central locations are undertaken by public transport, such policies will have had some benefits in reducing car travel and supporting the viability of public transport. In some cities, such as Portland, this was clearly a specific objective of urban regeneration policies.

The use of pedestrianisation to enhance city-centre retailing is important in many European cities, such as Freiburg. Such actions and related environmental improvements are used as part of a town centre management strategy to counter pressures for decentralisation. The Portland Case Study stresses the importance of encouraging retail uses, and limiting "blank walls", in the creation of a pedestrian-friendly environment.

Planning also plays an important role in underpinning public transport for trips to central areas, by limiting parking provision at new developments. In the UK, the *maximum* amount of parking at office developments has been specified in London since the mid-1960s, although the majority of other cities have been specifying *minimum* amounts to avoid creating problems connected with on-street parking. The volume of privately-owned off-street parking that has, as a result, been created in city centres is now an obstacle to demand management.

Urban containment policies

Measures to limit low-density sprawl are a focus of increasing interest in Ontario and Vancouver in Canada and have been applied in Davis, California in the United States (Owens and Rickaby, 1992). In the UK, many cities have long-standing Green Belt controls which support urban regeneration, as well as protecting open country. Such policies seem to be an essential part of any policy package designed to maintain or create compact cities, and many European cities pursue policies which are intended to have similar effects. For example, policy in Helsinki and many other cities, favours infilling rather than opening up new areas for residential development. Reuse of vacant or derelict land within existing urban areas is a key principle in the UK's policy on new housing development.

Urban containment policies in many European cities involve resistance to peripheral shopping centres and business parks. There are even indications of a policy shift in this direction in North America. Changing patterns of accessibility, associated in particular with new orbital routes, have increased pressure for urban containment policies – resulting in a market-driven trend for some cities, such as Birmingham in the UK, to begin to turn inside-out. Resistance to out-of-town shopping is part of national planning policy in France and the Netherlands, and in the UK, national planning policy proposes much tougher tests for new out-of-town retail development, including not having an adverse impact on vitality and viability of existing town centres, being accessible by a choice of means of transport (not just by car) and not adding to the overall level of car travel (UK DOE, 1993). However, the primary motivation tends to be the preservation of existing retail centres, rather than concern about the high levels of car travel at out-of-town malls, brought about by their distance from residential areas, lack of public transport and lavish parking provision.

Maintaining and developing the role of urban sub-centres

The potential advantages of a polycentric urban structure, in which facilities are decentralised in order to be closer to the residents which they serve and to their workforces, are clear. Such structures can shorten journey lengths and increase the proportion of the population which can access frequently-used facilities without resorting to motorised travel. If sub-centres involve a mix of uses, they also widen opportunities for people to make multi-purpose trips. If they are well served by public transport, and/or offer a safe and attractive environment for walking and cycling, they can be potentially helpful in reducing car dependence. These potentials partly explain the current interest in the urban village concept in Europe – as reflected, for example, in the Malminkartano development in Helsinki. A similar planning philosophy underlies the so-called neo-traditional developments in Australia and North America, as well as in the principles of concentrated decentralisation in Danish planning.

Many European urban regions are naturally poly-centric – reflecting the limited transport available at the time of their development. Sometimes, as in the Basin des Mines in Belgium, the coalescence of a network of villages has led to a multi-centred structure. In the United States, the scale and form of many urban sub-centres – "down-towns for cars" (Cervero, 1991) – affect their role. The creation of a sense of community, public space and pedestrian-friendly environments are clearly important potential elements, if such sub-centres are to be effective in reducing car dependence. Reston, Virginia, a suburb of Washington DC, has been retrofitted with a centre. There has also been a trend towards denser, more mixed-use suburbs, such as Denver Technological Centre.

In several major cities, important new centres have been developed to overcome constraints on, or deflect pressures from, existing centres. The La Defense complex, Creteil and Velizy, all of which are well served by public transport, are major examples in Paris. A number of Italian cities have sought, or are seeking, to develop alternative centres for economic activity to relieve their historic cores.

The government of the Tokyo Metropolitan Region, the largest and densest of all OECD city regions, is seeking to reduce congestion on the railways serving its central wards by moving towards a poly-centric structure. By promoting the move of firms outwards to growth points outside the existing city, and by creating space for residents to move into the city, there is a prospect that commuting travel will be reduced. Hiroshima and Seoul are likewise promoting poly-centric structures, but in neither city is reducing car travel an objective.

Intermixing land uses

Mixing homes and jobs (as was once characteristic of town centres) takes the process of seeking to minimise trip lengths a stage further. Whether it will prove effective in reducing travel under current circumstances is an open question, but the European Union's Green Paper on the Urban Environment advocates it, and there are signs that thinking amongst many policy makers is moving in the same direction. To be fully effective in reducing travel it will be necessary to mix opportunities for living and working with opportunities for recreation, shopping and local services. This may be achieved by ensuring that homes themselves and their neighbourhood offer scope for exercise, sport, home entertainment, walking, bicycling and opportunities for eating, drinking and meeting people.

Historically, of course, one of the key concerns of planning has been to separate uses, but the rationale of this separation has declined with the shift from manufacturing to services and other less objectionable economic activities. It is noteworthy in this context, that Houston, a city with no zoning controls, is said to have the most mixed-use suburbs in the United States (Cervero, 1991).

New towns

In cities such as Paris and London, some decentralisation has taken place to a ring of peripheral new towns, established through national policy initiatives. Part of the philosophy behind these towns was to achieve a balance between population and employment, enabling high levels of self-containment to be achieved. However, these new towns are typically served by a high standard of infrastructure, including good links back to the main metropolitan area. The potential for self-containment has not therefore been entirely realised in practice – and, at least in the case of London's new towns, self-containment has declined over time (Breheny, 1990). A key factor has been the closeness of these towns to the capital, so that distance has become a less significant barrier to commuting, as (in common with other major Metropolitan centres) the labour market catchment area of London has extended outwards over time.

Other policies

The quality of facilities for pedestrians and cyclists can influence the extent of non-motorised travel. In Norway, cycleways and cycle parking are accordingly being provided at transit stops in the ten largest cities in order to encourage people to "cycle-and-ride". Traffic calming, pioneered in the Netherlands and Germany, likewise has potential to encourage walking and cycling. However, it needs to be borne in mind that the extensive city cycleway systems found in Denmark, the Netherlands and Germany are a result, as well as a cause, of high levels of cycling.

The location of public facilities is also an important issue. In Switzerland, planning laws require health, leisure and education facilities to be located so as to reduce the need for mobility – although not necessarily car travel as such. The new policy package in the Netherlands, described below, emphasises the importance of siting public facilities in locations which are well served by public transport. Similar policies have also been adopted in the UK.

Many of the measures described above are not, of course, mutually exclusive. In the example of Portland, the success of the policy was due largely to the use of a number of measures brought together within an overall package designed to limit car travel and dependency. Shifts towards such an integrated, strategic approach are now also evident elsewhere.

2. Recent policy initiatives

The Netherlands

The Netherlands' Government gives prominence to land-use policies as a means of influencing travel behaviour. The key aim, as set out in the Fourth Report on Physical Planning (NL, 1991), is: "to ensure that businesses and services with a high potential of public transport utilisation by employees and visitors are sited on locations which are easily accessible or which can be made easily accessible by public transport."

The siting of labour-intensive or visitor-intensive services at locations easily accessible by road vehicle, but poorly accessible by public transport, is discouraged. Such locations are to be reserved for car-dependent activities or, where appropriate, road haulage.

The cornerstone of the approach called "The Right Business in the Right Place" (NL MOH, PP and E, 1991), is the development of accessibility profiles for different locations and mobility profiles for different types of business. Locations are categorised A, B or C based on their accessibility by public and motorised transport. Mobility profiles are assessed on the basis of the labour and visitor intensity of each type of business, its dependence on car for business purposes and the extent to which road is used for deliveries and the distribution of goods. The planning process then seeks to match the accessibility characteristics of locations with the mobility profiles of different activities in such a way as to meet the basic requirements for accessibility for different types of business, whilst maximising public transport utilisation.

These measures form part of an overall policy package which is designed to halve the increase of 70 per cent in car usage, which was previously projected as likely by 2010, and to double the usage of public transport. Its other elements include planned investment of Gld 14 billion (ECU 6.6 billion) in public transport over the period to 2010 and a range of supporting policies in relation to road and public transport pricing, as well as parking policy. The principle of concentration also plays an important role in Dutch planning policy in the establishment of recreational facilities as near as possible to large concentrations of population.

The United Kingdom

The UK Government issued new planning policy guidance to local authorities in March 1994 (UK DOE, 1994). The objective of the guidance is to:

"address ... the role of land-use planning in reducing the need to travel and encourage ... use of means of transport other than the car, the interactions between land-use planning and transport planning, and the importance of co-ordination, and other transport considerations in development plans and development control."

The land-use policies set out in the policy guidance follow from a commitment in the 1990 Environmental White Paper to reduce economy wide CO_2 emissions to 1990 levels by the year 2000. They form part of a wider policy comprising: a decision to raise road fuel duties by at least 5 per cent a year in real terms in successive budgets; studies into the effects of urban congestion pricing; a commitment to introduce motorway tolls when the technology becomes available; and moves to integrate road and public transport investment planning.

The major land-use elements of the draft guidance relate to:

- maintaining or increasing residential densities, particularly in areas well served by public transport;
- focusing residential development in larger settlements;
- concentrating employment and other trip-attracting activities in urban and suburban centres well served by public transport, and increasing the juxtaposition of residential and employment development;
- incorporating local facilities and attractive provision for walking and cycling into neighbourhood planning; and
- favouring locations outside congested areas, with good access to transport infrastructure, for freight-transport-intensive activities.

The guidance provides specific recommendations designed to influence travel to work; travel within work; freight transport; and travel relating to shopping, social activities, entertainment and tourism, and education and public facilities. The work-related travel policies stress the importance of: linking employment development to public transport, making provision for walking and cycling, and encouraging the juxtaposition of complementary land uses. The policies in relation to social activities, entertainment and tourism – which as discussed below are particularly important – emphasise both the need to provide facilities locally and the advantages of town-centre locations, which are well served by public transport.

Most of the measures proposed in the UK policy guidance are not individually radical. What distinguishes the policy is the holistic approach to reducing both the need for travel and car dependency. The UK's renewed attempt to achieve greater integration between land-use and transport planning is also important.

3. The results of studies

An assessment of the role of land-use policies in reducing car travel is based on evidence from three types of sources, each of which is reviewed in turn.

After studies

Few of the OECD/ECMT Case Studies contain evidence of the effects of the policies pursued. There are a number of reasons for this. Few study areas have prolonged experience of implementing land-use policies designed to reduce car travel. Many of the land-use policies which will have influenced travel behaviour have been implemented with other objectives in view. And attributing the changes which have occurred to specific policy measures is difficult. The results of the Case Studies are discussed in more detail in Chapter 7, which looks at the impacts of the overall package of policies adopted in the Case-Study cities – not just land-use policies – and considers a wider range of objectives than reducing car dependence.

The Case Study which offers the most convincing evidence is Portland, Oregon (Bartholomew, 1993). Car dependency remains high, but the policy package of urban regeneration and support for public transport appears to have resulted in:

- an increase, since 1972, of over 30 000 jobs in the downtown area, without an appreciable increase in numbers of parking spaces or vehicle trips;
- an increase of over 50 per cent in public transport trips to the downtown area, with a 43 per cent mode share for public transport in travel-to-work trips;
- a high level of usage of the LRT system, with a substantial volume of development having taken place along the line; and
- a fall, from more than 100 per year to zero, in the number of violations of CO standards – a change, to which other factors, such as three-way catalysts, will clearly have contributed.

Before studies

Before studies take two forms: simulations of expected travel behaviour in idealised cities; and simulations of alternative policies for new development, based on interactive land-use/transport models, which are designed to replicate travel and urban development in particular areas. Needless to say, the results from both should be treated with caution, in the absence of further supporting evidence.

One simulation by Steadman and Barrett (1990), suggests that savings of 10 to 15 per cent in fuel for passenger transport might be achieved over a 25 year period, through land-use changes at the city-region scale. The key policy in this saving is the centralisation of population into the cities and their surrounding settlements in order to shorten trip lengths.

Land-use and transport modelling of the type carried out in the major ISGLUTI International Study [Webster et al. (eds.), 1988], typically suggests that travel behaviour is relatively insensitive to land-use changes alone. However, simulations for one UK sub-region indicate that co-ordinated land-use planning policies combined with public transport investment could reduce projected CO_2 emissions from transport by 16 per cent over a 20 year period, broadly in line with the conclusions of more theoretical work (UK DOE/DOT, 1993).

There are grounds, however, for supposing that, for technical reasons, some of this modelling work may understate the potential scope for land-use measures to affect travel behaviour. Most obviously, some of the available models do not consider non-motorised modes, which therefore understate the extent to which a shortening of trip lengths could provide a basis for inducing transfers to walking and cycling, particularly in conjunction with measures to improve the attractiveness and safety of such options. The more advanced ISGLUTI models [Webster et al. (eds.), 1988] did, however, take account of non-motorised modes.

Efforts have also been made in, for example, Portland (Bartholomew, 1993) to represent more realistically the potential sensitivity of transport behaviour to land-use changes. New modelling work suggests that policies of favouring high-density residential development, linked to public transit, will have significant favourable effects, including, in the case studied, reducing car-ownership levels, relative to alternative strategies, by 4 per cent, and increasing public transport ridership and the roles of walking and cycling.

Comparative studies

Most of the evidence from this type of study is based on comparisons of travel or related indicators, such as energy consumption, in different places at particular times. Kenworthy and Newman (1989) show a strong, non-linear negative association between gasoline consumption per head in different cities and population density (Figure 5.2). There is a clear rank order, at the opposite ends of which, are North American cities, which show the lowest densities and highest gasoline consumption, and Asian cities which exhibit the highest densities and lowest gasoline consumption.

Similar results flowed from a comparison by the Norwegian Institute for Urban and Regional Research of energy consumption in 97 towns in Sweden (NIURR, 1993). The NIURR found that when urban land per person increased from 500 to 1 000 sq.m. the average annual fuel consumption for transport increased by about 25 per cent. However, no correlation was found between energy consumption and either city size (measured by population) or average income.

In a related study of 15 small city regions (defined by commuting trips of up to 35 km), the NIURR found that decentralised, multi-nuclear urban patterns are the least energy demanding – even where the component centres are small. Energy consumption per capita in the most centralised regions was found to be 25 per cent higher than in the most decentralised. Energy consumption was also found to increase with the degree of urbanisation.

A study for the UK Department of the Environment (Breheny et al., 1993), which reviews British evidence, came to different conclusions. The researchers found that in British towns, petrol consumption went up as population density went down and that car dependency was highest in small towns and rural districts. Another study (UK DOE/ DOT, 1993), reviewing evidence in the UK, confirmed the importance of population density, but differed in its conclusions from the Norwegian work. Small settlements and rural areas are associated with the greatest levels of travel and car dependency (Table 5.1). However, no systematic relationship between travel behaviour and the size of the urban area is evident so far as the largest cities are concerned. Neither self-containment in commuting terms, nor intermixing of land uses, emerges as a significant explanation of the observed differences in travel behaviour between urban areas. The centralisation of work places and other facilities is shown to be a powerful factor encouraging the use of public transport, rather than car, with the availability, or otherwise, of parking, and ease of access to a railway station, also important influences on mode of travel. The conclusion, however, is that central locations are important as much in frustrating the use of the car, as in encouraging the role of public transport alternatives.

Figure 5.2. Fuel use per person versus population density, 1980

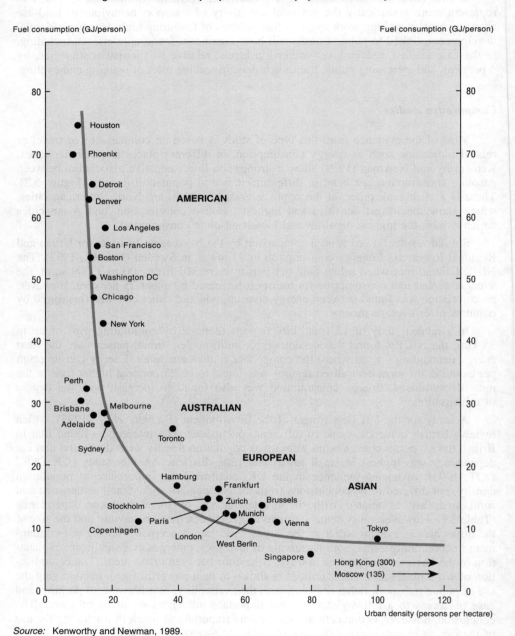

Source: Kenworthy and Newman, 1989.

Table 5.1. **Total distance travelled by mode and settlement population size in the United Kingdom, 1985/86**

Area	All modes km[a]	Car km[a] (%)	Local bus km[a] (%)	Rail km[a] (%)	Walking km[a] (%)	Other[b] km[a] (%)
Inner London	141	76 (54)	12 (8.5)	34 (24)	2.5 (1.8)	17 (12)
Outer London	167	113 (68)	8.9 (5.3)	23 (14)	2.6 (1.6)	19 (11)
Conurbations with populations over 250 000 (average)	117	74 (63)	16 (14)	5.2 (4.5)	3.5 (3.1)	18 (15)
Urban areas with populations:						
100 000-250 000	161	115 (72)	8.6 (5.4)	11 (7.0)	3.2 (2.0)	23 (14)
50 000-100 000	155	110 (72)	7.2 (4.7)	13 (8.4)	3.7 (2.4)	20 (13)
25 000-50 000	151	111 (73)	5.7 (3.8)	13 (8.3)	3.7 (2.5)	18 (12)
3 000-25 000	176	133 (76)	7.2 (4.1)	8.0 (4.6)	3.0 (1.7)	24 (14)
Rural areas	211	164 (78)	5.7 (2.7)	11 (5.2)	1.7 (0.8)	29 (14)
All areas	160	114 (71)	9.3 (5.8)	11 (7.1)	3.2 (2.0)	22 (14)

a) Kilometres per person per week – excludes trips under 1.6 km.
b) "other" refers to two-wheeled motor vehicles, taxis, domestic air travel, other public transport and other types of bus travel.
Source: UK DOE/DOT, 1993.

Such evidence is a better guide to the *type* of effect which can be expected to follow from land-use changes, than to the likely *scale* of the impact. There are complex inter-relationships between factors such as density, location, car ownership and a range of socio-economic influences, making it difficult to be confident of their individual effects, or to project from cross-sectional data. It is clear too, that the effects on travel of population decentralisation may be far larger and more complex than simple comparisons of travel data for residents of urban and non-urban areas can account for alone (Breheny, forthcoming).

4. Effectiveness of land-use planning policies in practice

The effectiveness of indirect policy instruments is always, to some extent, uncertain. The impact of land-use planning measures, which are designed to limit the level of car travel, will be influenced by a range of factors, including the following.

Rates of development and redevelopment

Land uses in mature economies tend to change only slowly. For example, annual levels of new housing construction in the United States and the UK represent less than 1 per cent of the existing stock (UK DOE/DOT, 1993). However, rates of change for offices, shops and leisure establishments are higher than for housing: such uses can change within existing buildings. They also attract more travel than houses. Nevertheless, the scope for radical change to mature cities is limited. Land-use policies in mature economies are therefore primarily concerned with incremental growth in what may, or may not, be travel-efficient built environments. New policy directions may also take time to have effect, because of existing development commitments. Existing decentralisation is both a constraint on new policies and an influence on what policies are likely to be effective.

Property costs

Patterns of land use designed to reduce car travel are likely to have different cost characteristics from those associated with traditional urban and suburban development. Developments comprised of mixed land uses involve more investment (and more entrepreneurial skill) than producing the same accommodation in a series of single-use parcels. Raising the residential density of existing suburbs may, likewise, involve diffi-cult political judgements, particularly if the most suitable sites are occupied by the expensive villas of wealthy residents.

Implementation

Planning involves trading-off conflicting objectives, and in most countries pragmatic considerations result in departures from plans. For example, the Danish Overview reports that a significant proportion of development does not take place in strict accordance with the strategic principles of the plan. Greece provides a more extreme example: one fifth of new housing development takes place without planning permission (Papayannos and Assoc., 1992).

Focus on travel to work

The primary focus of the majority of the land-use policies intended to reduce car travel is on travel to work and, to a lesser extent, shopping. This is partly because of the way congestion influences the debate on urban travel, but also because travel to work is perhaps, along with shopping, the easiest potential target for such policies. However, it is important to recognise that travel to work typically accounts for less than 30 per cent of travel and that, where data is available, the dominant source of growth appears to be leisure-related travel (UK DOE/DOT, 1993). Leisure travel will be influenced to some extent by, for example, measures to alter residential densities, but it is clearly mainly associated with trends in incomes and lifestyles which are only very loosely, if at all, related to land-use changes.

Congestion effects

Many of the policies which have the strongest potential to shorten trip lengths or improve the viability of public transport and non-motorised modes are likely to add to congestion through their effects in concentrating travel demand. This raises three issues:

- the slowing down and re-routing of vehicles may outweigh the benefits of shorter trip lengths on energy efficiency (UK DOE/DOT, 1993), unless the measures are part of a policy package which includes measures to manage private demand for road space. Indeed, they may well prove counter-productive;
- aside from issues of energy efficiency, the resultant concentrations of traffic will reduce air quality and other urban environmental conditions. Indeed, it is precisely to counter these effects that the Case-Study city regions in, for example, Japan and South Korea have opted for policies of dispersal. This emphasises the potential sensitivity of policy choices to the importance accorded to particular objectives, as well as to local circumstances; and
- there could be a potentially substantial impact on the efficiency and competitiveness of businesses. Some of the adverse effects of these policies could be tackled through a comprehensive demand-management package, although aspects of this might also have adverse implications for commercial and industrial activities which depend on accessibility by car or commercial vehicles.

Interaction with surrounding areas

Land-use policies for the cities cannot be formulated in isolation. There are at least two important aspects of this issue:

- in the absence of uniform regional policies, accessibility by car may act as an instrument of competition for economic development between locations. The greater ease of providing parking in suburban and non-urban areas, together with the improved accessibility provided to such locations by new orbital and intra-urban roads, have been important contributory factors in the dispersal of employment from inner city areas in the UK and many other countries. In urban areas where there is a need to attract activity, but development interest is weak, fear of dispersal and competition from other centres acts as a significant constraint on demand management policies. Such policies need to be harmonised over a wide area; and
- urban containment policies and efforts to raise densities may, by raising the relative cost of space in urban areas, intensify population dispersal. Within the UK, for example, there is evidence that Green Belts have increased migration from the cities to beyond the area of restraint, increasing travel-to-work distances in the process (UK DOE/DOT, 1993). Even if such development pressures were controlled, migration from the cities could continue, with substantial impacts on surrounding rural housing markets. Whether policies can be simultaneously introduced, which will make higher density and urban lifestyles relatively more attractive to potential outmigrants, is therefore crucial.

It is important to bear in mind too, that wider national policies, in relation to the distribution of people and economic activity, can have important effects. For example, both the London and Paris Case Studies suggest that regional policies might have had the effect of increasing travel, particularly inter-urban travel. Policies to retain population in rural areas might also add to total travel, although the issue is not clear-cut, since, in some cases, they might help maintain the critical mass of people necessary to support local services. Some policies, such as park-and-ride facilities at suburban rail stations, might shift some urban car trips to rail but, as the Paris Case Study notes, they might also promote long-distance commuting.

Linkages to complementary policies

Some mention has already been made of the potential importance of seeing land-use planning policies as just one part of an integrated package, rather than as a self-standing solution to the problems associated with growth in car travel. Two overall points need to be made:

- land-use policies can help generate the concentrations of trip origins and destinations, which improve the feasibility of public transport provision. Increasing the actual quality and use of public transport is also likely to depend on policies to finance, or stimulate, new public transport investment, and on measures to constrain car use within urban areas. The effective *separation* of responsibilities for planning and transport investment in many countries is clearly unhelpful in this context, as is recognised in the initiatives to co-ordinate these responsibilities more closely in countries such as Norway; and
- the effectiveness of land-use policies is likely to depend on the adoption of policies which increase the real costs of car travel substantially, and perhaps also raise travel costs more generally. Indeed, the extent to which this is done will, to some extent, determine which land-use policies are most appropriate to the objective of reducing car travel. These issues require some expansion.

The form of cities reflects to a large extent the transport technology and real travel costs prevailing at the time that their different phases were developed (Newman, 1992). Dense cities, with a juxtaposition of complementary land uses, were, at least in part, the result of the external economies of agglomeration, at a time of high real travel costs – and such cities clearly have a strong potential to be efficient in travel terms under a high-real-travel-cost scenario. However, as transport infrastructure has improved and travel costs have fallen, the external economies, which shaped the development of such cities, have diminished in importance, being to some extent replaced by congestion-related diseconomies. The result has been the observed dispersal of people and economic activity. An important associated driving force has been the exploitation by outmigrants of reduced travel costs back to job opportunities in the city, to facilitate their acquisition of greater, lower cost, residential space in locations further from the city centre.

The problems of urban sprawl, which are found in countries as different as the United States, France and Belgium, need to be seen in this wider context, rather than as solely a recent product of increasing car ownership. Historically, it was development of the rail, tram and bus services which was responsible for much of the process of suburbanisation in the nineteenth century. It was public transport which drove much of the expansion to Los Angeles in the early part of this century. More recently, similar effects were evident in cities such as Munich, which have benefited from major investment in LRT systems (Kreibich, 1978). This again points to the risk of tensions between land-use policies which seek to constrain sprawl and raise densities, and pressures for residential decentralisation – unless the policies are accompanied by much higher real travel costs. Whilst the benefits of high-density, urban lifestyles have their advocates (EU Green Paper, 1990), the pervasiveness of outwards migration raises concerns about the private costs of such policies.

The non-linearity in the observed relationship between residential density and travel, in the work of Kenworthy and Newman (1989), suggests that there is considerable scope for raising densities in US and Australian cities to perhaps 40 persons per hectare, a relatively low level by the standards of major European cities. This could be combined with initiatives to develop flexible (bus and shared taxi) and fixed link (LRT, busways, etc.) public transport systems. Within much of Europe the major benefits could well be achieved through maintaining or increasing the proportion of the population which lives in large urban areas, rather than necessarily seeking to raise the densities of the existing developed parts of the cities.

Whether policies to intermix land uses and decentralise work places and other facilities to improve access from residential areas, will succeed in reducing trip lengths and car travel, is likely to depend heavily on the extent to which people elect to make use of local opportunities. The risk is that, within an environment of low real travel costs, they may not. The results of such decentralisation may then be the growth of diffuse patterns of suburb-to-suburb car journeys and the sorts of suburban congestion increasingly seen in the United States (Cervero, 1991). This risk is underlined both by prevailing market trends towards the exercise of choice and specialisation, and evidence (UK DOE/DOT, 1993) that the processes of residential and job search and choice within cities, are not currently much influenced by concerns for proximity. Jorgensen, (1993), in a study of travel to work in Copenhagen, also makes the point that such concerns for proximity tend to decline as education levels increase, jobs become more specialised and incomes rise. Under these circumstances, policies of centralising facilities in order to increase the role of public transport may well perform better in relation to minimisation of car travel, than policies to bring together homes and work places.

There is, of course, an important argument for seeking to retain, or create, urban structures which have the potential for reduced car dependency, even if this potential is unlikely to be realised in practice under prevailing conditions. It offers a form of contingency planning against the consequences of dramatically higher fossil fuel prices or severe traffic restraint measures in the future, which might be brought about by either policy choices reflecting increased environmental concerns, or by economic or international political developments. An escalation of energy prices could be countered partly by the use of more energy-efficient vehicles (as in Italy, which has Western Europe's most expensive petrol), rather than through lower levels of car use, but would clearly still pose some major problems of adjustment for the dispersed forms of development now prevalent in or around many cities. Moreover, the prevalence of low-density development in, for example, US cities arguably already represents a major political constraint on policies to internalise the environmental externalities associated with the transport sector, through higher energy prices.

5. Concluding remarks

The evidence, from which to form judgements on the scale of the impact which land-use policies can have in reducing car travel, is much less comprehensive than might be wished. However, it seems useful to group policies into three categories:

- the first set comprises what might be termed *"no regret" policies,* which are either beneficial for other reasons, or which are at least unlikely to have any wider adverse consequences. These policies include, for example: urban regeneration initiatives; steps to ensure that the location of public facilities takes account of the potential costs of access by users; steps to steer trip-attracting activities, where a reasonable choice exists, to areas where journey lengths and car dependency are minimised; provision of the most frequently-used local facilities in or near new residential developments; and ensuring that developments in general provide an environment which is as pedestrian- and cyclist-friendly as possible. The contribution of such policies to reducing car travel, however, will probably be modest, especially in the absence of complementary policy initiatives;
- the second group of policies includes the bulk of measures now being implemented, or under consideration, in the countries considered, including: measures to focus new trip- attracting developments in city centres or in more or less concentrated forms in the suburbs; efforts to focus travel demand in particular areas and corridors; maximum parking standards; and overall urban containment policies. These policies carry some risks either of exacerbating urban environmental problems and/or of weakening the competitiveness of the areas in which they are implemented. Conversely, in the right circumstances, their potential to reduce car travel is probably reasonably significant. Success and the wider impact of such policies are likely to depend heavily on the extent to which the wider policy context (in terms of the costs of car travel and demand management measures, public transport investment and planning policies in the wider region) is supportive. Effectively, these policies make most sense when used as a supportive part of a larger policy package; and
- the third group includes policies for urban intensification and increased residential densities. Again, the effectiveness of such policies will depend on whether or not other instruments are being used to pursue the same objectives. However, the tendency for households, when able to do so, to adopt suburban and rural lifestyles, argues that the private costs of raising densities may be substantial, even leaving aside concerns about their implications for public health and social stress.

In view of the acknowledged weakness of most land-use policies when used in isolation, and also of the long time lag between the drawing up of metropolitan plans and their implementation through building permits, it is clear that the goal of sustainable development requires the combined application of reinforcing land-use and transport policies.

6. TRANSPORT POLICIES

This chapter looks at transport policies adopted by OECD countries in an attempt to overcome the problems discussed in Chapter 3. The various measures, which have been grouped into a small number of categories, are by no means exhaustive. Environmental measures, where appropriate, have also been included in this chapter. The bulk of the information used has come from the National Overviews, the Case Studies and the papers presented at the Dusseldorf and Basle conferences (OECD, 1993b; and Frey and Langloh, 1992).

1. Public transport

Investment in public transport has been widespread in recent decades, with rail construction featuring most in the metropolises and larger cities and service improvements in smaller cities. Almost all the National Overviews stressed the importance of public transport improvement as a major plank of transport policy. Higher frequencies, improved regularity, more effective communication with passengers, the provision of new LRT or underground systems and lower fare levels, where appropriate, were the main elements of the various packages of policies.

Effects of public transport measures and investments

The beneficiaries of improved public transport are the users themselves, other travellers, the urban environment and city-centre activities. Investment in public transport helps, in particular, those who are dependent on public transport, many of whom have seen services deteriorate and fares rise. By reducing car traffic (though reductions tend to be small and short-lived), they confer benefits on other road users through reduced levels of congestion and pollution. Public transport improvements are often an essential component of any policy to restrain car use but, even if they are not, they might help to make such a restraint package more palatable. Perhaps the most important aspect of improving public transport, especially rail systems, is that they help to retain employment and other activities in city centres or, in the case of rapidly expanding cities, to allow a higher proportion of new jobs and facilities to be located in the centre.

A study of metros and tramways in five French cities (Walmsley and Perrett, 1992; and Walmsley and Pickett, 1992), indicated that the average rate of growth of public transport trips rose from 1 per cent p.a. to 3.5 per cent p.a. following the opening of the various systems. After 7 or 8 years, the metros in Marseilles, Lyon and Lille had increased total public transport journeys by 30, 21 and 58 per cent respectively. Care should be taken in interpreting this sort of patronage data, however, because some journeys which were previously made entirely by bus are sometimes recorded as bus-rail journeys, with each leg counting as a separate journey. In these particular French cities a quarter to a third of all public transport journeys involved a rapid transit leg, even though most of the systems consisted of only one or two lines. A study in Germany, by Hall and Hass-Klau (1985), concluded that rail investments "strikingly halted or even reversed" the decline in public transport patronage, as shown in Table 6.1.

Hall and Hass-Klau noted that in three British cities which invested in urban rail, patronage *fell* by 10 per cent (Tyne and Wear), 27 per cent (Glasgow) and 19 per cent (Liverpool) between 1977 and 1982. However, in cities which did not invest in rail, larger falls occurred: 36 per cent in Leeds and 34 per cent in Manchester. Only in Sheffield, which pursued a low-fares policy, was there a rise (1.1 per cent).

Not all the new rail systems have come up to expectation, however. The new Metrolink in Los Angeles is carrying only 3 000 passengers per day, for example, far fewer than forecast (Wachs, 1993). Even in the rapidly growing city of Seoul, the first phase of the new underground system captured only 19 per cent of the total traffic instead of the expected 30-40 per cent. By contrast, the new light rail system in Manchester is carrying more passengers than expected.

The various National Overviews make it clear, however, that improvements to public transport systems, while bringing in *more* passengers, tend to have only a limited effect on the use of private motor cars, congestion, CO_2 and toxic emissions, even if transit travel is increased substantially. Most of the new public transport users tend to be former pedestrians, cyclists or car passengers.

Table 6.1. **Patronage changes in selected German cities before and after the introduction of metro systems**

	Annual percentage growth/decline in public transport use	
	Before	After
Munich	−0.3	+2.0
Cologne	−0.9	0.0
Hannover	0.0	+3.1
Essen	−2.0	+1.4
Nuremberg	0.0	+3.4

Source: Hall and Hass-Klau, 1985.

Railways generally offer a more attractive alternative to car users than buses, though this is not always the case (see, for example, the Zurich Case Study, Annex 2). The largest impact is naturally on car commuters to the city centre. In most cases, however, the majority of the new users come from bus (some still using bus for part of their journeys). Table 6.2 shows the modes formerly used by metro and tramway passengers in those cities which have carried out surveys.

Former car users in these cities constitute about 20 per cent or so of the ridership of the new systems – about 6 or 7 per cent of all public transport journeys. In a city like Manchester, with 25 per cent of all journeys made by public transport, the reduction in car traffic on this basis would be only 1 to 2 per cent. Since there is a suppressed demand for car travel in most large cities, such a reduction would very soon be eroded. It is not surprising, therefore, that most studies find there is no noticeable effect on car travel and congestion. A study of metros in developing countries also concluded that in none of the cities studied was there a notable reduction in traffic congestion (Fouracre *et al.,* 1990).

An assessment, carried out for the Danish Action Plan suggested that *doubling* the level of bus operation in Danish towns and cities (using existing technology) would result in only a 3 per cent reduction in total transport energy consumption, with emissions of NO_x, SO_2 and particulates actually *rising*. If the buses were run on natural gas with catalytic converters, the reduction in energy consumption would be even less, but emissions of NO_x, SO_2 and particulates would *fall,* as indicated in Table 6.3.

In circumstances where public transport services are substantially increased, without a corresponding fall in car usage, total emissions and energy consumption would, of course, rise. As far as energy and CO_2 emissions are concerned, one car passenger-km is equivalent to only 2 to 4 bus or rail passenger-kms, on average, for the same proportionate occupancy. If the buses or trains are full and the car carries only the driver, then the ratio could be as high as 10 or 12 (EU Green Paper, 1992).

Table 6.2. **Previous modes used by users of new metro and tram systems**

	% of passengers who formerly travelled by:		% new journeys[a]
	Bus	Car	
Marseilles[b]	74	15	11
Lille	56	28	16
Lyon	71	12	17
Nantes	67	17	16
Grenoble[c]	53	20	27
Calgary[d]	72	20	7

a) New journeys might include passengers who had changed home, job or school and so were making journeys different from those made previously.
b) Survey of only one line of the system.
c) Approximate figures only.
d) Peak hour: average of three lines.
Source: Walmsley and Pickett, 1992.

Table 6.3. **Effect of doubling the level of bus operation in Danish towns and cities**
Percentages

	Total transport energy consumption	CO	NO$_x$	SO$_2$	Particulates
Using existing technology	−3	−6	(———— +6 ————)		+4
Buses running on natural gas with catalytic converters	−2 to −3	−7	−5	−2	−4

Source: Danish Overview.

One of the conclusions of a study of 14 metros and tramways in France, Canada and the USA (Walmsley and Perrett, 1992), is that these systems can facilitate pedestrianisation of the city centre, enabling people to walk about unhindered by traffic. This has been done in Lyon, Grenoble, Nantes, and to a lesser extent, Lille, and in some German cities also, to good effect. By contrast, the metro in Marseilles has had little effect on the attractiveness of the city centre, where there has been only a small amount of pedestrianisation. With regard to urban development, rapid transit might well accelerate any expansion which is taking place or halt any decline, though in some circumstances it could hasten the decline.

Urban rail investment

Substantial sums of money have been spent, and are still being spent, in OECD countries on urban rail systems. One of the most striking examples is in Sweden, where SKr 5.5 billion (ECU 0.6 billion) is being invested in public transport improvements (mainly rail and LRT) in the major metropolitan areas. In Stockholm, the *Dennis Agreement* will provide SKr 16 billion (ECU 1.7 billion) over a 15-year period, mainly for new rail lines, modernisation of the metro system and a new rapid tram line round the inner city (Malmsten, 1993).

In the Netherlands, Dutch Railways are planning to invest in a coherent network of rapid urban tram, express bus and Underground lines, with the intention of reducing door-to-door journey times by public transport to less than 1.5 times that by car by the year 2010. It is recognised that cars, except in heavily-congested conditions, will almost always provide faster door-to-door travel than public transport, but these new measures should improve the competitive edge of public transport.

In Turkey, major construction programmes include the building of a new Bosphorus rail tunnel, a new metro in Istanbul (about 30 km in length) and a rail transit system in Ankara (about 55 km in length), all of which are expected to relieve congestion on the roads and improve the general urban environment through reduced emissions. In Seoul, five new underground rail lines have been built in the last 20 years and a second phase of rail development will add seven more lines, which should be in service by 1997. As the underground system develops, buses will increasingly play a complementary role to the underground. In Canada, new LRTs have been built in Edmonton and Calgary, and new linear induction systems in Vancouver and Scarborough (Toronto).

Rail systems and segregated busways are seen as the way forward in France. In the French provinces there were only 26 km of segregated urban public transport in 1973, but by 1988 this had quadrupled and it is expected to double again by the year 2000. It is in cities with such systems where public transport use has actually risen (but so has car use).

While there was a spate of urban rail construction in the 1970s and 1980s in many countries, including the United States, the rate has now slackened off. This is partly due to tighter economic controls over public expenditure, but might also be due to the fact that the more urgent systems have already been provided and only the more marginal ones remain. It is also true that some of the systems, such as the Los Angeles Metrolink have failed to live up to their expectations from the patronage point of view.

Bus and tram systems

Over the past decades, many tramway systems have been replaced by bus systems in cities throughout the world. This has been partly because of the inconvenience and perceived danger caused by vehicles running on fixed tracks on ordinary streets and partly because of the flexibility which bus systems offer. This policy, however, is now being reversed in many cities, because of the pollution caused by buses and the apparent popularity of tram systems, which nowadays are increasingly being given segregated tracks to avoid the problems experienced earlier. In some cases, for example in Brussels, tramway systems act as pre-metro systems, eventually becoming full metro systems, when segregation is available for their whole routes.

In the Ottawa-Carleton region of Canada, an extensive system of dedicated busways has been introduced. In other Canadian cities field tests of alternative transportation fuels for buses are being carried out – methanol in Windsor, natural gas in Hamilton and Toronto, and the hydrogen fuel cell in Vancouver.

In Stockholm, as part of the *Dennis Agreement,* a core network of bus and tram services in the inner city will be allocated exclusive street space, where practicable, and given priority at traffic signals. Only buses with catalytic converters and particle traps, or operating on clean fuels, will be allowed to operate in the core network. Such measures as bus lanes and bus priority at traffic signals will be used as a deterrent to car use and to encourage greater bus patronage, through improved regularity and journey speed.

In Zurich, the introduction of bus lanes, bus-only access to pedestrianised areas, segregated tram and trolley routes, computerised operational control systems and selective vehicle detection at 80 per cent of the traffic signals on bus and tram routes, has enabled public transport patronage to remain buoyant, while systems in many other cities have been in decline (see Case Study Summary in Annex 3 and Figure 3.8). In Seoul, with well over a hundred private bus companies operating in the metropolitan region, with 9 000 buses between them, bus priority has become an essential component of traffic management. Some streets have as many as four lanes completely occupied by buses. Flows of buses in bus priority streets in Helsinki are of a similar magnitude.

Fares, ticketing and information

Measures to make public transport systems easier to use also attract more passengers. Forty transport operators in the Zurich conurbation have formed an association which requires all operators to work to a common timetable and fares system, so that door-to-door journeys are possible on a single ticket. Travel cards have been introduced and communication improved between the operators and the users. All these measures were part of a SF 250 million (ECU 157 million) programme to improve public transport. As a result, patronage levels reached 470 trips per person p.a. in 1991 (a 30 per cent increase over 1986 levels). This is a higher level of usage than that in most other major cities (290 in London and 150 in Cologne) and it was achieved without the need to build expensive metro systems.

In the Netherlands there has existed a national tariff system for tram, bus, metro and urban rail since the late 1970s. High levels of subsidy have enabled a quality service to be offered at low fares (only 30 to 40 per cent of the operating costs are recovered from the fare box). In Helsinki too, generous subsidies have enabled fares to be kept low, but only a half of the operating costs come from the fare box. High operating subsidies in Paris have allowed the system to evolve and have made it cheap to use. In France, public transport is supported by a transport contribution tax which, at the discretion of the local authority, can be levied on all firms with more than nine employees in towns with over 20 000 population. The maximum levy in towns with fewer than 100 000 inhabitants is 1 per cent of wages; in larger towns it is 1.5 per cent, but if the town has a tramway or underground railway system, the levy is 1.75 per cent. In the Ile de France region (Greater Paris area) the levy is 2 per cent (French National Overview). However, most of the countries with high operating subsidies have recently become concerned about the escalating costs of public transport, but only a few countries, such as the UK, have taken action to reduce operating subsidies. "Smart" card technology could ultimately allow subsidies to be focused more specifically as fares concessions to particular groups of people, for travel at particular times of day and on particular routes.

If public transport is to retain (or increase) its ridership, it has to become more attractive. One way of doing this is to make all the information which a would-be passenger is likely to need widely available through the use of telematics. This information should include delays, time of next bus or train, routes, time-tables, fares, etc. and should be available in real time, through the use of view-data systems and computer terminals in the home, stations and other public places. Such information will depend on accurate information being available on the location and real-time schedule of buses and trams within the system. The SCOPE project (a pilot project within the framework of the DRIVE research programme of the EU) is developing and implementing such a system, demonstrating its usefulness and assessing its value.

Land-use planning linked to public transport

The use of public transport is greatly affected by density of development: many cities in many countries are limiting development to places which are already well-served by public transport, or which could become so. The Swiss, in particular, have adopted this approach and the Dutch policy of "The Right Business in the Right Place" pays special regard to access by public transport in the location of new businesses. Chapter 5 gives more details of these and other strategic policies which link land-use planning to public transport.

2. Cycling and walking

Walking is usually the most important means of transport for short journeys (ie less than 1 km) in all cities, but travel by bicycle varies greatly, as can be seen in Table 6.4. Even in the same country (with the possible exception of Holland), travel by bicycle differs from city to city, mainly because of tradition and culture. In the case of Holland and Denmark the flatness of the land (as in East Anglia in Britain) has helped to give cycling a popularity that subsequent provision of cycle tracks has helped it to retain.

The Dutch and the Danes have perhaps done more than any other people to promote the use of environmentally-friendly modes. In the Netherlands bicycle-km are comparable to train passenger-km and in Denmark they outnumber them (Table 6.5). In Copenhagen, for example, where there are 300 km of cycle tracks (equal to half the road network length), 25 per cent of trips are made by bicycle. Cycling has increased by 50 per cent over the 1980s in central Copenhagen, but accidents to cyclists remain a problem, particularly at junctions (see Section 9 of this chapter). New cycle routes are being planned in an attempt to increase the amount of cycling between home and work place and for local and weekend trips.

Table 6.4. **Variation in mode use in different cities and countries**

	Population (thousands)	Percentage of all trips by:			
		Foot	Bicycle	Public transport	Car
Netherlands (1990)		17	29	5	47
Germany, Fed. Rep. (1990)		27	10	11	53
United Kingdom (1979)		39	3	14	45
Groningen (NL, 1990)	160	17	48	5	30
Delft (NL, 1986)	85	25	40	10	25
Vasteras (S, 1981)	117	17	33	10	40
Munster (D, 1990)	253	21	34	7	38
Copenhagen (DK, 1982)	580	27	20	20	33
Salzburg (A, 1982)	128	29	11	20	40
Bologna (I, 1990)	176	23	8	34	35
Grenoble (F, 1985)	170	36	3	10	51
Stuttgart (D, 1986)	561	31	3	22	44
Madrid (E, 1981)	4 400	56	0	29	15

Source: Krag, 1993.

Table 6.5. Bicycle use in a selection of countries

	Total travel (billion pass-km)	Bicycle use (billion km)	Bicycle use (per cent of all travel)	Train use (billion pass-km)
Netherlands (1984)	137	11	8.0	12.8
Denmark (1987)	71	5	7.0	4.8
Germany (1986)	674	17	2.5	44.9
Great Britain (1985)	519	5	1.0	31.9

Source: Krag, 1993.

According to a national survey on travel behaviour, cycling in Norway increased by 60 per cent (passenger-km) between 1987 and 1992 and is now equal to half the amount of travel by train. Table 6.6 shows how cycling has developed over the last 30 years in Norway. In the ten largest urban areas overall transport plans are now being formulated which will specifically include provision of cycle tracks.

In the Netherlands, 40 per cent of all car journeys are less than 5 km, making cycle a reasonable alternative (see Figure 5.1). The Dutch national plan aims to increase the amount of cycling by 30 per cent by 2010 using a combination of measures that favour cycling, such as the provision of new cycle routes, facilities at railway stations and principle bus and tram stops, and other aids to make cycling both safer and more pleasant. It is all the more a challenge because the increase is being pursued with respect to an already very high level of cycling (see Table 6.4). These measures will be complemented by measures which make travelling by car less convenient. *Car-free residential areas* are even being considered, where cars are kept on the perimeters of the areas, rather than adjacent to individual homes.

In Canada and Australia, extensive cycle path networks have been introduced in several cities. Many other countries have included cycle paths and priority facilities too, but progress in this direction has, in general, been slow and even when provisions have

Table 6.6. Trends in cycling in Norway

	Cycle-km (1964 = 100)
1964	100
1975	108
1980	124
1987	89
1992	146

Source: Norwegian Overview.

been made, their use has often been disappointing. It should be remembered also, that promotion of cycling tends to attract travellers from public transport, with adverse effects on its viability.

The creation of *pedestrian priority areas* is one of the most widely-used measures to bring about local reductions in noise, air pollution and danger. This treatment has been applied mainly to shopping streets, and occasionally to streets in the business quarter also. The results of studies in Germany show that pedestrian priority measures are now regarded as being of benefit to local businesses (Hass-Klau, 1993). The comfort that can be experienced by those not in cars in the centres of cities, such as Munich, Lyons, Leeds and Minneapolis, shows what city centres can be like. Japan has initiated historic street-improvement programmes and neighbourhood schemes to emphasise the culture and identity of the locality. In Warsaw, traffic is being concentrated on to selected peripheral streets so that suitable streets in the centre can be converted for pedestrian use only.

Traffic calming was initially applied to inner-city residential streets in Holland. It was then adopted in particular cities in other countries and is now beginning to be used more widely (see de Wit, 1993). During the 1980s, the German government commenced a major 10-year demonstration project and monitoring programme to test traffic calming measures in different types of areas and in different sizes of cities. The results are being used in the design of traffic calming schemes for German cities (Doldisson, 1988). The technique has been used mainly in residential areas using chicanes and road humps to reduce speed and transfer some of the road space to pedestrians and cyclists. Speed limits (usually less than 30 km/h) are frequently imposed. Tree planting and other measures are used to provide a more attractive environment. Where traffic calming measures have been introduced in the UK, child casualties have fallen by 80 per cent.

Measures have been taken by Birmingham City Council in the UK, and by Berlin and other cities in Germany, to calm traffic on some of the main radial roads where they pass through shopping centres or other sensitive zones. Calming has also been introduced on main roads in villages in Denmark, Norway and France: an example can be seen at Goulancourt in the Somme. In the UK, Kent County Council has pioneered calming techniques on a trunk road, the A253 at Sarre between Canterbury and Ramsgate.

While safety of pedestrians and cyclists was the predominant reason for most of the earlier schemes, and still is the main reason in most cases, environmental issues and pedestrian convenience are now playing an increasing role.

3. Traffic restraint

Despite the lack of effective action in most countries to reduce car use, it is widely believed that private transport costs too little, because the user does not pay the external costs, which are borne by others in the form of road casualties and collisions, noise, pollution, taxation to provide the necessary infrastructure, etc. In France, a new system called the Passenger Transport Account has been introduced to isolate the economic and social costs of both public transport users and private car users and to identify the various sources of finance which pay for the infrastructure and services provided (French

National Overview). It is also generally recognised that increasing car travel costs has a greater effect on car use, and hence on vehicle emissions, than lowering fares or improving public transport service. Much thought has therefore been given to the appropriate economic instruments to achieve a reduction in car use and how they might be put into practice. However, it must be realised that the application of severe restraint measures might, in some circumstances, have unwanted side effects, *e.g.* in driving out businesses and encouraging out-of-town developments. Such systems need to be introduced as part of a coherent, internally-consistent, package of policies (see Chapter 5).

Internalising the external costs of mechanised travel

Few studies have been carried out to indicate how road users could be made to pay for the external costs of their journeys and what the magnitudes of the costs might be. One such study is by the Swiss government (GS EVED, 1993). This study distinguishes between three components of external costs: environmental costs, congestion costs and uncovered infrastructure and operational costs.

Tangible components of environmental costs, such as accidents, noise and damage to buildings from air pollution amount to some SF 1.8 billion per year (ECU 1.1 billion). This is SF 270 per resident (ECU 170). Over 90 per cent of this is due to car and truck traffic. In order to cover tangible environmental costs, the price of fuel would have to be raised by 30 cents/litre (ECU 0.2). Less tangible components of environmental costs due to the negative impacts of infrastructure on landscape and the urban fabric and impacts of air pollution on health, agriculture and climate (due to CO_2 emissions), etc., might add a further SF 4 billion per year (ECU 2.5 billion), *i.e.* about SF 600 per resident (ECU 375). Congestion costs are estimated at SF 100-300 million per year (ECU 65-190). Uncovered infrastructure and operational costs arise mainly from public transport and amount to almost SF 2 billion per year (ECU 1.3 billion).

Environmental costs of car traffic are to a large degree concentrated in urban areas. In the metropolitan region of Zurich, total environmental costs (tangible and less tangible) are estimated to be over SF 1 billion per year (ECU 630 million). Considering also the negative impacts on health and climate, the price of fuel would have to be raised by something like SF 2.5 per litre (ECU 1.6). Congestion costs in the urban area are estimated at over SF 100 million (ECU 63 million). The uncovered cost of infrastructure and operation of public transport exceeds SF 300 million (ECU 190 million). Thus, the environmental costs make up 70 per cent of the total costs, congestion costs 7 per cent and uncovered costs 23 per cent.

The Zurich study (Maibach *et al.*, 1992) illustrates how a differentiated strategy for the internalisation of external costs could be applied to individual drivers. The charges would be as follows: a carbon tax on fuel of SF 0.2/litre (ECU 0.12) to cover the costs of reforestation, a SF 200 (ECU 125) tax on new cars to cover the environmental costs of waste and a SF 1 000 (ECU 630) tax to comply with new regulations on noise. A further SF 0.1/km (ECU 0.06) would be required as a general environment/accident charge [or SF 0.14 (ECU 0.09) if the car does not have a catalytic converter] plus SF 0.03/km (ECU 0.02) as a congestion charge for peak-period journeys. To this should be added a daily parking charge of SF 8 (ECU 5.0).

Such an environmental tax would favour energy-saving vehicles and energy-conscientious drivers and would increase the use of public transport. This, in turn, would reduce the uncovered costs of public transport: the remaining deficit should be internalised at a later stage. Sweden has also been considering ways to internalise the external costs of travel and has introduced measures to implement the "polluter pays" principle (see Section 2, *Sweden,* in Annex 2 for more details).

In practice, there is an array of taxes on motoring in most countries, ranging from a purchase tax on new vehicles, an annual vehicle-licence fee (which might or might not vary with the type of vehicle), a tax on fuel and sometimes a tax on use (*e.g.,* tolls). All these affect the type of vehicle purchased, how much it is driven, the way it is driven, in which areas, and the use of other modes. Whereas, originally, some of these taxes were imposed mainly to raise revenue for road building and maintenance, they have since ceased to be hypothecated taxes in most countries and now contribute to general revenue. Recently, however, the idea of using taxation to reduce vehicle use, conserve energy and reduce CO_2 emissions has been at the forefront of political debate. The effects of taxation measures of this type are discussed in Section 8 of this chapter on "Measures to reduce fuel consumption and CO_2 emissions", though they have obvious uses as restraint measures.

Congestion pricing

The use of economic instruments in urban travel management was the subject of a conference held in Basle in June 1992 (Frey and Langloh, 1992) and one in Dusseldorf in June 1993 (OECD, 1993*b*), both organised by the OECD/ECMT project group. This section draws heavily from these two conferences, the Overviews and the Case Studies.

Fiscal restraint measures have been in use for decades in the form of *parking charges.* The only other long-standing fiscal restraint measure in use is in Singapore where drivers are charged on entry to the central area (Behbehani *et al.,* 1984). Charging vehicles to use congestedc streets on a per-km basis was successfully tested in Hong Kong, but not proceeded with for political reasons (Dawson and Catling, 1986).

Road pricing is, however, mentioned as a possibility in most of the National Overviews: in the Netherlands, for example, plans are being made for the introduction of electronic road pricing on certain congested sections of the road network at certain times and for fuel taxes to be raised. The Swiss are working on possible road pricing schemes for Berne and other cities, but it will be several years before they can be implemented. Another scheme, which uses a "smart" card to automatically impose a charge when the vehicle is stationary in a traffic queue within the controlled area, is being tested for the central area of Cambridge, UK (Oldridge, 1992). *Toll systems* in several cities in Norway have the potential for restraining traffic, but have not been used for this purpose so far, though the idea is being considered. Stockholm is planning to introduce road pricing, as part of the *Dennis Agreement*, using a toll ring surrounding the inner area. Reductions in city-centre traffic of about a third are expected (Section 5 of this chapter). The UK Department of Transport is carrying out research into the likely impacts of urban congestion charging in London (Larkinson, 1992).

In Singapore, where S$ 1 billion (ECU 0.55 billion) has already been spent on new or improved roads and a further S$ 1.5 billion (ECU 0.8 billion) is committed over the next five years, the Government is to introduce electronic congestion pricing by 1997 (Teik, 1993). The new restraint mechanisms will regulate traffic on the network, reducing it where necessary, but traffic levels over the city as a whole are unlikely to be reduced significantly, especially with such a large increase in the road network.

Road pricing is being widely discussed in the United States, where metropolitan planning organisations are authorised to incorporate congestion-pricing pilot programmes in their plans under the air quality provisions of the Intermodal Surface Transportation Efficiency Improvement Act, 1991 (ISTEA). The US Department of Transportation has allocated $ 25 million (ECU 20) a year for the six years up to 1997 to support congestion-pricing pilot projects in polluted metropolitan areas. The Federal Government will pay 80 per cent of the cost of agreed projects (US DOT, 1992*b*).

The increasing use of road tolls in general could establish a tradition of paying for the use of roads, which might facilitate the introduction of urban road charging, leading eventually to a fully-integrated road user charging system affecting all car journeys.

Other restraint mechanisms

Limiting the parking supply (usually in conjunction with raising the cost) has been one of the most common methods of restraint in almost all cities. While this method has been accepted by both public and politicians alike in many countries, it wastes resources through queuing or searching for a space. Using the price mechanism to ration scarce parking facilities, as explained in Chapter 4, is more efficient. Limiting parking supply to company employees, however, is a different matter: this can be a very effective way of influencing the modal split.

In Zurich, car movements have been restricted by *redistributing road space* in favour of public transport and pedestrians, as mentioned earlier. The effect has been strengthened by allocating more time at traffic signals to pedestrians and public transport also. Segregated tram tracks, bus lanes and bus priority at traffic signals, combined with a reduction in parking supply, have resulted in the number of trips by private car (as a proportion of all trips) falling to about half the level of most other cities in Western Europe. Despite this, the economic viability of Zurich has not suffered, though jobs are still decentralising to the fringe area (but this is happening in almost all cities). It is noteworthy that this result was merely a by-product of measures taken, as a result of a referendum, to support improvements to public transport.

In Italy, *reducing air pollution* is the driving force for traffic restraint in the major metropolitan areas. Two thresholds have been fixed for the presence of CO, SO_2, NO_x and ozone and when the lower one of these is reached, the municipal authorities are required by law to reduce the amount of traffic until the level of pollution falls below this limit. If the upper limit is reached, no traffic is allowed to enter the area until emission levels have fallen below the upper limit. The scheme has been tried in Milan, where so far, it has been necessary to impose only "alternate day" working, which has reduced traffic by 20 per cent and kept pollution below the upper reference point. If the scheme is successful, it will be extended to the whole country (Milan Case Study, summarised in Annex 3). Even though "alternate day" working has operated satisfactorily in these trials, it is regarded as an emergency measure only, since some drivers would find ways round the prohibition, if it were to become permanent. Other methods will be tested. In 1991, new legislation allowed Gothenburg to restrict all motor traffic when air quality standards were not met.

In 1985, vehicle access to Milan's historic centre was restricted to halve the number of vehicles entering daily: public transport was improved to enable residents and others to circulate freely and new off-street car parks built in other parts of the city centre to allow streets and public places to be freed of parked cars, many of them parked illegally (Tessitore, 1993). Rome has also imposed restraints on entry to its central area. Restricting vehicle access to particular areas has also been tried in Japan, using the technique of voluntary no car days, but without much success. In Seoul, car use at certain times has been limited to alternate days, as was tried in Milan (more details in Case Study summaries in Annex 3). In Munich, BMW has suggested that access to an area about four times the size of the present city centre should be severely restricted under the "Blue Zone" plan. BMW propose that a new ring road surrounding the area be equipped with ten automated car parks, each one connected by free bus to the main public transport network and the principle urban facilities using low-polluting buses (Janssen, 1993).

In the financial centre of London, entry restrictions have recently been placed on all vehicles, except buses, taxis and those with special permits, following a spate of terrorist bombings. What politicians had previously thought was impossible, has become a reality as a result of a disaster. Traffic now flows freely and air quality has improved, with no obvious adverse effects, either within or just outside, the affected area.

In the United States, where reducing vehicle-km travelled has generally been felt to be detrimental to the economy, measures to reduce travel in cities through Transport Demand Management are now being implemented in many areas. Under the 1991 transport efficiency act (ISTEA), all metropolitan planning organisations are obliged to file, "Congestion Mitigation and Air Quality Improvement Programs" whenever Federal air quality standards are not attained. In some air quality non-attainment areas, employer trip reduction programmes are required under the Clean Air Amendments of 1990 (US DOT, 1992b and 1992c). More details of the acts are given in Section 7 of this chapter and Annex 2. The Southern California Air Quality Management Board is pledged to reduce region-wide (not just CBD) commuter vehicle-km travelled (VKT) by an amount sufficient to bring air quality within acceptable limits. Commuter travel will still be predominantly by car, however, and since work journeys form only about a third of all travel, the impact on total car travel will not be dramatic, though specific areas at certain times of the day will experience significant reductions.

The Dutch government plans to reverse the trend to longer travel distances between home and work and reduce unnecessary car traffic in cities by constraints on parking supply, by pricing means and by making certain sectors of the city less accessible by car. It is even proposed to limit the amount of car parking space available on company premises in outlying areas if suitable public transport facilities are available. Sites near motorway junctions will be reserved for production, transport and distribution companies in accordance with the "Right Business in the Right Place" policy.

4. Making more efficient use of the road system

Car sharing and car pooling

The average occupancy of cars is less than 1.5 in most cities. An obvious way to improve the carrying capacity of the road system is to increase this through car sharing (giving lifts to other car drivers) and car pooling (taking it in turns to drive with other drivers as passengers).

There have been many experiments in car sharing and car pooling over the last few decades, but mostly without a great deal of success. In general, the extra trouble of picking up and setting down passengers and keeping to agreed times of travel tend to outweigh the monetary benefits of sharing, though a car left at home for other members of the family to use may be a sufficient incentive for some people (though this arrangement will not necessarily reduce energy consumption and vehicle emissions). Much more success has been obtained in the United States where commuting distances are relatively great and concessions of one sort or another can provide the necessary incentives. These often take the form of special lanes for the use of car poolers at toll booths and on motorways and the offer of special car park spaces much closer to the work place than are available to non-car-poolers.

In Australia, car pooling has had a generally poor success rate, but where high-occupancy vehicles have been allowed access to priority lanes on motorways and given special car parking spaces, car pooling has become more popular. As a result, the total length of motorway lanes which give priority to high-occupancy vehicles is increasing.

One effect of supplementary licenses in Singapore was to increase the level of car pooling – including the giving of lifts to bus passengers. As a percentage of all car journeys to the CBD between 7.30 a.m. and 10.15 a.m., car pooling levels were (OECD, 1988*b*):

Before supplementary licensing (1975)	23 per cent
Immediately afterwards (1975)	40 per cent
Some time afterwards (1980)	50 per cent

Pooling has subsequently declined for a number of reasons: the bus service has been improved; CBD employment has increased; downtown parking charges have been raised; and in 1989/90, the Mass Rapid Transit system was commissioned.

Car pooling and car sharing are the essential elements of Transport Demand Management used in Southern California to attain the required environmental standards in particular areas. Legislation obliges employers to file plans showing how they propose to increase commuter car occupancy levels. These in turn lead to company-based measures to promote car pooling. Whether cities include employer-organised car pooling in such programmes depends on a comparative assessment of such measures with the available alternatives.

116

It seems that where employers are given responsibility for organising car pooling; where there are clear-cut goals for them to aim at; and where there are penalties for failing to increase commuting car occupancy rates, car pooling does happen. In the UK, at least one county (Avon), in its Transportation Plan for the next 20 years, is aiming to put more responsibility on employers for more environmentally-sound travel.

Road transport telematics

Large research budgets have been committed to applying information technology to road transport in Japan, the United States and the EU. Over the coming ten years the output from these programmes will upgrade the quality of information available to travellers and traffic managers and give rise to intelligent highway vehicle systems.

Traffic management will benefit from integrated systems incorporating real-time, adaptive computer programmes that will optimise traffic-signal timings and give buses priority, making use of information from incident and congestion detector systems. These new techniques will extend tried-and-tested computer-adaptive systems, such as SCOOT (developed at the UK Transport Research Laboratory). The technique, used to manage and control the transport system, will be to determine theoretically the best strategy to implement at any particular time, by modelling the effects of different strategies prior to implementation. It has been estimated that traffic management measures, which remove much of the "stop-go" from urban driving, coupled with congestion pricing, could reduce NO_x emissions from trucks by up to 70 per cent (ACEA, 1993), quite apart from any savings in fuel consumption. Telematics also has an important role to play in public transport operation. The application of techniques of this type in Zurich has already brought about significant improvements to public transport speed, reliability and service quality in general.

Information is also at the heart of route planning. Accurate, timely and widely-disseminated information will enable travellers to make well-informed choices about their particular journeys. This information can be used for pre-trip planning through the use of view-data systems and computer terminals in the home, the work place and in public places. In-trip information will be available through variable-message signs, special radio message channels and other systems aboard buses, trains and ferries.

At full deployment (perhaps 30 years hence), all the sub-systems will be integrated and able to complement each other. Such systems will give travellers knowledge of conditions ahead before they set out, enable them to switch modes en route, allocate priority to vehicles deemed to justify it, and reduce collisions – first by warning drivers of hazards and, perhaps later, by taking over control. These technologies promise to make important contributions to reducing congestion, emissions and casualties.

5. Investment in roads and parking

Most cities have invested in new roads and off-street parking space, but many are having difficulty in deciding how much investment they need to make to attract industry, services, educational and cultural institutions, without serious effects on public transport and the environment. No satisfactory measure has been devised to indicate at what point further investment becomes counter-productive.

Increasing the overall capacity of the road network and/or parking facilities (by building new car parks or by reducing parking duration) will inevitably lead to higher levels of traffic, unless offset by reductions in capacity elsewhere. New links which bypass sensitive areas, however, can be of local environmental benefit, especially if they are in tunnels. In Oslo, for example, a new tunnel under the city centre removes 70 000 vehicles a day from the city streets and has allowed a new park to be created. This and other road projects are being financed by tolls collected at points surrounding the city, using an electronic toll-collecting system. Drivers have the option of purchasing period tickets, which allow an unlimited number of journeys within the controlled area. While the scheme could in principle be used to reduce city-centre traffic, the primary objective at the moment in Oslo, Bergen and Trondheim is simply to raise revenue for new road construction.

The toll ring in Trondheim differs from that in Oslo, because it discriminates by time of day, amongst other things. There are no period tickets, but 85 per cent of the drivers use electronic tags. Drivers have to pay the toll only between 6 a.m. and 5 p.m. on weekdays, but for drivers with peak-period (6 a.m. to 10 a.m.) electronic tags, the charge is higher. So far, there has been no loss in sales for businesses in the inner city. An evaluative report on the first two years of the toll ring, including statistics from detailed surveys on travel behaviour, will be published in 1994.

In Sweden, the *Dennis Agreement* of 1992 provided for the most comprehensive transport package ever contemplated for the Stockholm region. In its original version it involved a financial commitment of SKr 36 billion (ECU 3.8 billion) over a 15 year period, divided roughly equally between roads and public transport. The objectives of the road proposals were to improve access generally, while reducing car traffic in the inner area of Stockholm. A ring road round the inner area (mostly in tunnel) and an outer cross-link will steer traffic away from sensitive areas. The tolls collected will be used to finance the construction loans. Impact studies made after the agreement suggests that by 2005 there will be a slight reduction in overall traffic growth of 5-10 per cent compared to a situation where the package is not launched (the actual growth will be 15-30 per cent). The greatest benefits will arise in the inner areas of Stockholm, where traffic will be down by 25 per cent. This effect is largely due to the tolls. Air pollutants will be down by about 50 per cent, largely due to cleaner engines, while CO_2 emissions will remain about the same. This example illustrates the combined effect of road building and congestion pricing. More details of these schemes are given in the Stockholm Case Study report (summarised in Annex 3) and in Malmsten (1993).

In Istanbul, new orbital roads are being built to divert through traffic from the centre and new multi-storey car parks are being provided for vehicles with destinations in the centre. New off-street parking facilities in both Milan and Hiroshima are part of the package of measures designed to improve traffic flow and enhance the urban environment by removing parked vehicles from the streets (see Case Study summaries in Annex 3).

6. Urban freight distribution

Urban residents and the business community tend to have strong and opposing views on goods distribution. According to a study by the Federal German Office for the Environment, residents reject trucks in cities and see "an increasing acute conflict ... between road freight traffic and quality of life", while businessmen see no alternative to moving goods by road. The attitudes of residents are also in conflict with those of their elected authorities who have a strong interest in attracting new businesses on account of their promise of jobs and tax revenue.

This German study underlines the need to reduce the environmental impacts of trucks and identifies the following measures:

- reduce gas and noise emissions at source;
- build bypasses;
- locate goods traffic centres in industrial areas;
- promote combined road/rail transport;
- tighten exhaust gas tests; and
- expand the use of pipelines.

Restrictions on heavy goods vehicles are being imposed by an increasing number of cities, in some cases for the whole day, while in others for just certain hours of the day. From 1992, it has been possible for communities in Sweden to restrict heavy vehicles (buses and trucks) from entering their inner areas: restrictions are based on an environmental index, which requires all heavy vehicles in Sweden to be registered in three environmental classes from July 1994. In the UK, there is a London-wide night and weekend heavy lorry ban, which, apart from those exempted because of an acknowledged need to deliver or collect at those times, bans all lorries over 16.5 tonnes. In Poland, restrictions apply to selected residential and other sensitive areas. The Netherlands plan to reduce goods vehicle movements in city centres by 50 per cent through the use of freight distribution centres located close to good transport connections. New distribution techniques are being tried too: in Bremen, trucks are allowed to use certain bus lanes and, at a pilot depot, the trans-shipment and concentration of loads has cut goods traffic by 60 per cent. At Bad Reichenhall, there has been a switch to quieter lorries following a ban on access by noisy ones.

Over the years, rail has been losing out to road in the movement of goods, but there have been determined efforts from time to time to try to redress the balance, in order to reduce the harmful effects of long-distance road goods traffic and to free towns of transit traffic. Some progress, for instance, has been made with transferring goods to rail in Germany and Switzerland. Volkswagen receives some just-in-time deliveries by rail and Migros, the largest Swiss retail chain, has located its warehouses on railways and distributes 56 per cent of its consignments by rail. Switching from road to rail and barge in the main, however, has not been realised (see Figure 2.10). Such modes are, it seems, better suited to coal and other minerals than to fragile, low-weight, high-value consumer goods. These goods require fast, flexible, short-distance transport, for which road haulage is ideally suited. It is also relatively cheap, so there has been little incentive for industry to choose rail.

A Swiss study suggests that combined road/rail transport can be competitive even if the rail leg of the journey is as little as 80 km, and logistical systems of chains of transport are currently being studied. Two thirds of goods movements in the EU, however, are over distances of less than 50 km. In Europe, there is considerable interest in distribution by pipeline and in using spare capacity in the NATO network.

7.   Environmental standards and targets

The problems of noise and pollution were discussed in Chapter 3. To combat these problems, most countries have set targets for the reduction of noise levels and noxious emissions. These targets can be achieved through less vehicle usage or by reducing emissions at source. In practice, there has been a mixture of the two, though most of the success in this area, so far, has tended to come from technology improvements to vehicles. Even those countries which have not set targets will have experienced changes in noise and pollution levels as a result of technology improvements, which may well have been initiated through other countries' actions.

Many of the standards and targets adopted by individual countries have been prescribed by the United States and international organisations, such as the EU, and it is in areas like noise and pollution where international pressure and agreement can be most effective. EU regulations have specified limits on noise and exhaust emissions since the late 1960s. Over the years these have become stricter, though consistently lagging behind US standards. There is scope for tighter controls still, but it is important also that vehicles continue to meet the requirements after they have been in service for a long time. Badly maintained vehicles are responsible for a proportionately greater share of noise and exhaust emissions.

Reducing noise levels at source

Over the past decade the amount of noise that European vehicles may emit at low speed (mainly from the engine and exhaust) has been progressively reduced as a result of stricter EU regulations. Vehicle noise will be further reduced as a result of a new EU directive, which will come into force in 1995. Even though the permissible level of sound energy emission is now only about one-tenth of what was permitted in the 1970s, the vehicles are still perceived as being about half as noisy as previously. Moreover, there are now more of them.

One of the biggest changes, which has taken place recently, is in the speed and acceleration of vehicles and in the way they are driven: all these tend to increase noise levels, even if the engines are inherently quieter. At higher speeds most of the noise comes from the tyres on the road surface and there is a limit to the reductions possible from this cause, because quieter surfaces tend to be associated with lower skid resistance. Research is being undertaken into quieter road surfaces with satisfactory skid resistance.

As far as motor cycles and scooters are concerned, noise limits have applied in many countries since 1970, with stricter limits since 1987 following an EU directive, but much more could be done to reduce noise to tolerable levels. With heavy vehicles, engine noise still predominates throughout most of the speed range in urban areas, but attempts are being made to reduce noise levels from heavy goods vehicles in a number of countries. The "Quiet Heavy Vehicle" research programme in the UK has demonstrated that a limit of 80 dB(A) for the heaviest vehicles is feasible. Prototype vehicles developed during the programme were up to 5 dB(A) below the current legal limit of 84 dB(A). Tyre noise begins to become dominant at constant speeds of over 50 km/h.

From 1995 light vehicles in Norway will be subject to a 75 dB(A) noise limit and heavy vehicles to a 80 dB(A) limit, if standards now under consideration are adopted. This would be expected to reduce noise disturbance by 40-50 per cent by the early part of the next century. In general, the task of reducing noise levels in most countries is being left largely to the motor manufacturers, who are under pressure from governments working to EU, US or other directives.

Reducing vehicle emissions at source

The United States, as the most car-oriented society in the world, has done more than most countries to clean up vehicle emissions, so that their standards are now adopted by many other countries. Emissions of CO and hydrocarbons from the average car in the United States have fallen by about 70 per cent since 1970, NO_x by about 30 per cent and lead has practically disappeared altogether. Nevertheless, a large number of urban areas in the USA still fail to meet the national ambient air quality standards (NAAQS). The Clean Air Amendments (1990) to the Clean Air Act of 1970 are setting even more stringent emission standards for cars and light goods vehicles to be produced between 1996 and 2003. Japan also has had strict emission standards for well over a decade. In Europe, the situation is not as well advanced. As from the beginning of 1993, catalytic converters have been obligatory on all new petrol-driven cars sold in the EU and more stringent standards will be introduced in 1995. They are expected to reduce emissions of CO, HCs and NO_x from such vehicles by about 75 per cent. The improvement will be gradual, however, because vehicles which are not fitted with catalytic converters will be on the roads for many years to come. Not until most of the vehicles have cleaner engines, will the atmosphere be noticeably different and even then the result will depend on how well vehicles already in service are maintained. In the USA, for example, the cleanest 50 per cent of cars produce only 3 per cent of HCs, while the dirtiest 6 per cent produce 50 per cent of HCs. In Finland, emissions from older cars, not fitted with catalytic converters, will be reduced through changes in fuel quality.

By the year 2005, most of the present vehicle fleet will have been replaced and pollution levels should be reaching a minimum. In 30 to 40 years time, however, unless more stringent standards are applied, traffic growth could have largely eroded the benefits. By then, NO_x emissions from road traffic will be predominantly from heavy goods vehicles.

Most countries now have a differential price for leaded and non-leaded petrol: for example, in Norway it is NKr 0.53/litre (ECU 0.063) and in Finland Mk 0.45 (ECU 0.072). Since leaded petrol cannot be used in vehicles which are fitted with catalytic converters, and these are becoming obligatory in more and more countries, the use of leaded petrol is diminishing, and lead in the atmosphere is ceasing to be a problem in many countries. Under Australian regulations, effective from 1986, all new petrol-fuelled vehicles are required to run on unleaded petrol and Diesel engines are subject to exhaust smoke limits. There have been some trials of buses running on compressed natural gas (CNG) and liquefied petroleum gas (LPG). Already 90 per cent of taxis in Australia have the capability to run on LPG, which, like CNG, is tax free. In the Netherlands, 11 per cent of passenger cars in 1991 were equipped to run on LPG.

The motor industry is presently addressing the problems of cold starts (which are responsible for 50 per cent of vehicle emissions), the wider use of alternative clean fuels and ways of increasing the efficiency of combustion. The major pollutants are NO_x and particulates, but the three technologies best suited to reducing NO_x emissions all increase fuel consumption and have varying effects on particulates, as Table 6.7 indicates. The industry's view is that the key to reduced emissions is wide availability of high-quality/reformulated (very low sulphur) Diesel fuel; natural-gas-fuelled urban buses, municipal vehicles and delivery vans; and on-board diagnostic systems to ensure good lifetime environmental performance.

The EU 1995 standard for heavy Diesel vehicles will be introduced soon to reduce particulate emissions. New Diesel oil with low sulphur content is being introduced in Denmark and will be exempted from a new Diesel tax to encourage its use. Experiments are taking place with LPG and CNG and particle traps for city buses. Implementation of US 94 standards for heavy vehicles during the 1990s should halve noxious emissions and reduce particulates by even more.

It is widely agreed that vehicle exhaust emission control systems tend to deteriorate with age. Catalysts are sometime poisoned with leaded fuel: fuel/air mixing controls become maladjusted, and so on. The US and Swedish governments have responded to this problem by making car manufacturers responsible for the long-term performance of catalytic converters. The Swedish law makes manufacturers and importers liable for five years or 80 000 km – whichever comes first.

Table 6.7. **Interaction of emission control technologies and fuel consumption**

Percentages

	Fuel consumption[a]	NO_x	Particulates
Exhaust gas recirculation (EGR)	+1 to 2	–20	+15
EGR plus particulate filter	+6	–15	–70
Lean NO_x catalyst	+10	–40	..

a) A surrogate for CO_2 emissions.
Source: ACEA, 1993.

In 1992, the Swedish Motor Vehicle Inspection Company (Svenska Bilprovning) conducted tests before and after maintenance on 141 vehicles with mileages ranging from 30 000 to 50 000 km. While maintenance reduced the number of vehicles not complying with Swedish emission standards, 41 per cent still failed the test. The Swedish Environment Protection Agency required one car manufacturing company to replace catalysts and another to add insulation to exhaust pipes. Switzerland has adopted a different approach. It makes owners responsible for the performance of their vehicles, regardless of vehicle age, and enforces the law via an annual vehicle test.

The Swiss approach is designed to make owners keep their vehicles in a good state of repair, whereas the US and Swedish approach, by putting responsibility on car makers, encourages them to equip their vehicles with lasting emission-control systems (EFTE, 1993). Whatever method is used, regular emission checks are essential, with roadside sensors to detect high emitters and possibly random roadside checks as well.

Noise and pollution standards for cities and districts

The Australian Design Rule System (ADRS) makes it legally binding on states to ensure that air quality and noise levels meet the required standards. The Swiss government, too, has set precise targets for reducing the levels of local and overall air pollution, and it has instructed cantonal governments to outline related action plans. In the European Union, regulations are applied at the planning stage of new roads and building developments to ensure that levels of air pollution and traffic noise will be kept within acceptable limits.

In the United States, the Intermodal Surface Transportation Efficiency Act of 1991 (ISTEA) and the Clean Air Act Amendments of 1990 (CAAA) are innovative and aggressive efforts to move US cities toward integrated transportation and air quality planning. Under these two complementary laws, healthy air takes its place as a major national transportation goal. And in urban areas with serious air pollution, air quality will be a major consideration in determining the future shape of urban transportation. The CAAA and the ISTEA are complex national laws that deal with a broad range of aspects of transportation and air quality. It is in combination that the two laws provide an innovative national policy approach of potential interest to governments seeking to encourage sustainable development in urban centres. The CAAA mandates measurable and enforceable targets of healthy air for every city in the country. Among other requirements, nation-wide standards are set for acceptable levels of carbon monoxide, ground level ozone and small particulates. The regulations also require "higher oxygen" fuel to be on sale in cities with the most severe ozone problems and to be generally available in other areas to reduce winter CO pollution. The ISTEA provides directions that transportation planners and decision-makers must follow to reach the required air quality standards – transportation planning must emphasise maximum efficiency of the regional system, and for cities with severe air pollution, transportation must make measurable contributions to clean air. Each urban area has flexibility in how it applies this framework to reflect its priorities and solve its own problems. Strict federal sanctions provide incentives for compliance with both laws.

Newcastle in the UK has adopted air pollution standards which have helped to determine the local planning and transport strategy. Certain parts of cities in Japan are being designated as "low pollution" areas to encourage the use of electric and low-emission cars. The proportion of cars which do not satisfy the new standards for the area concerned will be progressively reduced as low-polluting vehicles become more common. In Italy, since 1992, only petrol containing 0.1 per cent sulphur, 2.5 per cent benzene and 33 per cent aromatic products has been permitted in the major metropolitan areas.

Under certain circumstances, city councils in Germany since 1992 have had to prepare noise reduction plans. The Lander commission has defined noise quality standards for residential areas of 59 dB(A) in daytime and 49 dB(A) at night and these are expected to be attained over the longer term.

8. Measures to reduce fuel consumption and CO_2 emissions

Past trends

Energy consumption in transport has been increasing at 3.8 per cent p.a. in the European Union over the past 20 years (Section 8 of Chapter 3), with consequential increases in the production of CO_2 and other emissions.

Fuel consumption per person for passenger transport in 1987 in four EU countries is given in Table 6.8, where it can be seen that Germany had the highest fuel consumption per person on transport and Italy the lowest. Between 1970 and 1989 fuel consumption rose by only 32 per cent in Italy, by 53 per cent in France, by 67 per cent in Germany, but by 77 per cent in the UK (Taschner, 1992). The differences are partly due to changes in car ownership and partly due to changes in fuel efficiency of the vehicle stock.

Table 6.8. **Energy consumption in passenger transport in four EU countries, 1987**

	West Germany	France	Italy	UK
Energy per person on car travel (GJ/person)	19.9	14.7	11.4	16.6
Energy per passenger-km (MJ/km)	2.31	1.53	1.47	1.90
% passenger-km by car in:				
1970	78	80	75	76
1987	83	82	78	86

Source: Taschner, 1992.

The role of different taxation policies

Fuel consumption and CO_2 emissions can be lowered by:
- reducing the number of vehicle-kilometres-travelled (VKT);
- increasing the fuel-efficiency of vehicles; and
- encouraging drivers to trade down to smaller and less powerful cars and to drive in a more fuel-efficient manner (less severe braking and acceleration and lower speeds on free-flowing roads).

Although different countries have imposed different levels of taxation on fuel for a variety of purposes (see Taschner, 1992), it is only recently that consideration has been given to increasing fuel tax specifically to reduce energy consumption and CO_2 emissions.

The implementation of a carbon tax on fuel is likely to change the vehicle stock over the longer term, as well as encouraging manufacturers to produce more energy-efficient and less-polluting vehicles. The magnitude of the effect would depend on the level of carbon tax chosen, but differential car purchase taxes and annual licence fees for different types and sizes of vehicles would also have significant effects on the type of vehicle acquired.

Italy, with the highest fuel taxes and petrol prices in the EU (Figure 6.1), and double the level of VAT on the purchase of large cars compared with small cars (38 per cent as opposed to 19 per cent), has the most fuel-efficient stock of cars in the EU (8.4 litres of petrol per 100 km): 37 per cent of Italian cars have engines of less than 1 litre capacity, compared with 12 per cent in the UK and 7 per cent in Germany (Taschner, 1992). In France too, high fuel taxes, coupled with the highest annual car tax in the EU (which is itself related to engine power), have encouraged people to buy cars which are economical to use (fuel consumption of 8.8 litres/100 km – in 1987). The total amount of tax paid annually (fuel tax plus license fee) in running a high-powered car in France is 2.5 to 3 times the amount paid in Germany or the UK (Taschner, 1992). In Luxembourg, Belgium, the UK and Germany, fuel is relatively cheap and consumption is high (ranging from 9.6 litres/100 km in Luxembourg to 11.1 litres/100 km in Germany). In the UK, where company cars make up over 50 per cent of new cars, there has been a tendency for engine size to increase over the years, thus offsetting some of the gains in engine efficiency.

Fuel price also affects how much each car is used. For example, annual car-km in the United States, with the cheapest fuel, is over 17 000, whereas in Germany, the Netherlands, and France, with dearer fuel, it is about 13 000, and in Italy, with the most expensive fuel, it is only 10 000 km/year on average (OECD, 1993a). There are exceptions to this simple relationship, however: in Japan, the annual car kilometrage is only 10 000, despite relatively cheap fuel – probably a result of the very high use of rail travel. In Sweden, on the other hand, annual kilometrage is over 16 000, even though fuel is very expensive – possibly a result of a sparse and spread-out population and a high ownership of second homes.

Figure 6.1. **Comparison of fuel prices,** 1990

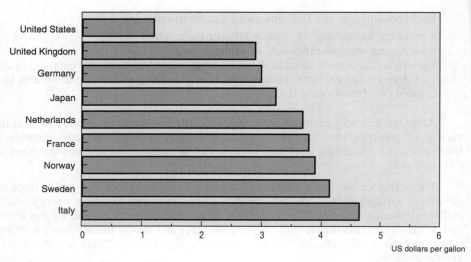

Source: Mackenzie et al., 1992.

The total amount of fuel used per car (specific fuel consumption multiplied by the average annual kilometrage) shows a similar falling trend with increasing fuel price. For example, in 1988 the average car in the UK, with fairly cheap fuel, consumed about 1 750 litres of fuel, in Germany about 1 400 litres, in the Netherlands and France (with dearer fuel) about 1 200 litres, and in Italy (with the dearest fuel) only about 850 litres (figures from Taschner, 1992 and OECD, 1993a). Once again, there are exceptions (Japan and Sweden, for instance).

These figures illustrate the important role of fuel tax and differential license fees on vehicle efficiency, but show how people's behaviour, through the choices they make, affect the amount of travel undertaken and hence the amount of fuel used. Despite the anomalies, there is a fairly clear relationship between fuel price and the amount used.

Unlike most countries, Denmark has taken steps to limit car ownership by imposing a tax on new cars of over 150 per cent of the manufacturer's price. Not surprisingly, car ownership at 310 cars/1 000 inhabitants is lower than that in other European countries with a similar standard of living. Severe measures are also being taken in Seoul to reduce car ownership growth: a high tax on households with two or more cars and a ban on households owning a car if they have nowhere to garage it (Seoul Case Study summarised in Annex 3).

Potential for improvement in the fuel efficiency of vehicles

In most countries there is a vast range in the energy efficiency of vehicles in the current stock of vehicles (quite apart from engine size). In Denmark, for example, it is estimated that, for the same engine size, some vehicles could be consuming between 50 and 100 per cent more fuel than others. Thus, a feasible upgrading of the present Danish car stock towards greater energy efficiency could readily lead to a 14 per cent reduction in fuel used. This is apart from any trading down from larger, more powerful, vehicles to smaller vehicles. Higher fuel prices would encourage owners to improve their vehicles.

Drivers themselves could save fuel and reduce vehicle emissions by driving more slowly and less erratically and avoiding heavy acceleration and braking. Driver information and training could, in principle, reduce car fuel consumption by 10 per cent or more with little increase in journey times. High fuel prices would help to make this happen. For commercial vehicle drivers, training and company rules could make fuel savings a more realistic objective. Combined with devices like speed limiters and gear change indicators, the savings could be as high as 10 to 15 per cent on the heaviest lorries (Waters, 1990). A greater use of Diesel-engined cars and light vans has the potential to reduce fuel consumption by 10 per cent or more, but this would lead to an increase in emissions of NO_x, SO_x and particulates. Down-sizing to smaller, less powerful cars has a much greater potential. The more fuel-efficient of the current small cars consume about 25 per cent less fuel than the new car fleet average. Fuel savings will eventually come from improvements to engine design which increase engine efficiency during the warming-up period and from advanced automatic gearboxes, which can be programmed for economical driving. Here again, appropriate pricing policies are necessary to encourage the development and adoption of new technology. For heavy goods vehicles, reducing aerodynamic drag would save fuel provided running speeds did not increase. The use of cruise control devices, gear change indicators and speed limiters would help drivers to save fuel.

Alternative fuels and electric vehicles have the potential for reducing energy consumption and CO_2 emissions. Fuels with lower CO_2/heat output (like compressed natural gas) may be a way forward to reduce CO_2 emissions, but there are difficulties in using them without cost and weight penalties. In the case of methanol, the advantage in CO_2 emissions from the vehicle is only about 7 per cent compared with petroleum, though the fuel has some attractions for efficient engine design. The total CO_2 emissions for the whole process needs to be taken into account to establish whether there is any net advantage. In the very long term, hydrogen may be the solution, as it contains no carbon. It could be burnt as a gas and stored in hydrides in the vehicle or used to produce electricity directly in a fuel cell. The production of hydrogen, without the use of fossil fuel, requires a breakthrough in photo-electric cells or the acceptance of large-scale nuclear power.

Present battery electric road vehicles are still some way from commercial viability, but may find some limited application, especially in urban areas. They would benefit from a fairly small improvement in battery performance. They do not seem likely to reduce CO_2 emissions in total when compared with Diesel vehicles, even when the electricity is generated from the right mix of fuel (for example, natural gas or 50 per cent nuclear or renewable resources). Electric vehicles do not solve any of the other problems of urban mechanised transport, such as congestion, accidents and severance.

Likely improvements in fuel efficiency

The specific fuel consumption of the stock of private cars in the EU is expected to improve from 9.3 litres/100 km at present to 7.8 litres/100 km in 2010 (EU Green Paper, 1992), but Waters (1990) suggests that, with present emission limits (which incur a fuel penalty), fuel economy improvements for private cars will be less than 15 per cent by 2010 and fuel economy of goods vehicles will remain static or, at best, improve only slightly. This is partly because improvements in engine efficiency are not always matched by reductions in overall fuel consumption of the car fleet. Car owners tend to take advantage of any improvement in fuel consumption to purchase larger and more powerful vehicles. This was particularly marked during the 1980s, when the cost of fuel was actually falling in real terms. In the UK, for example, fuel consumption of the average vehicle rose during this period, after having decreased sharply between 1979 and 1982, as a result of world-wide fuel crises.

In Australia, voluntary targets for fuel efficiency have been set, but those for 1983 and 1987 were not achieved. The 1990 new car fleet, with a fuel consumption of 8.9 litre/100 km, has now passed the 1983 target, but not yet the 1987 target.

The Danish Action Plan predicts that fuel consumption of all road vehicles (except Diesel-driven cars), passenger trains and aircraft will be reduced by 15 per cent for each of the periods 1988-2010 and 2010-2030. The corresponding figure for Diesel-driven cars, freight trains, ferries and cargo ships is 10 per cent. With the necessary incentives in place, it is believed that the efficiency improvements in cars could be 25 per cent over the next 15 years, instead of 10-15 per cent, but this situation is only likely to come about if there is sufficient international pressure to promote technological development, through, for example, the EU. The Danish overview supports the introduction of compulsory standards for energy efficiency of new cars, the imposition of vehicle taxes to encourage the purchase of more economical cars and the harmonisation of fuel taxes at a high level.

Fuel price elasticities

Many studies have been carried out over the years on the effect of fuel price changes on car-km travelled. These are summarised in Goodwin (1992). Short-term elasticities of car-km with respect to fuel price changes range from –0.1 to –0.3, *i.e.* if fuel price rises by 10 per cent, car-km will be reduced by between 1 and 3 per cent over the short term. In the longer term, people choose different travel destinations to reflect the increase in price, and over a much longer period (10 or 20 years), people take fuel prices into account when deciding where to live and where to work. Long-term elasticities with respect to fuel cost per km of travel should therefore be much greater than short-term elasticities, and values given by Goodwin (1992) suggest a range from –0.3 to –0.5. However, most studies are not able to measure these effects properly, so the true values may well be greater. It should be noted that, as a result of sustained high fuel prices, the fuel economy of vehicles is likely to improve through technology changes and drivers are likely to trade down to smaller, less powerful cars and drive in a more fuel-efficient manner. This would lower the fuel cost per km and it is to this value, and not to the fuel price per litre, that the elasticity relates.

In a study using a theoretical model to represent a town and its transport system, Bland (1984) estimated the effect of increased fuel prices on car trip making and car trip lengths. The changes in car travel took into account the long-term changes in where people live and work as a result of the fuel price increases and any changes in public transport service which resulted from increased patronage levels. The model was calibrated to reproduce observed travel behaviour as accurately as possible. The modelling predicted a long-term elasticity of car use (car-km), with respect to fuel cost per km, of about –0.5, comprising –0.3 due to changes in car trip lengths and –0.2 due to changes in car ownership, with a negligible contribution from changes in the number of journeys by car.

Bland also calculated how the elasticity would change if fuel price rose steeply. At twice the fuel cost per km, the elasticity would increase from –0.5 to –0.9, because fuel cost would become a far greater proportion of the generalised cost of travel (money plus time costs combined). At four times present fuel prices (*per km*) the elasticity would rise to –1.5, a third of which would represent changes in car trip making (due largely to changes in car availability), and two thirds to shorter trips. These results cover a much wider range of situations than those from which other elasticity measurements have been obtained, but where the situations are similar, the results are compatible.

Introduction of a carbon tax

In Sweden, a CO_2 tax on fuel was introduced in 1991. At present it amounts to SKr 0.74 per litre (ECU 0.08) of petrol and SKr 0.92 per litre (ECU 0.1) of Diesel oil. The fuel price in Sweden was already one of the highest in Europe (see Figure 6.1). In Norway, a carbon tax was applied in 1991 to the sale of petrol and Diesel fuel [NKr 0.8 per litre (ECU 0.1) for petrol and NKr 0.7 per litre (ECU 0.08) for Diesel]. In 1993, this CO_2 tax was applied to liquefied petroleum gas (LPG) and compressed natural gas (CNG). The Norwegian authorities estimate that to stabilise national emissions by the year 2000, the carbon tax would have to be increased by a further NKr 2.5 (ECU 0.30) per litre and to be applied to all fossil fuels according to their content of carbon. This would reduce the expected *growth* in car traffic by the year 2025 from 85 per cent to 60 per cent, but there would be little change in public transport patronage as a result. There would, however, be some improvement in vehicle efficiency mainly as a result of the change in vehicle stock.

A recent study by Virley (1993), using a time series model of road transport fuel consumption, estimated that CO_2 emissions from road transport in the UK could be returned to the 1990 level by the year 2000 (the government's commitment following the Rio Convention), if the real price of fuel were to be raised to 90 per cent above the 1990 price by 2000. The British Government has made a commitment to increase duty on fuel by at least 5 per cent in real terms every year over the foreseeable future.

The European Commission's advisory Motor Vehicles Emissions Group has concluded that the most effective method of reducing CO_2 emissions from motor vehicles would be a community framework, within which Member States might introduce a differential charge/credit based on new car CO_2 emissions per km, accompanied by increased fuel prices. The Commission has estimated that a combination of proven technologies and a modest weight reduction could enable a 40 per cent improvement in the fuel economy of new cars to be achieved by 2005.

Such an improvement in fuel economy would result in CO_2 in the European Union increasing by only 10 per cent over 1990 levels by 2010. If this improvement in fuel economy were to be accompanied by increases in fuel taxation (in real terms) of 15 per cent in 1995, 25 per cent in 2000 and 50 per cent in 2005 (all related to 1990 levels), CO_2 emissions from road transport could be stabilised between the years 2005 and 2010 at the 1990 levels (Samaras and Zierock, 1992). Stabilisation of emissions, however, would not, of course, stabilise the absolute levels of CO_2 in the upper atmosphere, which would continue to grow and contribute to global warming.

The European Environmental Bureau has recommended (Taschner, 1992) that fuel should cost ECU 1.5 per litre in the EU from 1993 and that the duty should be increased by 5 per cent over and above the rate of inflation every year, thus doubling the amount of duty paid after 14 years and trebling after 21 years. Even this is less than the rate of increase which would be required to reduce CO_2 levels to that recommended by the Intergovernmental Panel on Climate Change (IPCC, 1990).

9.   Road safety standards and targets

All the measures discussed in this chapter, such as building new roads, traffic calming and car restraint, have implications for safety, whether or not this was a primary consideration at the time of implementation. Changes to road safety, however, are not just a by-product of transport and land-use policies introduced for other purposes. Local authorities introduce measures specifically designed to reduce road casualties, and governments legislate on matters which affect safety and set targets for casualty reduction, by whatever means are available and seem suitable.

So far, the most successful changes have come from government legislation on drink-driving and on the wearing of seat belts, and there is more that can be done in these areas. There is always the problem, however, that greater safety for some (vehicle occupants, for instance) might be accompanied by greater danger for others (pedestrians, for instance) as vehicles become more powerful and manoeuvrable and driven with more verve. If ambitious targets to reduce road casualties are to be met in the future, the problem will have to be tackled on a wider front. This will inevitably mean confronting the problems of speed and aggressive driving, which seem to be at the heart of much of the safety problem in many countries.

In Poland, as in other countries of Central Europe, very high accident rates in urban areas have been attributed largely to the general 60 km/h speed limit. Although the latest amendment in traffic legislation provides for 30 km/h speed-limit zones and residential zones based on the Woonerf principle, city governments have been reluctant to implement them. In Zurich, on the other hand, extensive 30 km/h speed-limit zones have been introduced in selected residential areas and it is intended to implement similar schemes in other parts of the city by 1995.

The general speed limit for urban areas in Denmark in 1985 was changed from 60 to 50 km/h, with the result that actual speeds fell by 2 to 3 km/h, fatalities by 18 per cent and injuries by 6 per cent. It was estimated that for each one per cent reduction in speed the number of injuries fell by 3 per cent and the number of fatalities by 4 per cent. The Danish Action Plan seeks to revise all urban speed limits over a period of four years in order to make them more appropriate to the prevailing conditions. A yearly saving of 22 fatalities and 550 injuries (3 per cent and 5 per cent respectively of the national total) is predicted.

Controlling speed by means of speed signs only has, not surprisingly, been found to have had only a limited effect: it is hoped that a greater effect can be obtained by some redesign of the urban road system itself. The Danish Action Plan suggests that half of all urban roads should be converted into local (non-through) roads over a period of eight years and estimates that speeds would be reduced from 54 to 40 km/h: the plan also proposes that traffic calming measures should be applied to those areas (about 10 per cent of the total) with the worst casualty records. The combined effect is estimated to be a reduction of 18 fatalities and 510 injuries per year. It is suggested also that 20 per cent of all urban through roads should be narrowed over an eight-year period to make it easier for pedestrians to cross. This would be expected to reduce average speeds on these roads from 54 to 45 km/h and save 10 fatalities and 260 injuries per year.

Road safety is likely to continue to improve in most countries. In countries like the UK, which have experienced sustained reductions in road casualties over many years (despite increasing traffic) there is no sign of diminishing returns on safety developments. Moreover, there is a whole new range of opportunities opening up through the use of advanced electronics which could lead to greatly enhanced safety of both vehicle occupants and other road users. Speed enforcement using camera technology, should play an increasing role in the future. Eventually, it should be possible to automate the whole process of identifying offending vehicles (not only speeding, but crossing red lights and disobeying regulations) and issuing summonses. In the longer term, speed governors could be used to adjust maximum speed to the prevailing conditions (weather, traffic, darkness, roadworks, etc.).

In Denmark's National Action Plan, the government is aiming for a reduction of roughly a half in the number of people killed and injured each year by the year 2000, compared with 1987 levels. The Dutch government's target on road safety is to reduce the number of fatalities by 50 per cent and the number of injuries by 40 per cent by the year 2010. In the UK, the target is for a reduction of a third in the number of fatal and serious casualties by the year 2010, compared with the early 1980s.

10. Concluding remarks

The transport policies described in this chapter have been used to a greater or lesser extent in all the countries taking part in this project. Over the years there has been a gradual shift in emphasis in most countries from measures geared to increasing road capacity (in an attempt to reduce congestion) towards improving public transport. More recently, attention has been focused on environmental issues.

The case of Zurich is of particular importance in this connection, since it shows that the right combination of policies (car traffic constraints, upgrading of, and priority for, conventional bus/tramway systems, integration of all modes of public transport, parking policy, etc.) can bring about much higher public transport patronage than new capital-intensive systems serving only selected corridors (with other areas served by low-quality and often neglected public transport). Most city authorities, however, have not been as far-sighted.

The mainly short-term objectives of these policies seem to have been achieved, but until very recently, little thought had been given, in general, to the more fundamental and longer-term aspirations, such as reducing the need for travel, reducing dependence on the private car, conserving fuel supplies and protecting the planet. The next chapter looks at the various policies described in Chapter 5 and 6, to see what impact they have collectively had in dealing with the underlying causes, as well as the symptoms, of the problems set out in Chapter 3.

7. PAST ACHIEVEMENTS AND NEW OBJECTIVES

The previous chapters have described the various land-use and transport policies implemented in OECD/ECMT countries and have examined the effects of individual policies. This chapter uses the Case Study findings and other relevant information to see what the effects in practice have been of applying a whole package of possibly unrelated land-use and transport policies over a long period.

1. Policy objectives

The problems faced by OECD/ECMT cities are of two kinds. In the first are the familiar, long-established problems of congestion, casualties, emissions, the isolation of those without access to cars, and so on. Most existing policies have been geared to tackling them.

However, during the late 1980s, a second set of concerns began to crystallise in many Member countries. These included awareness of the impracticality of catering for forecast volumes of car travel, concern about resource consumption and anxieties about the possibility of climate change. This led in turn to the identification of a new set of policy objectives, which were not only more wide-ranging, but were concerned with the underlying causes rather than the symptoms of the problem – too much traffic in our cities.

It is the purpose of this chapter to consider how far existing policies have gone, and may be expected to go, in achieving both sets of objectives, which can be encapsulated as follows:

  i) reduce the need to travel;
  ii) reduce the absolute levels of car use and road freight in urban areas;
  iii) favour more energy-efficient modes for both passenger travel and freight;
  iv) reduce noise and vehicle emissions at source (*i.e.* make engines quieter, cleaner and more energy-efficient);
  v) encourage a more efficient and environmentally-sensitive use of the vehicle stock to reflect the goals of energy saving, higher vehicle-utilisation and less pollution;
  vi) improve the safety of pedestrians and all road users in urban areas; and

vii) improve the attractiveness of cities for residents, workers, shoppers and visitors.

Most of the measures described in the National Overviews and in the Case Studies cut across several of these objectives: for example, high parking prices could have a beneficial effect on all of these except *i)* and *iv)*. Table 7.1 indicates which objectives could be achieved by the various policy levers at the disposal of central and local governments, assuming they were applied in the most effective way.

It can be seen from Table 7.1 that it is mainly the *land-use planning* policies which have the potential to reduce the need to travel. How such policies should be applied to achieve this end is discussed in Chapter 5. Both transport and land-use policies have the potential to reduce the absolute levels of car use and favour the more environmentally-friendly modes, but the indirect effect of the land-use policies is almost bound to be weaker than that of the appropriate transport policies. Reducing emissions at source and improving the efficiency of the vehicle stock can be achieved mainly through the imposition of targets and standards and by some transport measures. Road safety and the attractiveness of the city are affected by both transport and land-use measures, as well as by the application of targets and standards.

The Canada Mortgage and Housing Corporation (CMHC, 1993) has also conducted a study of the major types of initiatives which could be taken to improve the sustainability of cities. A subjective assessment was made of the likely impact of each type of initiative against a set of objectives similar to the ones set out in Table 7.1. The study found that, while many of the measures were still at the talking or planning stage in most Canadian cities, some of them had actually been implemented. This assessment is described in Annex 2 under the heading *Canada* and summarised in Table A2.1 of Annex 2.

2. Policy impacts

Many of the policy impacts recorded in Chapters 5 and 6 are short term. Without a study carried out over a very long period (and few, if any, have been), it is impossible to sort out the longer-term impacts of any particular policy from background effects which have little or nothing to do with the policy in question. Nevertheless, despite these problems, the Case Studies provide a useful assessment of public policy for a range of cities at different stages of development.

Table A3.5 in Annex 3 summarises the main findings of the Case Studies. It shows the extent to which each of the cities has moved towards particular objectives, whether or not they were appropriate to the particular city concerned. Any assessment of this sort is, of course, subjective and does not take into account how cities rated particular goals, nor how much effort they exerted in order to try to achieve them. Table A3.5 in Annex 3 is summarised in Table 7.2, in which the cities have been categorised into three groups according to population size.

Table 7.1. Potential achievements of land-use and transport policies

Policies and measures [a]	Potential achievements						
	Reduce need to travel	Reduce absolute level of car use and/or road freight	Favour more energy efficient modes	Reduce vehicle emissions at source	Improve efficiency of vehicle stock	Improve road safety	Improve city attractiveness
Planning							
Strategic [b]	/	/	/	–	–	/	/
Regional [c]	/(?)	–	–	–	–	?	/(?)
Designated growth areas [d]	/(?)	–	–	–	–	/(?)	/(?)
Regeneration [e]	/(?)	/(?)	/(?)	–	–	/(?)	/
Density [f]	/	/	/	–	–	/	/
Green belts	?	–	–	–	–	/(?)	/
Decentralisation [g]	–	–	–	–	–	?	/(?)
Local facilities	/	/	/	–	–	/	/
Transport							
Road investment	–	–	–	–	–	/(?)	/(?)
Rail investment	–	/	/(?)	–	–	/	/
Improve P.T.	–	/	/(?)	–	–	/	/
Traffic management	–	–	–	–	–	/	/(?)
Bus priority	–	/	/	–	/	/	/(?)
Road tolls	–	/	/	–	/	/	/(?)
Parking control	–	/	/	–	/	/	/(?)
Park and ride	–	/	/	–	/	/	/
Car restraint	–	/	/	/ [h]	/	/	/
Entry prohibitions	–	/	/	–	–	/	/
Goods restraint	–	/	/	/ [h]	/ [h]	/	/
Pedestrian priority							
Cycle priority	/(?)	/	/	–	–	/(?)	–
Traffic calming	–	/(?)	/(?)	–	–	/	/
Car pooling	–	/	–	–	/	/	–
Targets							
Road safety	–	?	?	–	–	/	/(?)
Toxic emissions	–	?	?	/	/(?)	/(?)	/
CO$_2$	?	/	/	/	/	/	/
Noise	?	?	/	/	–	?	/

Notes: /   Attempts to fulfil objective.
       –   Does not fulfil objective.
       ?   Might go either way.
       /(?) Fulfils objective if implemented in the best way.
a) See Table 4.1, Chapter 4, for more complete descriptions of policies.
b) New developments linked to the provision of public transport.
c) Employment encouraged to move to other parts of the country.
d) Including new towns.
e) Usually of city centres and/or inner areas.
f) Density and zoning regulations to bring homes closer to jobs, etc.
g) Retail and other activities to edge-of-town locations.
h) If the measure includes higher fuel prices.

Table 7.2. **Policy impacts in Case-Study cities**

Objective	Metropolises (10 to 30 m)	Large cities (1.5-5 m)	Medium cities (0.5-1.5 m)
Planning			
Constrain main city's growth	+		
Promote multi-centric structure	+++	++	
Make city more attractive	+	+	++
Bring homes and jobs closer	−		
Promote cycling and walking		+	
Restrain out-of-town facilities	+		+
Transport			
Improve mobility	+	++	++
Reduce congestion	−		
Improve parking	+	+	+
Improve safety	+		
Improve public transport	++	+++	+++
Encourage modal shift to transit		+	++
Reduce financial burden of transit		−	
Reduce dependence on car	−	−	
Reduce need for mechanised travel	−	—	
Environment			
Reduce noise levels	−		
Reduce pollution levels	−		+
Reduce CO_2	—	−	—

Notes: + to +++ indicates the strength of the impact positively.
− to — indicates the strength of the impact negatively.

Many of the impacts of the Case Studies are discussed in Chapters 5 and 6. The results will be used here to see if these cities have moved significantly in the direction of the objectives listed above in Section 1 of this chapter.

Reducing the need to travel

There is very little in either the National Overviews or the Case Study reports to suggest that any city or country has specifically tried to reduce the need to travel. This was brought out clearly in Chapter 5. Several countries have set up bodies or drawn up plans to co-ordinate land-use and transport planning with a variety of aims, some of which could be construed to imply a reduction in the need to travel, but none of the policies which have been introduced for whatever reason seem to have had that effect. Only in Portland was there evidence that something had been achieved. In most of the other cities, journeys to work (and to other activities) have been lengthening over several decades. For example, average commuting trip lengths to Central London more than doubled between 1962 and 1987 (from 9 km to 23 km). Responses to the Questionnaire provided similar evidence: most of the cities questioned reported increasing trip lengths by each of the mechanised modes, car, bus/coach and metro/rail (see Figure A1.6 in Annex 1). Table 7.2 indicates that in all three city categories, the need for mechanised travel has been increasing, particularly in smaller cities.

The situation is, however, changing, and determination to apply policies to reduce car dependence and reduce the need to travel is growing. Studies of the likely effect of such policies have been carried out (see Chapter 5) and plans are being drawn up in various countries to reinforce land-use and transport policies with the aim of reducing the need to travel. What impact these policies will have in practice remains to be seen.

Reducing the use of cars and trucks

Attempting to reduce the *absolute* levels of car and truck use sparks off strong feelings in both environmental and road lobbies. None of the policies described in the Case Study reports, however, has done anything significant to reduce dependence on cars, which appears to be increasing almost everywhere (see Table 7.2). It seems there has been little desire to do so. Even in towns and cities, car use has continued to grow, though peak-period use to and from, and within central areas has been constrained. Some authorities, however, have instituted policies to reduce car use in particular parts of their cities. Amsterdam, Milan and Rome are examples and the number is growing.

Many of the policies aimed at reducing peak-period congestion appear to be concerned as much with promoting public transport use as with reducing car use. Zurich, for example, has reduced car use by giving priority to public transport and pedestrians on urban roads. Increasing investment in public transport, while reducing car use, might even be increasing dependence on mechanised modes to the detriment of walking and cycling. While large benefits accrue from public transport improvement (see below), it is possible that it could be increasing trip lengths and, in some cases, contributing to the risk of global warming from transport-related CO_2 emissions.

Favouring more energy-efficient modes

The efforts made in the Case-Study cities to improve public transport have, in most cities, resulted in excellent services and increasing patronage levels (though not necessarily an increasing *share* of the travel market). In expanding cities, the improved services have kept pace with population and employment growth and have allowed the city centres to remain strong and compact. The financial burden associated with providing public transport services has, however, been heavy as Table 7.2 indicates, and some of the increased patronage has been at the expense of cycling and walking.

Little has been done to encourage the use of non-mechanised travel, except in the Netherlands, Germany and Denmark and in a few cities in other countries, which, through history or topography, are particularly suited to these modes. The result is that walking and cycling, while still retaining a large share of trip-making, are continuing to diminish as car ownership increases and as public transport (itself a more energy-efficient system than car travel) is promoted.

Reducing noise and emissions

Despite all the technical progress to limit engine noise from vehicles, the situation on the ground, with some exceptions (see Section 6 of Chapter 3), does not appear to have improved. None of the Case Studies reported a general reduction in noise levels (Table 7.2).

Some progress, on the other hand, has been made in reducing gas emissions, particularly in the United States and the Netherlands, and there is good reason to hope that further progress will be made in the future. Results from the Case Studies, however, indicated little change in the perceived level of pollution (Table 7.2), possibly because of increasing traffic and the continued use of older vehicles (which are responsible for most of the pollution). Nevertheless, selected areas in some of the cities studied have benefited from some of the regulatory measures taken (see Annex 3).

The need to reduce CO_2 emissions (to minimise the risk of global warming) was not recognised until recently. Little has therefore been done about it, though discussion about how to do so is taking place and modest targets have been set in some countries and cities (see Section 8 of Chapter 6).

Encouraging more efficient road use

High fuel taxation in Italy (see Section 8 of Chapter 6) has led car makers and buyers to focus on economical cars, though the policy seems to have had other origins. The potential of fiscal instruments to encourage trading down, driving in a more energy-efficient way, carrying more passengers, increasing load factors in freight transport, etc., has otherwise been little realised.

Car pooling and high-occupancy vehicle lanes have been promoted in some countries (e.g., USA and Australia), but the impacts have been slight. Existing transport infrastructure and vehicle stock are as a general rule not, therefore, being used in the most effective way.

Reducing casualties

Some success has been achieved in casualty reduction (considering the enormous increase in motorisation), but the toll of deaths and injuries remains high (Section 2 of Chapter 3). While speed is acknowledged to be a dominant cause of urban casualties and of their severity, governments and local authorities have been reluctant to take steps to reduce speeds. Police in most countries have also been reluctant to enforce speed limits. Schemes for calming traffic in cities in the Netherlands, Germany and Denmark using 30 km/h speed zones have, however, reduced casualties and made the streets involved less frightening places for elderly pedestrians and children.

Improving the attractiveness of cities

Constraining the growth of large metropolitan centres for the benefit of *other towns and cities* is comparatively rare since few municipalities are willing to divert economic growth elsewhere. Encouraging growth in other centres *within* the metropolitan region, in order to produce a multi-centric structure, is more common. This was a popular measure in the larger cities and metropolises covered by the Case Studies. While such measures seem to have improved travel conditions and made the cities more convenient for people to carry out their activities, they are unlikely to have reduced car dependence or the need for mechanised travel (Table 7.2).

Over recent years, many (but not all) city centres have been made more attractive, through rebuilding programmes, renewal of derelict or decaying areas, pedestrianisation and other measures. There has been less success in curbing the growth of edge-of-town developments, though London, Portland and Helsinki have managed to constrain such developments to a remarkable extent (Annex 3). Out-of-town developments are less of an issue in some countries, *e.g.* the Netherlands, where policies now favour the location of facilities in existing centres (see Chapter 5). Such planning policies are now being adopted in more countries, for example, the UK.

Many of the measures which make cities more attractive places in which to live, work, shop and socialise are ones which also encourage mobility. They conflict therefore with the aims of reducing urban travel and vehicle emissions. Some cities, such as Stockholm and Zurich, have, however, succeeded in making improvements which are more in tune with sustainable development (see Chapters 5 and 6).

Other achievements

If progress could be made towards the objectives listed in Section 1 of this chapter, almost all the travel and environmental problems of concern to cities would be reduced. Clearly, insufficient progress has been made, and many of the cities' biggest worries remain, particularly that of congestion.

Attempts to reduce congestion have been at the forefront of transport planning for many decades, but with limited success, however bold the attempts. Table 7.2 indicates that even in the Case-Study cities, little progress has been made. Peak-period travel speeds in the central areas of the largest cities have remained at about 17 km/h for decades despite road construction and traffic management.

It is interesting to see from Table 7.2 that two of the most significant policy impacts noted in the Case Studies were improved public transport and increased mobility in general (see Section 1 of Chapter 6). Both these might well have been at the expense of some of the more fundamental aims listed in Section 1 of this chapter. The increases in mobility have arisen largely from more people owning cars and using them to travel to destinations away from the more congested areas and from people using improved public transport networks to travel to and from places hitherto poorly served. Parking has been made easier and more orderly, mainly through higher parking charges and the provision of more off-street parking. Thus, accessibility has improved for people with cars and for those able to use the improved public transport, but for those who have to rely on cycling and walking, it has in most cities probably deteriorated (see Table A3.5 in Annex 3).

3. Future prospects

Forecasts of overall traffic increases vary widely from one country to another. In OECD countries as a whole, car traffic doubled between 1970 and 1991 and goods vehicle kilometres increased by a factor of 2.5 over the same period. In the European countries of OECD, the goods-veh-km trend is almost identical to the car-km trend over this period. Figure 7.1 shows the trends for the number of cars owned, car-km, goods-veh-km and fuel used in road transport, all indexed to 100 in 1991. Car-km and the number of cars owned have had almost identical trends for the last 20 years. If this trend is projected to the year 2015, both these quantities would increase by about 50 per cent over 1991 values. The amount of fuel used has been increasing rather less than the growth in traffic and since more improvements in vehicle efficiency are in the pipeline, growth in fuel consumption might be about 40 per cent up on 1991 levels by 2015. All forecast trends are, of course, uncertain and this uncertainty is shown in the projections on the diagram.

Traffic in city regions is likely to grow at a lower rate than in the countries as a whole, and in the city centres, hardly at all (see Figure 7.2, which shows likely changes in a range of travel and environmental indicators for the year 2015, compared with 1991). If policies continue to evolve as they have, road congestion will probably be kept at bay through physical and economic instruments and with the help of technology, though congestion will spread in time and space. The reduction in road casualties will probably continue, particularly if governments are prepared to "grasp the nettle" with regard to control of speed in urban areas.

On the question of emissions, the present rate of progress is likely to continue as new vehicles replace old and standards are raised, but growing car and goods vehicle use will eventually offset any reductions in emissions. An OECD study of the long-term prospects for reducing emissions (OECD, 1994) suggests that the main pollutants (CO, HCs and NO_x) could be reduced by between a quarter and a half between 1991 and 2015, though by then, they would all be on a rising trend. Whether the reductions would, in practice, be as large as the amounts suggested, depends on the extent to which current standards and future revisions are adopted in OECD countries and on how well vehicles are maintained, since a large proportion of air pollution comes from a small proportion of vehicles. But almost certainly, there will be some improvement by 2015. Noise, on the other hand, will remain a problem and there is little hope of any respite until traffic volumes are reduced drastically, speeds are cut and noise emissions from heavy goods vehicles and motor cycles are further reduced at source.

Cities will only become more attractive to those on foot if full advantage is taken to introduce traffic calming and pedestrian priority measures and to promote redevelopment on a more human scale. With increasing car use, travel by public transport, walking and

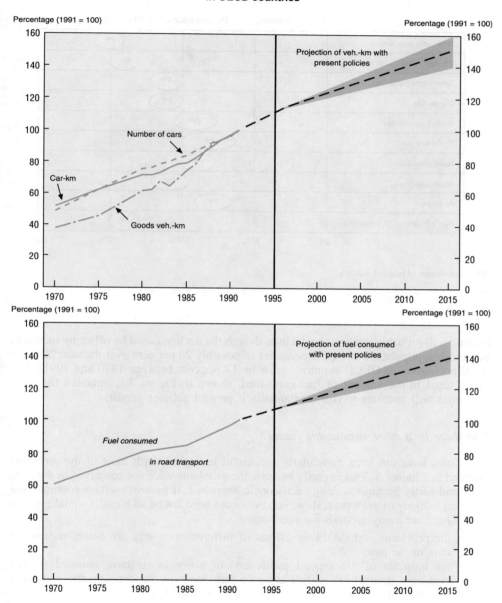

Figure 7.1. **Trends in vehicle-km and fuel consumed in OECD countries**

Percentage (1991 = 100)

Projection of veh.-km with present policies

Number of cars

Car-km

Goods veh.-km

Percentage (1991 = 100)

Projection of fuel consumed with present policies

Fuel consumed

in road transport

Source: OECD, for past trends.

Figure 7.2. **Likely impacts of the continuation of present policies by year 2015**

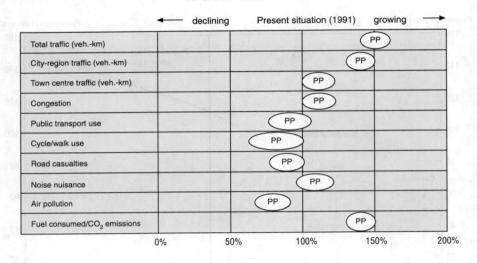

PP: Continuation of present policies.

cycling will probably continue to decline, though the decline could be offset by increases in the urban population of OECD countries of possibly 20 per cent over the next 20 years (total population of OECD countries grew by 17 per cent between 1970 and 1991). The likely trend in the amount of fuel consumed, shown in Figure 7.1, indicates that CO_2 emissions will continue to rise substantially if present policies persist.

Can there be a more sustainable future?

Cities have not been particularly successful in dealing with most of the problems outlined in Chapter 3. This is partly because the problems were not perceived as they are now, and partly because nothing catastrophic happened. If present policies continue, the situation is likely to get worse. However, the future need not be so bleak if we take action now. There are many grounds for optimism:

- the problems and the likely effects of different measures are better understood than in the past;
- the attitudes of the general public and of governments have matured so that measures impractical a decade or so ago are now on the agenda, and most governments are setting out strategies for sustainability;
- recent advances in technology, particularly in telematics, have brought sophisticated solutions to some of the more difficult problems much closer;

- despite the present recession, GDP in OECD countries is expected to grow in the 1990s. This will provide additional resources to devote to improving the infrastructure and appearance of cities, which in turn, will help them to regain some of their lost vitality and pleasantness; and
- countries are now beginning to act in unison on some of these matters, particularly those problems which are not confined within national boundaries (*e.g.,* air pollution). Suggestions are being made for standards which should be adhered to, and targets which should be met at specified dates in the future.

4. Concluding remarks

There is no easy way to achieve a safe, quiet, peaceful, visually-attractive urban environment with clean air and efficient access to all facilities. Improvements can be made to the urban environment and destinations, such as shops and work places, can be made more accessible to those without cars, but the benefits will not be without costs, in particular to people living mobile lives and dependent on cars for practically all travel. It is unclear how far politicians will be prepared to go in the pursuit of these objectives. However, with the social, economic and environmental costs of vehicular travel running at between 6 and 16 per cent of GDP in OECD countries and the benefits of sustainable travel and development far outweighing the costs suffered by those whose lifestyles would have to change, there is no justification for delaying the appropriate action. It appears that the politicians are lagging behind public opinion on these issues in many countries.

The next chapter outlines a possible policy package for the future, indicating what types of measures might be required and at what strength to achieve the necessary goals.

Part 3

POLICIES FOR THE 1990s AND BEYOND

8. COMBINING LAND-USE AND TRANSPORT POLICY

The policy analysis in Part 2 of this report shows that present land-use and transport policies will not solve the urban travel and development problems faced by Member countries. In particular, increasing the capacity of urban road networks, hitherto the single most highly-rated solution to urban travel problems, has grave defects: it encourages spatial change and car travel and adds to the extent and intensity of car dependency, congestion and associated environmental problems. *Widespread agreement exists about the need for a new approach.*

1. A new approach

Key policy instruments

A wide range of policy instruments exists to redirect urban travel through land-use planning and transport policy, and these instruments are set out in Table 8.1. An indication is given of the level of government responsible. The list includes:

- *land-use planning and development control policies* that influence settlement patterns and increase the accessibility to jobs, shops and other facilities, without the need to travel by car;
- policies affecting the *pricing* of fuel, car purchase and licensing, parking and road use to influence vehicle design, the location of activities, modal choice and the growth of teleworking;
- measures making use of *telematics* to integrate signal control, parking and public transport management to raise the efficiency of urban travel systems and promote shifts from car to other modes;
- policies making employers responsible for *commuter planning* to reduce peak traffic flows;
- policies concerning subsidy, privatisation and the use of upgraded information systems and marketing to *increase the efficiency and attractiveness of public transport;*
- measures to set up car-free zones, traffic calming and cycle and pedestrian priority to *assist pedestrians and cyclists,* reduce the risks to these modes, and improve the attractiveness of cities;

147

Table 8.1. **Policy instruments for sustainable development**

	Level of government responsible for implementation		
	Local	National	International
Land-use Management			
Urban containment	+	+	
Mixing land uses	+		
Density standards[a]	+		
Parking standards in commercial and residential areas	+		
Car-free zones	+		
Location of park and ride sites	+		
Promoting city-centre development	+		
Road Traffic Management			
Bypassing sensitive areas	+	+	
Priorities for bus, tram and HOVs[b]	+	+	
Segregated rights of way for transit	+		
Commuter planning	+		
Telematics standards and application	+	+	+
Traffic calming	+	+	
Cycle lanes and paths	+		
Pedestrian facilities	+		
Casualty reduction targets		+	
Lower speed limits and enforcement	+	+	
Environmental Protection			
Vehicle noise and emission standards/targets		+	+
Lowered fuel consumption goals for cars and trucks		+	
In-use vehicle inspection standards		+	+
Noise screening	+		
Noise minimising road surfaces	+		
Maximum allowable traffic levels for residential and shopping streets		+	
Pricing Mechanisms			
Carbon taxes			+
Vehicle purchase tax/annual licence fee		+	
Fuel duty		+	
Parking charges	+		
Transit pricing (subsidy policy)	+		
Urban road tolls	+		
Congestion pricing	+	+	

a) Higher densities (*e.g.* plot ratio/floor area ratio) allowed at selected locations, *e.g.* in the vicinity of railway stations – low densities in areas of low public transport availability.
b) High occupancy vehicles.

- measures to promote goods trans-shipment depots and city-friendly delivery vans to *suit logistics to urban conditions.*

Combining policies to make a more effective package

All the policy instruments listed in Table 8.1 are potentially helpful, but no single one of them has the power to achieve the objectives of sustainable development: to do this, governments need to introduce packages of policies that are mutually reinforcing. Packages embracing land-use and pricing instruments are particularly appropriate, since they have the capability of reducing car travel and improving accessibility for those without cars.

Travel and traffic conditions in different cities are far from uniform. Hiroshima, Zurich, Bristol and San Diego possess widely differing characteristics. Variations in size, topography, land-use patterns, income levels and public policy underlie such differences. Japanese cities are dense and served by very extensive transit systems. North American cities are diffused and largely car-based. European cities are somewhere in-between, though moving towards the American model.

No two cities are therefore likely to require precisely the same measures to make their development sustainable. Moreover, they are all starting from different positions and, quite probably, view the same problems in different ways. Willingness and ability to tackle the problems are likely to vary from country to country. It would be inappropriate, therefore, to define a precise package of measures which should be applied to all cities regardless of their size and state of development. It is more helpful to identify policy directions and leave the choice of individual measures, the extent to which they are used and the way in which they are applied, to the discretion of the cities and countries concerned.

A three-pronged attack

The Group has accordingly designed a policy package with three strands:
- the first is to use the best of the techniques which have been tried and shown to be effective. Use of *best practice* on its own will, however, not result in sustainable urban development;
- a second *innovative* strand of more sharply focused measures is needed to do this. Some of these innovative measures are not yet fully tested, although enough experience exists to show that they will reduce car dependence;
- the third strand, the *sustainable development* strand, is the only component of the package to tackle CO_2 emissions and, in so doing, reinforce all the other measures and make them fully effective.

All these strands are important and work on implementing them should start as soon as possible. Strands 1 and 3 can be introduced without delay. Strand 2, which converts best practice into a coherent set of measures designed to reduce car dependence, is of crucial importance, though some aspects of it will have to await the results of research and development.

Some countries, *e.g.* Switzerland, are already exponents of best practice and many others, *e.g.* the Netherlands, are experimenting with the innovations in Strand 2. Countries that find difficulty in going further than best practice should, however, introduce Strand 3 even if they need time before introducing Strand 2. The main instruments from which policy makers may choose in designing a strategy to suit their countries are set out in Table 8.1. The packages which form the three main strands are outlined in the following sections.

There is always resistance to new policy initiatives and implementation of land-use and transport policies aimed at reducing car dependency will be no exception. Implementation of such policies requires a great deal of preparatory work conveying the necessary information to the public and encouraging both public and private participation in policy formulation. Experience in Switzerland has shown how even tough measures can find acceptance if the measures in question are related to clearly-defined objectives, and there is sufficient co-ordination between the different levels of authority.

2. Strand 1: The adoption of best practice policies

The priority for governments and city administrations is to raise their current practice to the level reached by the best-managed cities in countries such as Sweden, Switzerland and Germany:

Land-use management

Current best practice in land-use management involves:

- limiting the spread of cities to keep up residential densities and protect open land;
- steering offices and shopping to city centres or other locations that are well served by public transport;
- limiting the amount of car commuting to new office developments by imposing low maxima on the number of car parking spaces that can be provided;
- increasing the supply of city-centre and inner-city homes, as in Portland, Oregon;
- shifting the supply of parking from central and inner districts to suburban and ex-urban park-and-ride interchanges, as at Oxford, UK; and
- reserving locations for freight distribution close to existing transport networks (whether rail, water or road).

Road traffic management

Best practice involves:

- limiting road investment to bypasses (possibly in tunnels, as in Oslo) of sensitive areas, combined with traffic calming measures and other improvements, such as the provision of parks and open spaces (as in Oslo and Portland), applied to the areas which have been bypassed;

- investing in lanes for high-occupancy vehicles, as in Amsterdam;
- using reserved lanes and telematics to give widespread priorities over other traffic to trams and buses, as in Zurich;
- extending pedestrian precincts and creating traffic cells, as in Gothenburg;
- providing improved facilities for cyclists and pedestrians;
- enforcing 30 km/h speed limits (or lower) in residential streets and other areas, as appropriate;
- using telematics (responsive urban traffic control systems) to minimise congestion, improve air quality and facilitate pedestrian movement;
- providing drivers with real-time information about park-and-ride and off-street parking availability; and
- providing bus and tram riders with real-time information about services at all stops.

Environmental protection

Best practice involves:
- tightening regulations to reduce emissions of gas and noise from new vehicles;
- introducing progressively lower fuel consumption targets for new vehicles;
- introducing more frequent and stringent tests for emissions from vehicles already in use;
- promoting the use of low-polluting buses; and
- banning/restricting road freight movement, *e.g.* in sensitive areas at night.

Pricing mechanisms

Best practice involves:
- using fuel taxes, vehicle purchase taxes and annual licence fees to promote the purchase and use of vehicles with low fuel consumption, as in Italy and France;
- using on- and off-street parking charges to balance demand and supply for road use;
- using toll rings, as in Oslo and Bergen, to pay for new infrastructure; and
- making businesses which benefit from improvements to public transport contribute towards the cost of those improvements.

3. Likely effects of best practice

Packages of best practice policies are expected to have little effect on traffic outside the main metropolitan areas, which is expected to grow by 50 per cent or more over the next 20 years in OECD countries and to almost double over the next 30 to 40 years. Growth rates in built-up areas, on the other hand, are likely to be close to nil and traffic in inner-city areas and city centres might even decline.

Inner city congestion levels should therefore be lower under best practice and accessibility to city-centre jobs should improve for those with and without cars, but access to suburban and rural destinations would continue to be predominantly by car and congestion in these areas would be largely unaffected. While decentralisation of both population and employment would be less than it would be under present policies, it would still continue, so that more and more journeys would be made in suburbs and rural areas surrounding the main cities. Total travel by public transport is likely to increase steadily, mainly due to improvements to the quality of service, the information provided, new LRT systems and priorities over car traffic. The growth in ridership, however, would be nothing like as fast as travel by car, so its share of the travel market would continue to fall. Walking would increase in central and inner-city areas, but probably decline elsewhere. Cycling would increase in areas where special provision was made for it, but would remain a minority form of transport.

Toxic emissions are likely to fall even more than under present policies as more stringent emission standards are adopted in a wider range of countries and as the proportion of "clean" vehicles increases, but in about ten years time, emissions will start to rise again as the increasing volume of traffic begins to outweigh some of the gains from exhaust catalysts. Noise levels in city centres and other protected areas are likely to diminish substantially, but noise levels in other areas could increase slightly with increasing traffic, despite quieter vehicles. Road accidents will probably continue to fall in most Member countries, perhaps by as much as a third in some, but higher levels of traffic will increase the risk of accidents to pedestrians and cyclists, and make travel more difficult for them.

Transport-related CO_2 emissions would be likely to grow overall by about a third in OECD countries over the next 20 years and by almost twice that amount over the next 30 or 40 years, with more than a doubling in some countries, where car and goods vehicle travel is increasing rapidly from a low base.

4. Strand 2: Innovations in policies

The adoption throughout OECD of current best practice policies is a high priority, but it will not achieve sustainable urban development. Innovations in land-use, transport and travel management will therefore be needed as well.

Land-use management

Innovations include:

- land-use policies designed to promote mixed uses or "urban villages" and improved facilities in local centres, as in the UK's current planning guidance;
- new tramways threaded through existing suburban districts, with residential densities raised in the vicinity of stations and new travel attractors located near them;
- measures to encourage development around existing transit routes and stations by the offer of higher permitted densities to developers (density bonuses);

152

- provision of networks of foot and cycleways with priority over vehicle roads; and
- establishment of car-free areas.

Road traffic management

Innovations include:

- limiting urban road construction to serving new development areas and to providing opportunities to improve the quality of public transport, through the provision of extra space for bus lanes and segregated tram and bus ways;
- using telematics to integrate all aspects of urban transport management, to keep demand for road space in balance with supply (through advanced signal control techniques) and to provide a wide array of real-time information services for travellers;
- using area and city-wide traffic calming measures;
- enforcing speed limits using video analysis and recognition techniques and ultimately through the use of speed governors or sensors on vehicles in order to reduce the risk posed to walkers and cyclists; and
- obliging employers to introduce commuter plans as in many US cities.

Environmental protection

Innovations include:

- using an array of regulatory and pricing mechanisms to promote the use of low-polluting fuels and low-polluting, city-friendly cars, buses and goods vehicles;
- setting deadlines for cities, tied to the receipt of national grants, to reach defined noise and air quality goals; and
- using telematics, regulations and engineering techniques to keep traffic levels within defined environmental limits in residential streets and urban roads.

Pricing mechanisms

Innovations include:

- electronic congestion pricing for city centres and inner cities and other areas where congestion, safety or air quality requires a reduction in traffic; pricing mechanisms could practically eliminate congestion and improve the quality of tram and bus services at the same time; and
- the replacement of operating subsidies for transit, where appropriate, by user subsidies. This could be facilitated by "smart" card technology.

Revenues from the various pricing mechanisms could be used for a variety of purposes. Additional local taxes could, for instance, be used in more innovative ways than taxes from fuel, which would probably go straight to national exchequers to enable other forms of taxation to be lowered in order to keep the total tax burden constant. Local income from charging for road space and parking could be used to fund public transport and environmental improvements (as, for example, in the City of Westminster, London). Using revenues in this way helps to make the pricing mechanisms more palatable.

5.   Likely effects of the policy innovations strand

The combination of best practice with policy innovations would increase the scope for working, shopping and satisfying other needs locally, and would thus help to arrest the trend towards longer urban trips by car. The growth in total car-km in built-up areas could actually be reversed, with consequential gains for walking, cycling and public transport use. Car-km in city centres and inner areas could fall dramatically, with public transport use both within, and to and from, such areas, increasing substantially. Overall car use would, however, continue to grow, even in the wider city regions (much of it devoted to leisure travel).

Traffic congestion could become a rarity in inner cities; teleworking would become more common and while urban transport-related CO_2 emissions would diminish, overall CO_2 emissions and energy consumption would continue to grow – though more slowly than under present policies. Improvements in fuel efficiency, as a result of targets and standards set by governments, would be offset, at least partly, by drivers trading up to larger, more powerful vehicles and making longer trips (even within the city regions).

City air would become noticeably cleaner, as exhaust emissions and the level of city traffic declined. Noise levels in city centres and protected areas would be greatly reduced, but in the vicinity of main roads, noise could become a greater problem, as traffic calming diverted vehicles away from residential streets. Road casualties in urban areas could be expected to fall appreciably with greatly reduced urban traffic levels, provided complementary measures are taken to keep speeds low and to offer better protection to cyclists and pedestrians.

6.   Strand 3: Sustainable urban development

Strand 3 goes further than the other two strands in order to reduce the risk of global climate change. It is designed to influence lifestyles, vehicle design, locational decisions, driver behaviour, choice of travel mode and the length of car journeys. Its aim is to reduce car use, fuel consumption and emissions. All three strands need to be implemented *as soon as possible*, but the nature of the third strand means that only in the long term will it become fully effective.

The key to the sustainable development strand is a substantial and steadily-increasing fuel tax coupled with all the measures included in Strands 1 and 2. Strand 3 is designed to reduce vehicle-kilometrage significantly over a period of two or three decades. This tax should be part of a comprehensive taxation policy affecting all fossil fuels, so as to ensure a high level of cost-efficiency. This is the main principle in the UN's Framework Convention on Climate Change. The principles of cost-efficiency and comprehensive approach mean that targets for reduction of CO_2 emissions should be decided at international level. The distribution of reductions in CO_2 emissions between countries and economic sectors will depend on the varying costs of such reductions.

Sustainable urban development measures involve:

- implementing steep year-by-year increases in the price of fuel to conserve fuel and reduce CO_2 emissions to recommended target levels. These would be set by national governments, but influenced by international bodies such as the EU and UN;
- implementing additional taxes on the purchase, licensing and use of vehicles to ensure that road users pay the full external costs of their journeys; and
- ensuring that the use of specialised, high-efficiency, low-weight, low-polluting urban cars, vans, lorries and buses becomes the norm in cities.

7. Likely effects of measures to achieve sustainable development

An increase in fuel price of the order of 7 per cent p.a. in real terms over two or three decades would be required to reduce CO_2 emissions to the levels considered necessary by the Intergovernmental Panel on Climate Change (IPCC, 1990). The assessment which follows is based on fuel price rising at this rate and is given for illustrative purposes only – the particular rate chosen should not necessarily be regarded as a recommendation.

The effect of a 7 per cent p.a. rise in fuel costs (in real terms) would be to almost quadruple fuel prices in 20 years. This would lead to lower car ownership levels compared with what they would otherwise be, fewer car trips and shorter trip lengths.

Effect on car fuel consumption

It would encourage motor vehicle manufacturers to increase the fuel efficiency of vehicles by up to 30 per cent, a change which is well within their reach, but might not happen to the same extent if the pressure is not there – the European Union estimates that 40 per cent is possible (see Section 8 of Chapter 6). It would encourage drivers to trade down to smaller and less powerful vehicles and drive in a more fuel-efficient manner, which could reduce fuel consumption by 15 per cent or so. The result would be that in 20 years time fuel cost per kilometre travelled would probably be just over two and a half times present prices, instead of four times, and the total fuel used, and consequently CO_2 emissions, would be down by much more than the reduction in car-km.

Effect on individual car usage

It is difficult to estimate the scale of the effect such a policy would have on car use. Fuel prices have probably never been subjected to such steep rises over such a prolonged period before. Elasticities of car use with respect to fuel price are extremely imprecise and a further uncertainty, when looking several decades into the future, is how rising incomes will affect people's travel choices. As incomes rise, the value of time rises, so that the monetary cost of travel becomes a smaller proportion of the generalised cost of travel (time plus money costs). Thus, by 2015, fuel price at four times present levels in real terms (*i.e.,* adjusted for inflation) would not be expected to have as great a deterrent effect on travel as it would have today, though how different it would be is not certain, particularly as by then, car ownership will have spread to lower-income sections of the population.

Calculations have been made using elasticities derived from Bland (1984), but with an allowance for rising incomes. The calculations suggest that car trip-making would probably fall by about 15 per cent compared with what it would otherwise be. This would be mainly due to a reduction in car ownership and availability and to changes in the modal split of those who still have a car available. In addition, car trip lengths would be expected to fall by about a quarter as a result of the rise in the cost of fuel *per km of travel* to just over two and a half times the present level. (These figures are estimated using an elasticity of car use with respect to fuel price per car-km of –0.5. This value is derived from Bland's work and is compatible with other long-term estimates [see Goodwin (1992) and Section 8 of Chapter 6]. The elasticity is a long-term value and takes into account changes in where people live and work, resulting from fuel price rises of this magnitude. It also reflects possible improvements to the public transport system as a result of increasing patronage. To include the effect of rising incomes, fuel costs were discounted by 2.5 per cent p.a. over the period to 2015. This allows people's travel choices to depend on how the fuel cost changes relate to their income, but it does not take account of the spread of car ownership to lower-income groups, which would tend to reduce the income effect.)

Effect on total car travel and fuel used

The overall effect of less car use and shorter car trip lengths is a reduction of about a third in total car-km travelled and nearly 60 per cent in the amount of fuel used (compared with what would otherwise have happened). If it is assumed that veh-km travelled in OECD countries would have increased by 50 per cent over the next 20 years and that Strands 1 and 2 of the policy package would have reduced this to 30 per cent above the 1991 level, then the application of sustained high fuel prices would be expected to bring car-km down to a little over 80 per cent of the 1991 level. With regard to the use of fuel, high prices would probably reduce the amount of fuel consumed by cars to about half the 1991 level, assuming Strands 1 and 2 reduced fuel used in 2015 from 40 per cent above 1991 levels (under a continuation of present policies) to 20 per cent. This calculation allows for improvements to the fuel-efficiency of vehicles, whether or not they are connected with the rise in fuel price. The rise in car ownership would be expected to be much less than the forecast 50 per cent or so for OECD countries over that timescale, but it would, nevertheless, still be a rise.

It should be noted that if manufacturers increased the fuel efficiency of cars in the absence of a rise in fuel price (say, as a result of government regulations), car-km would increase and offset some of the potential savings in the amount of fuel used. It has been calculated that at certain fuel price levels, the increase in car-km resulting from an improvement to engine efficiency could be so great as to practically nullify the potential fuel savings. This stresses the importance of making *fuel price* the instrument for reducing car-km to the required level, thereby ensuring that fuel savings materialise.

Effect on goods veh-km, total veh-km and fuel used

It is not at all obvious what effect such a rise in fuel prices would have on goods transport: it would certainly reduce the proportion of empty return loads and the number of just-in-time deliveries and would increase the number of distribution warehouses, so shortening trip lengths. It would transfer some freight to rail. There would also be some gains in engine efficiency, though probably not to the same extent as for cars. The assumptions made in this analysis are that the elasticity of goods vehicle-km with respect to generalised cost of travel is only half that for cars and gains in engine efficiency are likewise only half those for cars. Under these assumptions, total veh-km would fall to about 85 per cent of the 1991 level (this is a weighted mean for cars and goods vehicles, assuming car-km are five times as great as goods veh-km). With regard to fuel, the analysis suggests that total fuel used would fall to about 60 per cent of 1991 levels (this is a weighted mean of cars and goods vehicles, assuming cars in total consume twice the amount of fuel as goods vehicles).

This estimated reduction in fuel used by 2015 still falls short of the stated aims of the Intergovernmental Panel on Climate Change that "the nations of the world will have to cut CO_2 emissions by fully 60-80 per cent to stabilise atmospheric CO_2 concentrations" (IPCC, 1990), but is going a long way towards it.

The above analysis is very much at a preliminary stage and the results are tentative. While it takes into account a number of relevant factors, there are many others which are not considered. Much more research is required. However, under a sustained policy of rising fuel prices over several decades, errors in the analysis merely affect the *time* at which the target reductions are achieved.

Overall effects of the combined policy package on cities

High fuel prices would not, on their own, necessarily affect car travel within cities, because the benefits to motorists from using their cars for relatively short journeys might well be much greater than the costs (even with high fuel prices) – it is the other restraint measures of the policy package which are more forceful in reducing car travel to, and within, city centres and these are capable of eliminating most of the congestion from towns and cities.

Air quality would be high in all urban areas with the use of cleaner fuels, cleaner engines and possibly only half as much traffic as at present. Noise levels would be reduced considerably with quieter vehicles, stricter speed control and much less traffic, but the nature of noise nuisance is that the perceived improvement would not be as great as the changes in decibels might suggest.

Such increases in fuel costs would have a considerable effect on land use. Policies to raise densities and bring homes, shops and work places closer together would all be effective in a much shorter time than if they were left to operate alone. Similarly, public transport investment would be much more effective and drivers, priced out of their cars, would benefit from a more satisfactory alternative. Public transport use, cycle and walk are all likely to increase considerably from these policies.

Road casualties in urban areas could be reduced even more than with Strands 1 and 2 alone, but this is dependent on facilities being provided which give better protection for cyclists and pedestrians, as well as more effective speed control of motorised vehicles. Such measures are all the more important with greatly reduced traffic, because without these, speeds would automatically rise.

Downsizing of vehicles, which would be expected under a high fuel price policy, also has implications for safety. Injuries to occupants could be more serious as a result of impacts with fixed objects and heavy goods vehicles, but for collisions between cars, downsizing might have little effect if almost all drivers trade down to smaller cars. In any case, there is ample scope for designing small light vehicles which offer greater protection to their occupants and also to other road users, especially the more vulnerable ones, and such measures should be included as part of the policy package.

The importance of high car travel costs

Sustainable development policies combined with *innovative* and *best practice* policies could bring about:

- a land-use pattern that would place activities close to each other;
- a public transport system that would offer unimpeded travel for work and leisure trips; and
- a transport infrastructure which would be designed as much for safe and comfortable walking and bicycling, as for motorised vehicles.

The key is *high travel costs*. This financial pressure would ensure substantial take up of the other main strands of the package. It could ensure that:

- the accessibility of those without cars would be dramatically increased;
- the urban environment would be improved;
- CO_2 emissions would be substantially reduced and the levels in the upper atmosphere could, after 30 to 40 years be stabilised; and
- people would be able to exercise more choice in how, where and when to travel.

The study has not looked, however, into the effects of higher fuel costs and high road pricing charges on industry and countries' economies – this would be a major research project in itself. However, while it is accepted that some people will have to pay more for their travel, all road users – car and goods vehicle drivers, public transport users, cyclists and pedestrians – should see an improvement in the quality of their journeys. Moreover, the revenues collected could be used by governments to reduce other taxation or provide improved services.

8. Comparative assessment of the various strands of the package

Changing trends

The three strands of the recommended policy package have to be judged against a scenario in which none of them is adopted, *i.e.* against a scenario in which policies continue to evolve in much the same way as they were doing in the 20 years to 1991, with no special provisions made towards achieving sustainable urban development and a stabilisation of greenhouse gases in the upper atmosphere. Figure 7.1 in Chapter 7 shows how total veh-km and fuel used are likely to increase by 2015 under a continuation of past and present policies. Figure 8.1 shows how the various strands of the sustainable development package might change these trends. Best practice is unlikely to change these amounts by very much – perhaps 10 per cent at the most. Innovations will reduce car travel in urban areas generally and this might reduce the overall level of traffic and fuel consumption by another 5 to 10 per cent, but Strand 3, as we have seen, should reduce veh-km travelled to about 85 per cent of 1991 levels and fuel used to about 60 per cent of 1991 levels.

Timing

Figure 8.2 gives target dates for full implementation of the Group's proposals, together with the likely effects on VKT (Vehicle-Kilometres Travelled) for city centres, built-up urban areas, city-regions and national levels. Best practice, which could be fully implemented in OECD countries by the end of the century, would almost stabilise VKT in built up areas, but VKT would still be increasing in city regions and nationally. Innovations, which require research and development before some of the techniques and policy packages are available off the shelf, may take longer to be *fully* implemented, but even these should *all* be fully operational long before 2015. This strand of the package would vastly reduce urban car traffic, slow down the growth in city regional traffic, but nationally car travel would still be increasing. Only the sustainable development strand, combined with the other policies, lowers urban car travel generally and reduces overall car travel, allowing CO_2 emissions to meet the IPCC target value by about 2030.

A snapshot of 2015

Figure 8.3 gives a snapshot for the year 2015 of the likely effects of the three policy strands and compares them with present policies. It represents the collective views of the Project Group and shows likely changes in VKT at city-centre, city-region and national levels; air pollution; noise; casualties; fuel used and CO_2 emissions. While these esti-mates are tentative, they are placed within a quantitative framework of likely changes in overall VKT over the next 20 years, both in the absence of sustainable policies and with such policies in place. Efforts have been made to make all changes in modal choice consistent internally and with changes in veh-km travelled. Uncertainty, nevertheless,

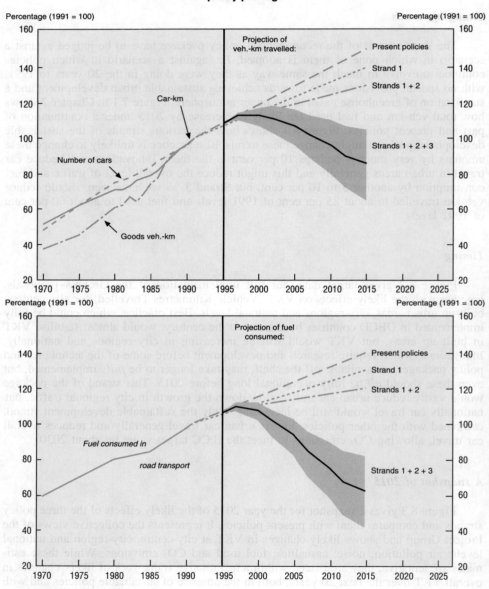

Figure 8.1. **Effect on vehicle-km and fuel consumed in OECD countries of the joint OECD/ECMT policy package**

Percentage (1991 = 100)

Percentage (1991 = 100)

160

160

140

140

Projection of
veh.-km travelled:

Present policies

Strand 1

Strands 1 + 2

120

Car-km

120

100

100

Strands 1 + 2 + 3

Number of cars

80

80

60

60

Goods veh.-km

40

40

20

20

1970   1975   1980   1985   1990   1995   2000   2005   2010   2015   2020   2025

Percentage (1991 = 100)

Percentage (1991 = 100)

160

160

Projection of fuel
consumed:

140

Present policies

140

Strand 1

Strands 1 + 2

120

120

100

100

Fuel consumed in

road transport

80

Strands 1 + 2 + 3

80

60

60

40

40

20

20

1970   1975   1980   1985   1990   1995   2000   2005   2010   2015   2020   2025

Source: OECD, for past trends.

Figure 8.2. **Target dates and major effects of the three policy strands**

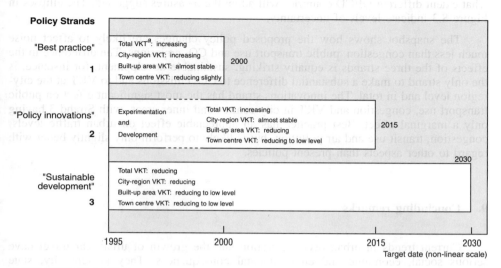

Policy Strands

"Best practice"

1

Total VKT[a]: increasing
City-region VKT: increasing
Built-up area VKT: almost stable
Town centre VKT: reducing slightly

2000

"Policy innovations"

2

Experimentation and Development

Total VKT: increasing
City-region VKT: almost stable
Built-up area VKT: reducing
Town centre VKT: reducing to low level

2015

2030

"Sustainable development"

3

Total VKT: reducing
City-region VKT: reducing
Built-up area VKT: reducing to low level
Town centre VKT: reducing to low level

1995   2000   2015   2030

Target date (non-linear scale)

a) VKT: vehicle-km travelled.

Figure 8.3. **Comparative assessment of proposed OECD/ECMT policies with a continuation of present policies for the year 2015**

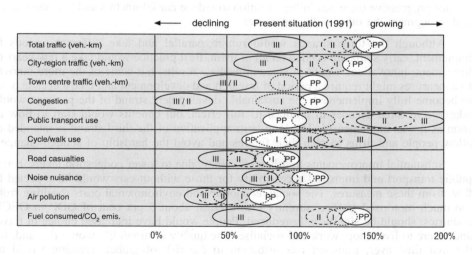

◄— declining   Present situation (1991)   growing —►

Total traffic (veh.-km)		
City-region traffic (veh.-km)		
Town centre traffic (veh.-km)		
Congestion		
Public transport use		
Cycle/walk use		
Road casualties		
Noise nuisance		
Air pollution		
Fuel consumed/CO_2 emis.		

0%   50%   100%   150%   200%

PP: Continuation of present policies.   I: Strand 1.   II: Strand 1 + 2.   III: Strand 1 + 2 + 3.

161

arises from inability to estimate effects so far in advance, as well as from not knowing to what extent different OECD countries will adopt the measures suggested. The ellipses in Figure 8.3 indicate levels of uncertainty.

The snapshot shows how the proposed policy changes are likely to affect noise much less than congestion, public transport use and CO_2 emissions. The difference in the effects of the three strands is equally striking: sustainable development, for instance, is the only strand to make a substantial difference to CO_2 emissions and to VKT at the city-region level and in total. The innovations strand has the most significant effect on public transport use, congestion and VKT in city centres and inner areas, with Strand 3 having only a marginal effect. Best practice has an appreciable effect on urban traffic levels, congestion, transit use and air pollution, but is likely to perform only slightly better with regard to other aspects than present policies.

9. Concluding remarks

Current trends in urban deconcentration and the growth of urban car travel have serious social, economic and environmental consequences. They present city, state and national governments with challenges which can be met only by moving towards sustainable development.

This report sets out three strands of a concerted policy aimed at that goal. The first relies on using the best practice in urban policy found anywhere in the world. The second builds on the first by using innovative land-use and transport measures to reduce the need to travel and converts best practice into a coherent structured policy package. The third applies progressive increases in fuel taxation to reduce car kilometres and CO_2 emissions, and to augment the other policy measures.

Although the three strands would run in parallel and take different periods to implement, early starts are needed on all of them. Best practice would take a few years to implement; innovations would produce immediate results, but some of the more innovative measures might require a period of research and development and take a decade or so to become fully implemented; the sustainable development strand of the package would take two to three decades to produce its full effect, but benefits would start to flow as soon as it was implemented. The long-term application of the third strand is intended to allow people and firms to plan their futures and avoid the hardship of sudden changes.

Substantial improvements to urban efficiency, due to lower congestion levels, better public transport and improved accessibility for those without cars would be expected to flow from these measures. The social, economic and environmental costs resulting from too much motorised traffic, currently estimated at about 5 per cent of GDP in OECD countries, should be significantly reduced. People would have increased choice in travel and where to live, shop, work and socialise. The quality of urban life would rise and, for the first time ever, transport's contribution to the risk of global warming would be significantly reduced.

Annexes

1. URBAN TRAVEL AND ENVIRONMENTAL TRENDS

2. SUMMARY OF NATIONAL STRATEGIC PLANNING
POLICIES

3. SUMMARY OF CASE STUDIES

Annex 1

URBAN TRAVEL AND ENVIRONMENTAL TRENDS

1. Introduction

To complement the information provided by the delegates in their National Overviews of their countries' policies (summarised in Annex 2) and the findings of the Case Studies of twelve large cities and metropolitan regions (summarised in Annex 3), a questionnaire was sent to a large number of OECD/ECMT towns and cities seeking information on urban travel patterns and trends on environmental indicators.

The UK Transport Research Laboratory was asked to participate in the design of the questionnaire and to carry out the analysis of the results. Information was requested on the trends in mode choice, trip lengths, traffic levels and speeds, and the provision of private and public transport. Quantitative and qualitative information was obtained on the severity, spread and trend over time of three types of urban nuisance: congestion, noise and pollution. The cities were then asked to list a range of transport and land-use policies that they had adopted in the last 20 years and to assess their effectiveness in tackling congestion. The cities were also asked to outline any further policies planned to reduce congestion and pollution.

The questionnaire was disseminated by the OECD delegates to the Member countries. In all, 132 cities (ranging in size from 27 000 people to 3.6 million) responded from 19 different countries. Two thirds of the cities were below 0.5 million. Table A1.1 gives the distribution of city sizes for each of the countries. The aim of the analysis was to assess the severity of urban transport problems and to investigate the effectiveness of possible solutions. The analysis has been carried out within the limitations of the information provided by the cities. This annex gives the preliminary results. First, it considers the background trends in travel and transport provision and examines the explanatory factors including the growth in car ownership and the changing nature of cities, which have shaped the nature of present-day travel demand. Following this is a description of the nature of the existing problems and the effectiveness of the policies adopted to date.

2. The changing pattern of travel and underlying trends

In most western countries, the rising level of affluence has been accompanied by growth in car ownership. The increased level of mobility offered by the car has given people more freedom to choose where to live, work, shop and carry out other activities. In turn, the widespread decentralisation of urban activities has encouraged people to travel further. As can be expected, the increase in car travel has contributed to the observed growth in traffic volumes. The consequences for congestion and CO_2 emissions are obvious. This section describes the extent to which these trends are present in the sample of OECD cities.

Table A1.1. **Number and size of cities responding from each country**

		Number of cities	Cities by size[a]			
			< 100	100-500	500-1 000	> 1 000
1.	Australia	5				5
2.	Austria	5	2	2		1
3.	Belgium	3		2	1	
4.	Canada	6	1	3	2	
5.	Denmark	4	1	2		1
6.	Finland	7	4	3		
7.	France	8	1	6		1
8.	Germany	10	2	6	1	1
9.	Great Britain	14		10	3	1
10.	Ireland	1			1	
11.	Italy	11	2	5	1	3
12.	Japan	20		14	3	3
13.	Netherlands	5	1	2	2	
14.	Norway	5	1	4		
15.	Poland	5		1	3	1
16.	Sweden	7	4	3		
17.	Switzerland	7	2	5		
18.	Turkey	1				1
19.	USA	8		1	3	4
Total		132	21	69	20	22

a) Population in thousands.

Car Ownership

There was wide variation in car ownership for the sample of cities. Figure A1.1 shows the distribution of car ownership in the period 1970 to 2000 for all the cities which gave information on car ownership. As the figure shows, in 1990, cars per person varied from 0.1 in Bursa in Turkey to 0.7 in Phoenix (USA). National differences are difficult to detect from the city data. In general terms, many of the cities in USA and Italy are clustered towards the highest levels of car ownership. In most of the European countries, the levels of car ownership were between 0.3 and 0.5. Most of the Polish cities had low levels of car ownership (below 0.3 cars per person).

Table A1.2 gives the number of cities at different levels of car ownership for 1970, 1980 and 1990. Clearly there has been a marked shift towards higher car ownership. Whereas in 1970, 57 per cent of cities had below 0.2 cars per person, by 1990 only 3 per cent of cities were below this level. For levels of 0.4 cars per person and above, the percentage of cities has increased from 9 in 1970 to 45 in 1990.

Despite the wide variation in absolute levels of car ownership, the trends over time show a consistent picture. As Figure A1.1 shows, with one exception, car ownership has risen everywhere in the 1970s and the 1980s. These trends are expected to continue in the 1990s in all cities. On average, cities are predicting further growth of 20 to 25 per cent.

Figure A1.1. **Car ownership: trends and forecasts**

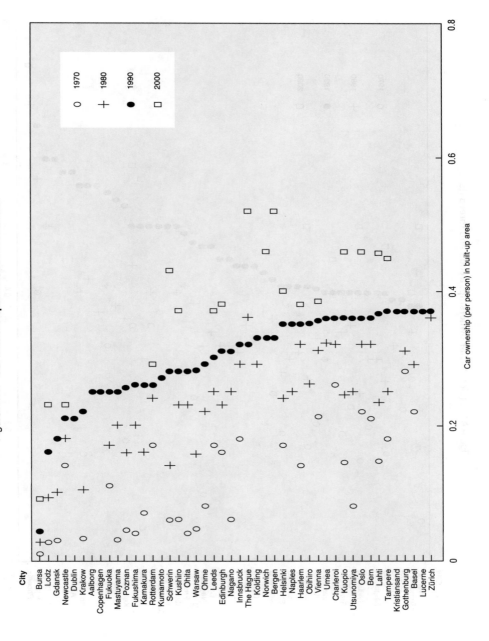

Figure A1.1. (*Cont.*) **Car ownership: trends and forecasts**

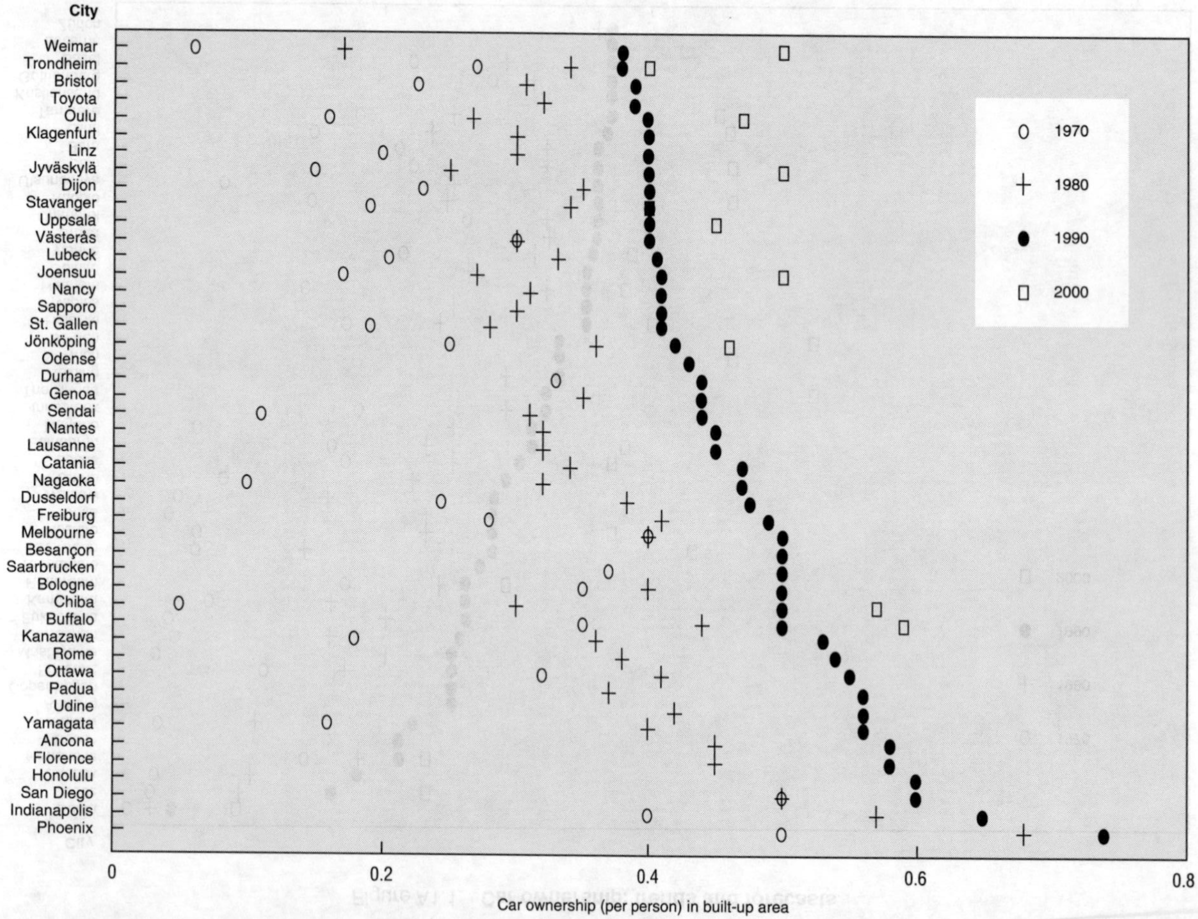

Table A1.2. **Per cent of cities at different levels of car ownership**

Percentages

Cars/person	1970	1980	1990
< 0.20	57	12	3
0.20-0.29	23	31	19
0.30-0.39	10	39	33
0.40-0.49	6	13	26
0.50-0.59	3	3	15
0.60+	–	1	4
Number of cities	68	90	92

Mode choice

The response rate for the mode choice question (question 8) was disappointing. Although half of the cities had given some information on modal split, the data was in many cases incomplete: only a third of the cities had data for the slower modes (that is, walk and cycle). Even where the slower modes were recorded, the data might not be comparable across cities.

The full modal share was available for only 33 cities. These are given in Figure A1.2. Among the cities which had a low (less than 40 per cent) modal share by car, Genoa, Kamakura, Bern, Fukuoka and Chiba had relatively high levels of public transport use. In the other cities which had low car use (including Bursa and the Polish cities), the slow modes were more prominent. In most of the cities, the public transport share is well below 20 per cent.

In view of the lack of data for the slower modes, an analysis was carried out for the car/public transport split. Figure A1.3 shows the car's share of mechanised modes of travel in 51 cities. In the vast majority of cities, the car/public transport split is overwhelmingly biased towards the car. In over half the cities, the car's share of mechanised modes was over 80 per cent, including many of the cities in Finland, Norway, France, Britain, Canada and the USA. In fact, the split was close to 100 per cent in the American cities. Many of the Polish, Swedish, Italian and German cities were below the 50th percentile. The car share of mechanised modes was below 50 per cent in only 6 cities (Krakow, Bursa, Genoa, Bern, Vienna and Kamakura).

There is of course a close association between car ownership and car use and this is reflected in the modal shares. At one extreme, Bursa and most of the Polish cities have low level of car ownership and car use. At the other end of the scale, the American cities have exceptionally high levels of car ownership and car use. In some of the countries the relationship seems to be less clear. In the Italian and the German cities for example, car ownership is very high but car use is relatively low. In many of the European cities (Genoa and Vienna are examples) the low levels of car use cannot be explained by their level of car ownership. In these cases, it is important to consider a much wider set of explanatory factors such as provision of public transport or the type of restraint policies adopted. These will be explored later in Section 5 of this annex.

It was clear from the analysis that, with the exception of a few cities (most notably – Vienna and Fukuoka, both of which have good metro/rail provision; and to a lesser extent, Krakow and Uppsala) the direction of modal transfer was from public transport and the slower modes of travel to the car. These trends have of course been driven by the consistent growth in car ownership. Since car ownership is forecast to grow significantly in the 1990s, it is likely that car use will increase in the vast majority of the cities sampled.

169

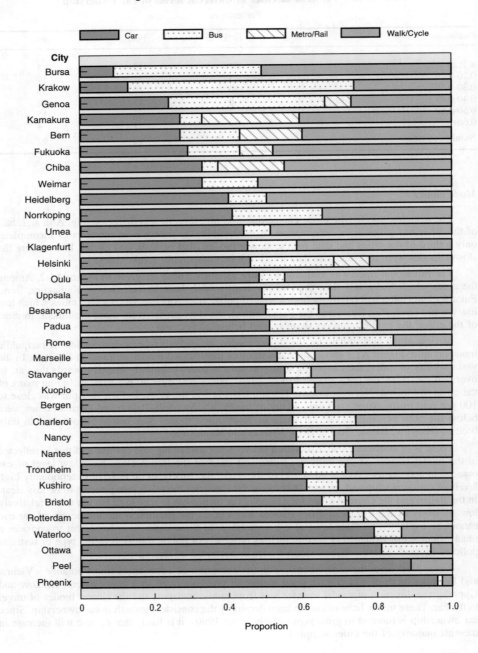

Figure A1.2. **Modal shares in transport,** 1990

Legend: Car · Bus · Metro/Rail · Walk/Cycle

City: Bursa, Krakow, Genoa, Kamakura, Bern, Fukuoka, Chiba, Weimar, Heidelberg, Norrkoping, Umea, Klagenfurt, Helsinki, Oulu, Uppsala, Besançon, Padua, Rome, Marseille, Stavanger, Kuopio, Bergen, Charleroi, Nancy, Nantes, Trondheim, Kushiro, Bristol, Rotterdam, Waterloo, Ottawa, Peel, Phoenix

Proportion

Figure A1.3. Car's share of mechanised modes

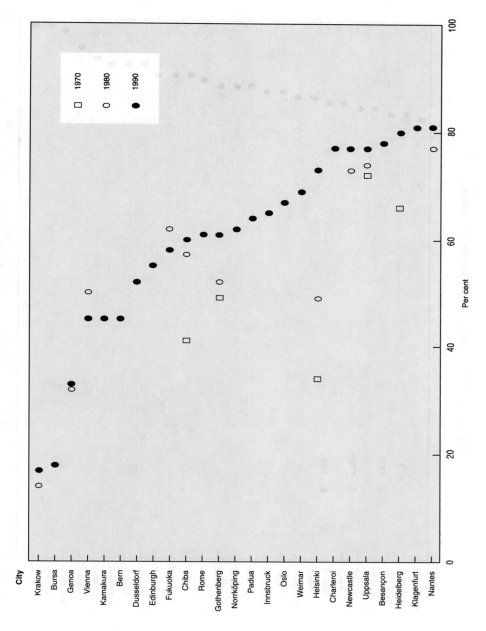

Figure A1.3. (*Cont.*) **Car's share of mechanised modes**

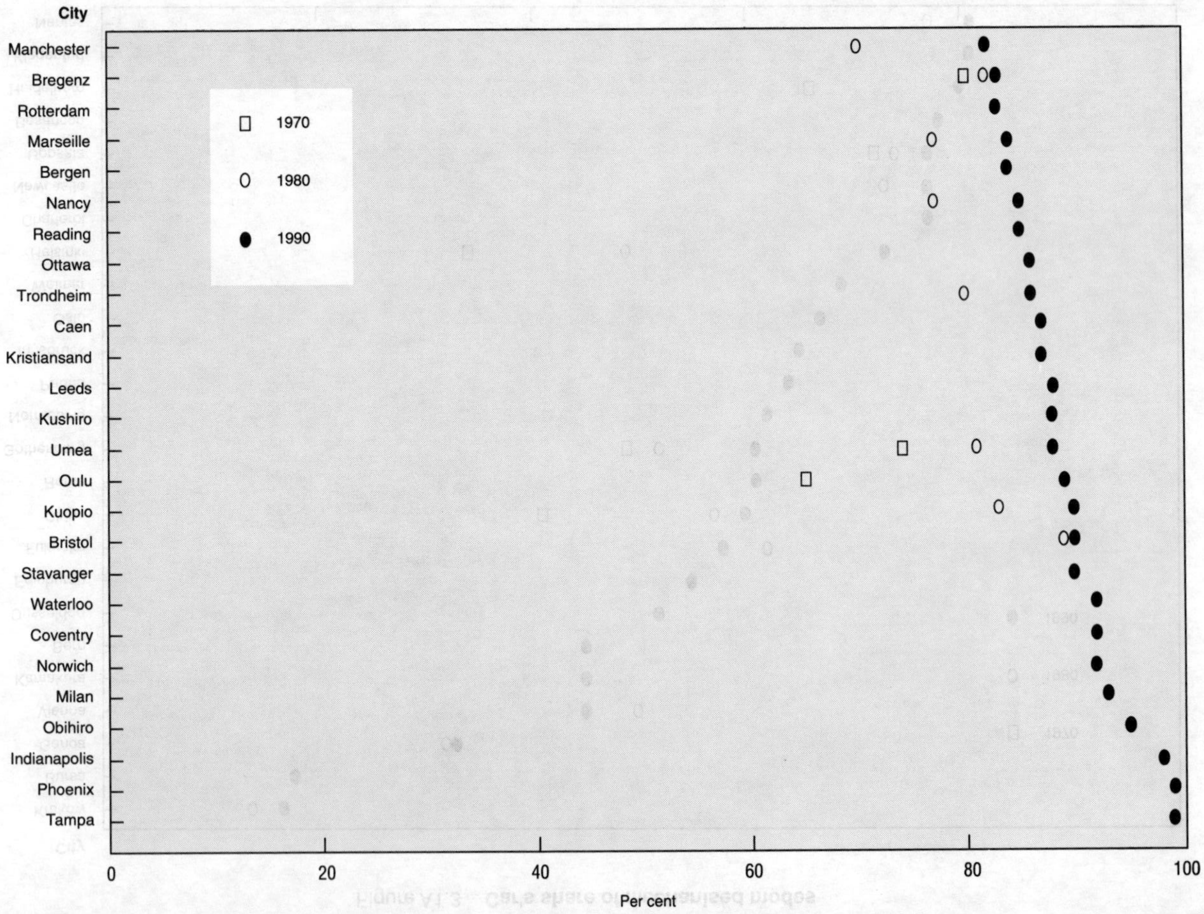

The cities were asked to provide information on changes in population and employment (questions 1 and 2 respectively). Finding a consistent definition for urban areas is a problem faced by most studies of this type. The two types of measures commonly used are − firstly, the contiguously built-up area of the city and secondly, the city region (which includes the commuting hinterland). The questionnaire had asked for population trend for both these areas. In addition, they had been asked for population trend data for the high density inner residential area to obtain a measure of internal structure and levels of centralisation/decentralisation. The response rate for question 1 was very high especially for the most recent year (98 per cent of the cities were able to provide data for the built-up area for the year 1990; about 65 to 70 per cent gave information on the breakdowns by area). For employment, they had been asked for trend data for the built-up area and for the Central Business District (CBD). Again, the response rate was high though not as high as for question 1.

Most cities have readily available data for administrative areas but not for built-up areas and in many cases the former has been provided. This does raise a problem when making cross comparisons specially for indices such as urban densities or route densities which are particularly sensitive to where the urban boundary is drawn. In some cases, the administrative boundary overbounds the built-up area, thus reducing the true urban density. More commonly, administrative boundaries are drawn too tightly (since they are historical in nature and in time the city overspills the boundary) and urban densities are seemingly too high. A consistent density criteria could only be derived for a small number of cities.

In all the non-European countries, that is, Japan, Australia, Canada and USA, the cities have been growing and population and employment are forecast to increase further. European cities show a mixed pattern. Most of the Scandinavian cities and cities in Poland, Turkey and Ireland are still experiencing population growth whereas in most other European countries, population is reasonably stable. In the British and Italian cities, the past trend is mostly one of decline. Switzerland shows a mixed pattern of growth. Many cities have estimated high levels of employment in 1990 and have high forecasts for employment in the year 2000. Given the severity of the current period of recession, some of the forecast growth in employment seems to be somewhat optimistic.

Whether a city is growing or in decline, there is a consistent trend towards decentralisation (from inner to outer areas) of both people and jobs in the vast majority of the cities. Figure A1.4 shows how the proportion of people living in inner city areas has changed in the 1970s and 1980s and gives the forecast for the year 2000. Only those cities for which trend data is available are shown. Clearly, the definition of "inner area" is not consistent across the cities: in some cities, the definition is too narrow and the proportion of population living in the inner area is given as less than 10 per cent (which corresponds more closely with population living in the CBD). In these cities, not surprisingly, there is very little change in the proportions. In other cases, particularly cities in Japan, the inner area boundaries have been drawn too widely and contain over 80 per cent of the city population. In these cases, the trends closely reflect population changes in the city as a whole, and not much weight can be given to interpreting these trends as valid measures of centralisation or decentralisation.

The consistent trend across most of the cities is one of a reduction in the proportion of people living in inner areas. The Japanese cities are exceptions because of the wide definition of their inner areas. In general, the level of decentralisation is more marked in the 1970s than in the 1980s. Where forecasts are available, most cities predict that decentralisation will continue in the 1990s.

Figure A1.4. **Changes in the proportion of people living in the inner area**

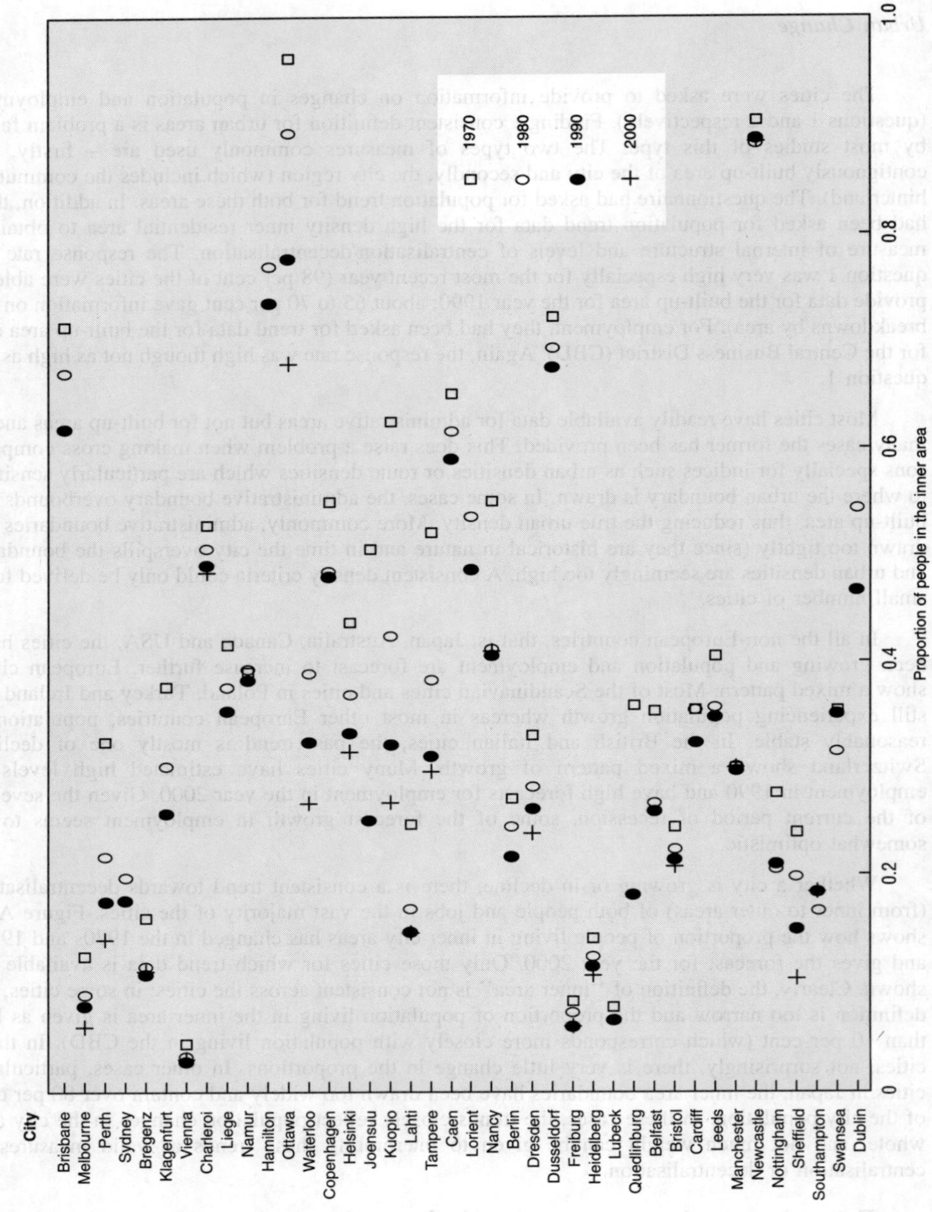

City

Brisbane
Melbourne
Perth
Sydney
Bregenz
Klagenfurt
Vienna
Charleroi
Liege
Namur
Hamilton
Ottawa
Waterloo
Copenhagen
Helsinki
Joensuu
Kuopio
Lahti
Tampere
Caen
Lorient
Nancy
Berlin
Dresden
Dusseldorf
Freiburg
Heidelberg
Lubeck
Quedlinburg
Belfast
Bristol
Cardiff
Leeds
Manchester
Newcastle
Nottingham
Sheffield
Southampton
Swansea
Dublin

1970
1980
1990
2000

Proportion of people in the inner area

0   0.2   0.4   0.6   0.8   1.0

174

Figure A1.4. (*Cont.*) **Changes in the proportion of people living in the inner area**

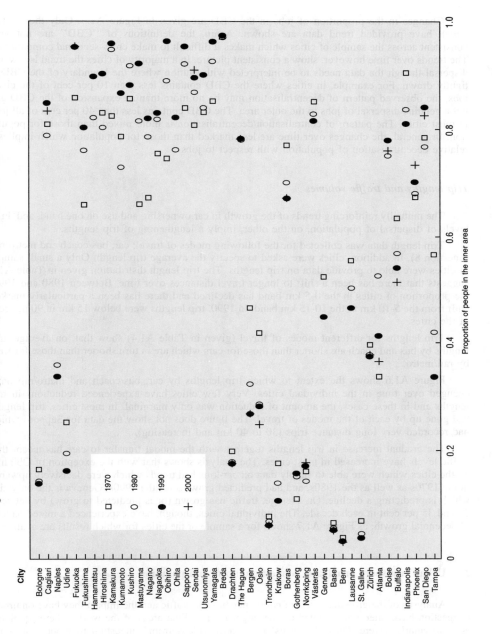

Changes in the proportion of jobs in the CBD are given in Figure A1.5. Only those cities which have provided trend data are shown. Again, the definitions of "CBD" are not very consistent across the sample of cities which makes it difficult to make cross-sectional comparisons. The trends over time however, show a consistent picture. In a majority of cities the trend is towards dispersal though the data needs to be interpreted with caution where the boundary of the CBD is tightly drawn. For example, in cities where the CBD contains less than 10 per cent of the city's jobs, the observed pattern of decentralisation may be no more than an expansion of the CBD and not a genuine dispersal of jobs to the outer area. The CBD contains less than 40 per cent of all jobs in most cities. The pattern of centralisation/decentralisation is more mixed than those for population. In general, the changes over time are less marked than those for population which implies a relative decentralisation of population with respect to jobs.

Trip lengths and traffic volumes

The mutually reinforcing trends of the growth in car ownership and use on one hand, and, high levels of dispersal of population, on the other, imply a lengthening of trip lengths.

Trip length data was collected for the following modes of travel: car, bus/coach and metro/rail (question 8). In addition, cities were asked to specify the average trip length. Only a small sample of cities were able to provide data on trip lengths. The trip length distribution given in Table A1.3 suggests that there has been a shift to longer travel distances over time. Between 1980 and 1990, the proportion of cities in the 0-5 km band has declined and there has been a particularly marked shift from the 5-10 km to the 10-15 km band. In 1990, trip lengths were below 15 km in 90 per cent of the cities.

Trip lengths for different modes of travel (given in Table A1.4) show that, on average, trip lengths by bus and coach are shorter than those for cars which are in turn shorter than those for trips by rail/metro.

Figure A1.6 shows the extent to which trip lengths by car, bus/coach and metro/rail have changed over time in the individual cities. Very few cities have experienced reductions in trip lengths and in these cases, the amount of reduction was only marginal. In most cities, trip lengths had gone up by each of the modes of travel. The figure does not show the data for Sapporo which had recorded very long distance trips (30 to 40 km and increasing).

The gradual increase in trip lengths together with the modal transfer to cars has meant that traffic levels have increased in most cities. The analysis shows that with the exception of Obihiro, all the cities which were able to supply data on car-kms had trends which were decisively upwards in the 1970s as well as the 1980s, and had predicted growths for the 1990s. Geneva is the only city which is predicting a decline. On average, traffic has grown (or is predicted to grow) by between 30 and 35 per cent in each decade. The individual cities, though, have experienced a mixed pattern of decennial growth, as Figure A1.7 shows for a sample of the cities for which results are available.

3. Urban transport problems: congestion, noise and pollution

Analyses of the growing levels of car ownership and traffic and the impact they have on urban congestion have often concentrated on the larger metropolitan areas of the world where problems are particularly severe. Once the focus of concern widens from congestion to global warming, however, it is necessary to consider the smaller urban areas also because the large cities, although they have severe congestion problems, only account for a small fraction of the national population.

Figure A1.5. **Changes in the proportion of jobs in the CBD**

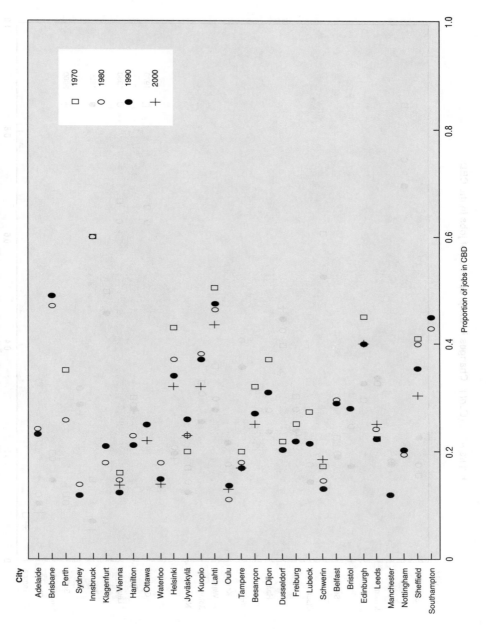

Figure A1.5. (*Cont.*) **Changes in the proportion of jobs in the CBD**

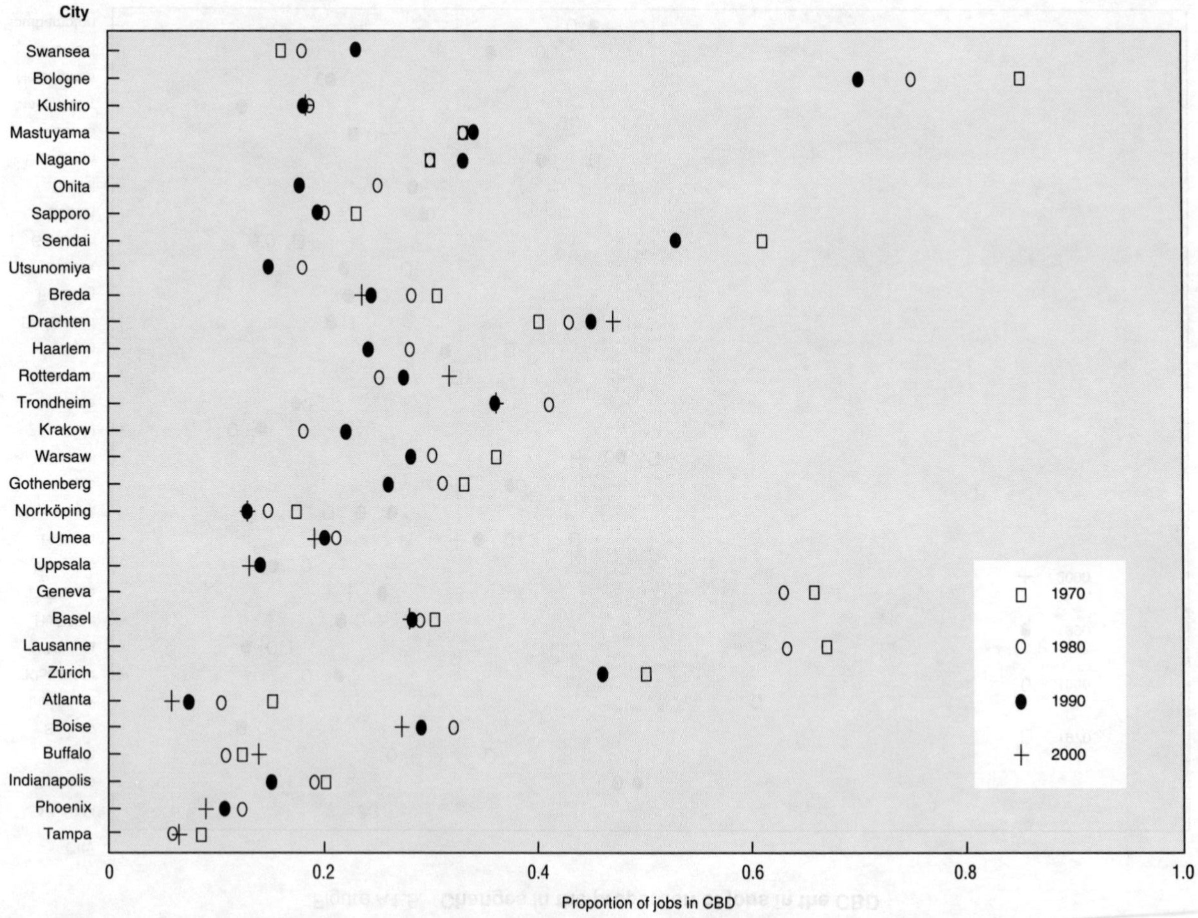

Table A1.3. **Cities categorised by average trip lengths**

Percentages

Average length (kms)	1970[a]	1980	1990
0-5	(56)	32	22
5-10	(33)	54	44
10-15	–	5	25
Over 15	(11)	9	9
Valid cases (= 100 %)	(9)	22	32

a) The 1970 data is for a very small sample.

Table A1.4. **Distribution of trip lengths by modes, 1990**

Percentages

Length (kms)	Car	Bus/coach	Rail/metro
0-5	8	28	13
5-10	49	44	13
10-15	35	23	34
Over 15	8	5	40
Valid cases (= 100 %)	37	39	15

An emerging issue therefore, is the growing level of traffic and the consequent environmental degradation (in terms of congestion and CO_2 emissions) in smaller as well as larger cities. This analysis of OECD/ECMT cities fills a gap in current knowledge with respect to the nature of urban transport problems in a wide spectrum of cities.

Perceived severity, spread and trend

In the questionnaire (question 11) each city had been asked to rate (on a scale of 1 to 5) the severity, spread and trend of three types of urban problems: congestion, noise and pollution. The scales used were:

For *severity:*   1 = no problem   5 = very severe problem
For *spread:*   1 = localised   5 = widespread
For *trend:*   1 = improving   5 = worsening

179

Figure A1.6. Changes in trip lengths by car, bus/coach, and metro/rail

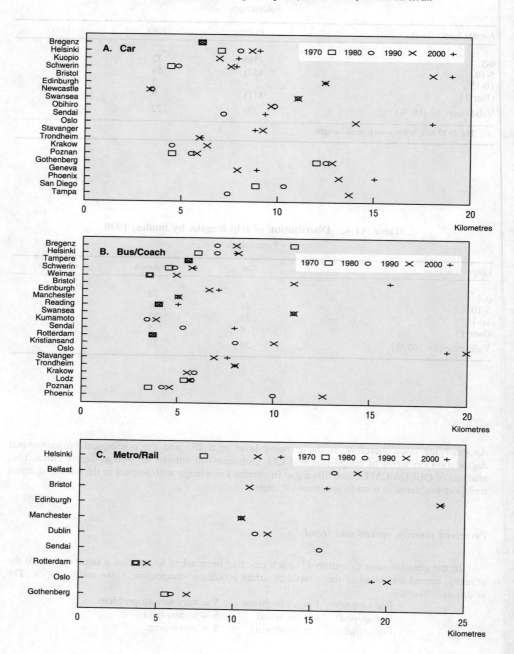

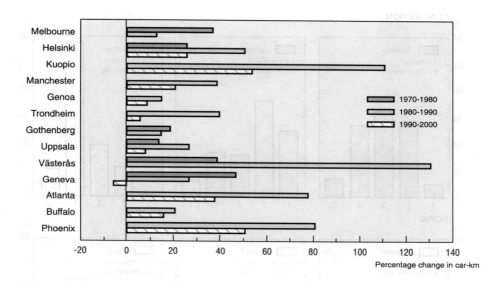

Figure A1.7. **Percentage change in traffic levels: trends and forecasts**

Legend:
- 1970-1980
- 1980-1990
- 1990-2000

Cities (top to bottom): Melbourne, Helsinki, Kuopio, Manchester, Genoa, Trondheim, Gothenberg, Uppsala, Västerås, Geneva, Atlanta, Buffalo, Phoenix

X-axis: Percentage change in car-km (-20, 0, 20, 40, 60, 80, 100, 120, 140)

This type of scoring system is of course highly subjective and the scores given are naturally dependent on the perception of the respondent. A comparison was made of the scores given for the severity of congestion with the traffic speeds recorded in the various cities. Unfortunately, the speed data is not complete – only 63 cities provided speed data. The results (given in Table A1.5) suggest that on average, there is a positive relationship between perceived congestion and speeds, though the standard deviation in some cases is quite high.

Table A1.5. **Perceived congestion versus observed speeds**

Score for congestion severity	Built-up area		CBD	
	Average speed km/h	Standard deviation	AM peak speed km/h	Standard deviation
1	65.0	– (1)	38.0	– (1)
2	41.0	14.4 (12)	22.9	6.2 (12)
3	36.1	10.3 (19)	23.7	9.7 (18)
4	32.9	11.8 (11)	17.9	9.2 (14)
5	27.0	20.0 (3)	16.7	10.6 (4)

Note: Number of valid cases are given in parentheses.

Figure A1.8. Perceived severity, spread and trend of transport problems

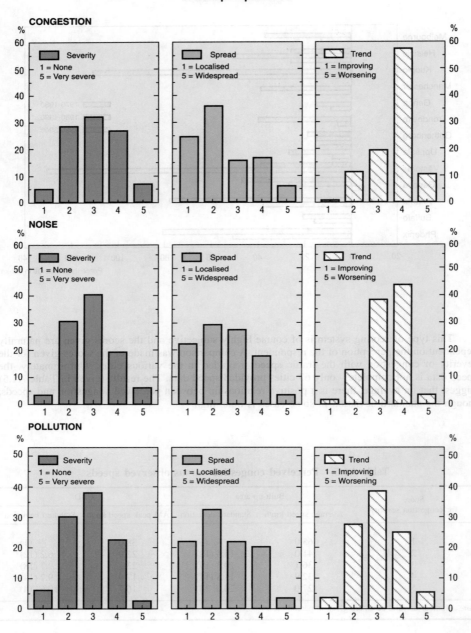

Figure A1.8 gives the summary results for the scores given for the severity, spread and trend of congestion, noise and pollution. Of the 114 cities which responded to the question, a third of the cities perceived congestion to be a severe or very severe problem (ratings of 4 or 5), a third indicated that congestion was not a problem and a third gave a rating of 3 (average levels of congestion. As to the spread of congestion, 60 per cent of the cities said that the problem was localised. However, most of the cities (68 per cent) felt that the problem was worsening over time. The problems of noise and air pollution were perceived to be slightly less acute than those of congestion. About 25 per cent of cities felt that noise and pollution levels were severe or very severe. Both these nuisances were localised over space. As to trend over time, 47 per cent of the cities said that noise levels were increasing. The cities were however optimistic about the trends for air pollution – only 30 per cent said that the trends were getting worse.

The results suggest that the majority of cities in the sample did not feel that they had very severe transport problems. This is probably a reflection of the fact that the sample included many small cities and towns where problems can be expected to be less severe. About two thirds of the sample had a population size of below half a million (see Table A1.1). The average score given for the severity of congestion by cities in different size classes are given in Table A1.6. The table shows that there is some relationship between perceived congestion and city size, the most severe congestion being associated with the largest cities and the least severe with the smallest cities. The relationship between city size and the level of noise is also reasonably clear though the average scores for pollution do not seem to be dependent on city size specially for the larger cities.

Clearly, city size alone does not explain the considerable variations in the scores given for the individual cities particularly for the medium to large cities. There is likely to be some national bias to reflect differences in urban densities, car ownership, provision of roads and so on. Information was collected on all of these parameters though in some cases the data given may not be strictly comparable across the cities. Wherever obvious anomalies exist, the data has either been cleaned as far as possible or eliminated from the analysis if the information given was either misleading or incorrect.

Table A1.7 gives the average scores for the severity of congestion in ascending order for each country. As the table shows, most of the Scandinavian countries are grouped near the top, possibly because the sample of cities responding from these countries tended to be small towns to medium sized cities. Other countries with average or below average scores include Canada and Australia (where low population densities are coupled with a good provision of roads), and Netherlands,

Table A1.6.   **City size and the severity of congestion, noise and air pollution**

City size (population)	Average "score" for the severity of:		
	Congestion	Noise	Pollution
25 000-100 000	2.5 (20)	2.8 (18)	2.5 (18)
100 000-500 000	3.0 (56)	2.9 (57)	2.6 (57)
500 000-1 million	3.2 (19)	3.2 (18)	3.6 (18)
1-3 million	3.2 (17)	2.8 (17)	3.4 (17)
Over 3 million	4.0 (2)	4.5 (2)	3.0 (3)
Total	3.0 (114)	2.9 (112)	2.85 (113)

Note: Number of valid observations are given in parentheses.

Table A1.7. **Perceived severity of congestion in different countries**

	Severity of congestion[a]		Average city size	Average population density	Provision of roads metres/head	Cars/head
Denmark	2.00	(3)	441	2 197	0.60	0.28
Finland	2.00	(7)	149	1 825	0.39	0.38
Sweden	2.00	(5)	155	1 274	0.53	0.39
Norway	2.60	(5)	206	2 119	0.47	0.37
Canada	2.60	(5)	411	1 783	0.48	0.50
Netherlands	2.75	(4)	410	4 269	0.27	0.31
Switzerland	2.83	(6)	199	5 682	0.31	0.38
Australia	3.00	(4)	1 594	938	0.74	0.50
Germany	3.00	(9)	223	4 797	0.29	0.42
France	3.20	(5)	372	4 348	0.26	0.46
Great Britain	3.23	(13)	516	2 736	0.34	0.31
Austria	3.20	(4)	445	6 701	0.27	0.36
Italy	3.27	(11)	941	5 273	0.22	0.51
USA	3.29	(7)	1 534	701	0.40	0.62
Japan	3.32	(19)	485	5 434	0.46	0.36
Belgium	3.66	(3)	410	1 541	–	0.36
Poland	4.00	(4)	663	2 925	–	0.21

Note: Number of valid cases are given in parentheses.
a) Average "score".

Switzerland and Germany where the average size of the responding cities was well below half a million. At the other end of the scale are countries such as Italy and USA where, on average, many large cities had responded. The perceived level of congestion was worst in Poland, probably because traffic and parking problems are relatively new experiences.

Observed levels of congestion

There are very few standard criteria for measuring the level of congestion in urban areas. Some of the common indices include the amount of delay at junctions, or the volume of traffic per route km, or the speed of traffic. Consistent data is rarely available on any of these measures. Few cities collect data on junction delay except in trouble spots and this information was therefore not requested in the survey. Instead, the cities were asked to provide information on the more commonly available data such as the length of the road network (question 4) and traffic flows and speeds (question 9). The response rate for question 4 was 86 per cent but for question 9 it was no more than 30 to 40 per cent. There were variations in the quality and comparability of the data on route km. In some cases, only the length of the main road network had been given. In other cases, the network length included all roads. Similarly, the speed information was not always compatible across all the cities. In some cases, the speed data was only given for measurements at one site.

The questionnaire had asked for four measures of speed: am peak and inter-peak speeds in the built-up area and am peak and inter-peak speeds in the CBD. The distribution of speeds (given in Table A1.8) shows that in a third of the cities which had given speed data, morning peak speeds in the CBD were 19 km/h or less (as a bench mark for comparison, Central London speeds averaged

Table A1.8. **Number of cities in different speed bands, 1990**

Percentage

Km/h	Built-up area		CBD	
	a.m. peak	inter-peak	a.m. peak	inter-peak
< 19	13	2	38	19
20-29	29	18	41	35
30-39	24	20	17	17
40-49	25	20	2	17
50+	9	40	2	12
Valid cases (= 100 %)	55	45	53	42

18 km/h in 1986-90). In contrast, speeds in the morning peak period were much higher in the built-up area as a whole. Indeed, in a third of the cities, the built-up area morning peak speeds were close to or over free flow speeds. In the inter-peak period, 60 per cent of cities had speeds of over 40 km/h in the built-up area.

As Table A1.8 shows, morning peak speeds are on average lower than inter-peak speeds (in the built-up area as well as the CBD) and the CBD speeds are significantly lower than the built-up area speeds (in both time periods). This strongly suggests that congestion is localised in time and in space.

Figure A1.9 confirms that congestion is localised in time and space in the individual cities. With few exceptions, the morning peak speeds are lower than inter-peak speeds in the built-up area as a whole. In the morning peak period, speeds in the CBD are significantly lower than those in the built-up area. In Figure A1.9, the cities have been ordered according to their morning peak speeds in the built-up area. Many of the Japanese and Italian cities are in the lower part of the scale (below 30 km/h) confirming the severity ratings given by the cities in these countries (see Table A1.7). The Scandinavian cities are mostly in the upper half of the scale, again, confirming their perceived ratings. There are, however, some mismatches between the perceived and the observed, particularly in the cities in USA and Poland where the average severity ratings were high but the observed speeds are also relatively high.

As was seen earlier, most of the cities felt that congestion was getting worse over time. This is amply confirmed by the deterioration of speeds in virtually all the cities studied as can be seen in Figures A1.10 and A1.11. The figures give the changes in speed between the period 1970 to 1990, for the CBD and built-up area as well as for the morning peak (Figure A1.10) and inter-peak (Figure A1.11) periods separately. Speeds had declined by about 10 per cent in most of the cities shown. This is in keeping with the trends in traffic given in the previous section. The only cities where speeds have gone up in the 1980s in both time periods and in both areas are: Jyvaskyla in Finland and Genoa in Italy. Speeds were also rising in Sapporo in the morning peak period.

To summarise, current levels of congestion (as perceived and observed) do not appear to be a major problem in many of the cities studied except in the central area where congestion is severe. The trends over time are however indicating that congestion has been getting markedly worse. Given the high forecasts for car ownership and traffic, congestion can be expected to increase significantly in the 1990s.

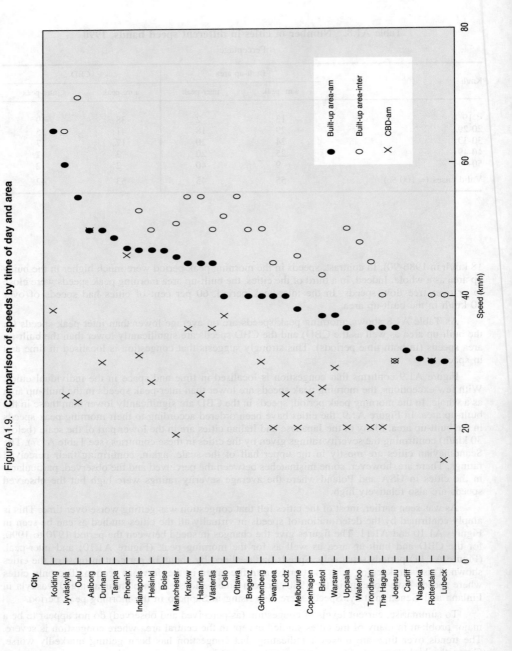

Figure A1.9. Comparison of speeds by time of day and area

186

Figure A1.9. (*Cont.*) **Comparison of speeds by time of day and area**

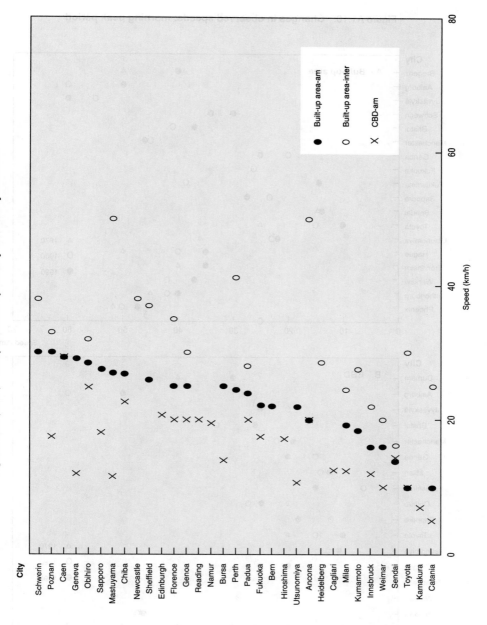

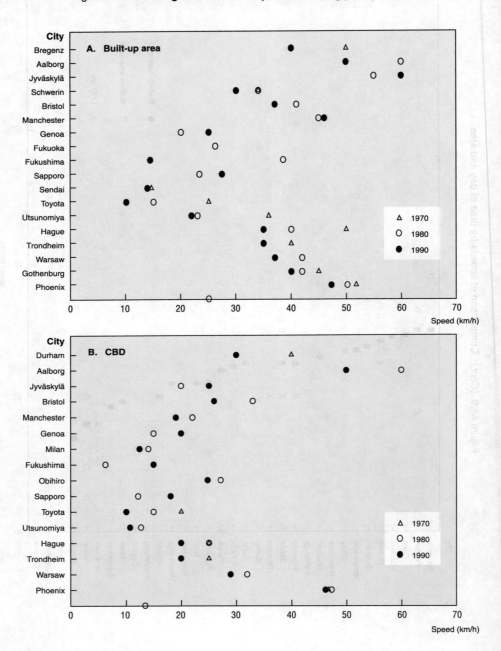

Figure A1.10. **Changes in observed speeds: morning peak period**

Figure A1.11. **Changes in observed speeds: inter-peak period**

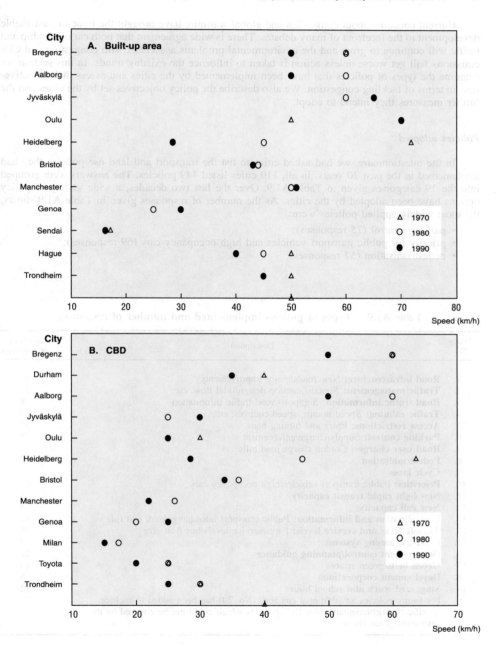

4. Urban transport and land use policies

Current concerns about congestion and global warming have brought the issue of sustainable development to the forefront of many debates. There is wide agreement that both car ownership and traffic will continue to grow and the environmental problems associated with congestion and CO_2 emissions will get worse unless action is taken to influence the existing trends. In this section we examine the types of policies that have been implemented by the cities and assess their effectiveness in terms of tackling congestion. We also describe the policy objectives set by the cities and the further measures they intend to adopt.

Policies adopted

In the questionnaire, we had asked cities to list the transport and land use policies they had implemented in the past 20 years. In all, 110 cities listed 449 policies. The answers were grouped into the 19 categories given in Table A1.9. Over the last two decades, a wide variety of policy options have been adopted by the cities. As the number of responses given in Table A1.9 shows, the most widely applied policies were:

- parking control (75 responses);
- priority for public transport vehicles and high occupancy cars (69 responses);
- pedestrianisation (57 responses);

Table A1.9. **Types of policies implemented and number of responses**

Policy No.	Description	Number of responses
1.	**Road infrastructure:** New roads/major improvements	11
2.	**Traffic management:** Signals/junction design/tidal flow, etc.	53
3.	**Road traffic information:** Signposts/road traffic information	8
4.	**Traffic calming:** Speed humps, speed controls, etc.	23
5.	**Access restrictions:** Entry and turning bans	42
6.	**Parking control:** Supply/charge/enforcement	75
7.	**Road user charges:** Cordon charge/road tolls	3
8.	**Pedestrianisation**	57
9.	**Cycle lanes**	7
10.	**Priorities:** Public transport vehicles/high occupancy cars	69
11.	**New light rapid transit capacity**	6
12.	**New rail capacity**	5
13.	**Co-ordination and information:** Public transport interchange/park and ride	11
14.	**Transit fares and service levels:** Fares/service levels/bus fleet size	26
15.	**Land use zoning systems**	9
16.	**Development control/planning guidance**	22
17.	**Green belts/green spaces**	15
18.	**Development corporations**	6
19.	**Staggered work and school hours**	2
•	For future policies an additional category (No. 20) has been added to include specific "environmentally friendly" policies which could not be covered by the categories given above	

- policies aimed at increasing the capacity of the existing network: junction design, signals etc. (53 responses);
- access restrictions (42 responses).

The only responses concerning road user charges were the toll rings in three Norwegian cities: Oslo, Bergen and Trondheim. The response to land use policies was somewhat disappointing. Clearly most cities operate within a framework for development control. In many cases, development control and planning guidance were mentioned as policies without further expansion. Fifteen cities cited green belts and nine cities mentioned land use zoning systems.

There were some interesting national differences (see Table A1.10) in the policies implemented. Most of the Australian cities, for example, had implemented measures to make public transport more attractive. In Germany, on the other hand, parking control, improvements to the capacity of the existing network and pedestrianisation were the more popular measures. British cities seemed to have a wide spread of transport and land use policies. Most of the British cities had implemented some form of parking control, pedestrianisation and bus priority. In addition, traffic calming was mentioned by 7 cities (higher than in any other country). More cities in Britain had cited land use policies than in any other country. Italian cities were biased towards parking policies, access restrictions and pedestrianisation (possibly related to the conservation of historic core areas). In Japan, public transport priority was the most commonly applied policy.

Table A1.10. **Policies implemented by cities in OECD/ECMT countries**

	1	2	3	4	5	6	7	8	9	10	11	12	13	14	15	16	17	18	19
Australia	0	2	0	1	2	1	0	1	0	4	1	1	0	4	0	2	2	1	0
Austria	0	4	0	1	1	3	0	3	2	3	1	0	1	0	0	0	1	0	0
Belgium	2	0	0	0	0	1	0	1	0	1	1	0	0	0	0	0	0	0	0
Canada	2	0	0	0	0	1	0	0	0	3	0	0	1	1	0	3	2	0	0
Denmark	0	2	0	3	2	4	0	2	1	1	0	0	0	1	1	1	0	0	0
Finland	1	5	0	0	1	7	0	4	0	5	0	0	0	2	0	0	0	0	0
France	3	1	0	0	0	2	0	5	0	2	1	0	2	2	0	0	0	0	0
Germany	0	7	1	3	1	7	0	7	0	1	1	2	1	0	0	0	0	0	0
Great Britain	0	6	0	7	5	11	0	11	1	12	0	1	3	4	3	7	5	4	0
Ireland	0	1	0	0	0	0	0	1	0	1	0	1	0	0	0	0	0	0	0
Italy	0	6	3	1	12	17	0	8	1	6	0	0	0	2	0	1	0	0	0
Japan	1	6	4	0	7	7	0	1	0	13	0	0	2	0	0	1	2	0	2
Netherlands	0	1	0	2	0	3	0	2	0	3	0	0	0	0	1	0	1	0	0
Norway	0	4	0	2	2	3	2	4	1	4	0	0	0	3	1	0	1	1	0
Poland	0	0	0	1	1	1	0	2	0	1	0	0	0	0	0	0	0	0	0
Sweden	1	2	0	0	3	1	0	1	0	3	0	0	0	1	0	1	1	0	0
Switzerland	1	2	0	2	3	4	0	3	1	5	0	0	1	3	1	1	0	0	0
Turkey	0	0	0	0	1	1	0	1	0	0	0	0	0	1	0	1	0	0	0
United States	0	4	0	0	1	1	0	0	0	1	1	0	0	2	2	4	0	0	0
Total	11	53	8	23	42	75	2	57	7	69	6	5	11	26	9	22	15	6	2

Note: Description of each policy is given in Table A1.9.

The cities were asked to assess the effectiveness of the policies they had adopted in terms of reducing congestion. The rating was given on a scale of 1 (not effective) to 5 (very effective). The results are shown in Figure A1.12. In general, transport policies were rated as being much more effective than land use policies. Averaged across the transport policies, well over 60 per cent of the scores were either 4 or 5. In comparison, the average for land use policies was 41 per cent.

Of the more widely applied policies, pedestrianisation was seen as the most effective measure (75 per cent gave a rating of 4 or 5). The second most effective group of measures were those concerned with public transport fares and service levels (68 per cent gave ratings of 4 or 5). Sixty-one per cent of the cities said that policies which increase the capacity of the network were very effective. In contrast, measures that restrict access (entry and turning bans for example) and measures that reduce capacity (bus priority and cycle lanes for instance) were considered to be relatively less effective (though even for these policies, over 50 per cent of cities gave ratings of 4 or 5). The other policies rated highly (though not as many cities had adopted them) were: provision of new roads; improved traffic information and traffic calming.

The effectiveness ratings given above can only provide a subjective guide. Quantitative measures of the impact of policies are much more difficult to derive because the causal influences are complex and the relevant interactions take place over long periods of time. Nevertheless, some anecdotal evidence can be drawn from the questionnaire data. There are some cities in the sample where there is an indication that either car ownership or traffic levels or modal split or speeds are not reflecting the general trends. Among these are the Hague, where car ownership is decreasing, but whether this arises from policies adopted cannot be determined because of the lack of data provided by the city. One of the few cities where the modal split has changed in favour of the non-car modes is Vienna, where there is a good provision of metro (which has been expanding steadily since 1970) and rail. Genoa had experienced an increase in speeds in spite of a 15 per cent increase in traffic levels. The city had implemented a wide variety of traffic measures including road traffic informatics. Another city where speeds had gone up (in the am peak) was Sapporo where there had been a large modal shift to metro/rail (from cars as well as other modes) for trips to the CBD.

Objectives, targets and further measures planned

Though many of the cities felt that their traffic management policies had been very effective, these had been aimed largely at solving local congestion. As we have seen earlier, the general consensus (confirmed by the observed trends for speeds) was that the overall level of congestion is getting worse. To assess whether future policies will influence existing trends, we had asked the cities to describe their traffic and environmental objectives and list what further measures they had planned to reduce congestion and pollution (question 13).

Of course, many countries already have objectives, guidelines and targets for reducing pollution. Most cities work within these national and/or federal frameworks. Examples of national legislation and targets include the Clean Air legislation in Switzerland, the national air quality standards (NAAQ) set in the USA, the targets for reducing accidents in the UK, and a variety of EU legislation with respect to emission of pollutants. Given their national frameworks, it was perhaps not surprising that few cities had mentioned the reduction of pollution as a specific objective. Cities which had set targets for the reduction of pollution included Innsbruck, Linz, Copenhagen, Berlin, Sapporo, St Gallen and Zurich. Only four cities (Linz, Copenhagen, Dusseldorf and Heidelberg) had mentioned the reduction of CO_2 emissions as an objective. Noise reduction was mentioned as an objective in Innsbruck and Berlin (which had set targets) as well as Copenhagen, Hague and Luzern.

Figure A1.12. **Perceived effectiveness of policies in tackling congestion**

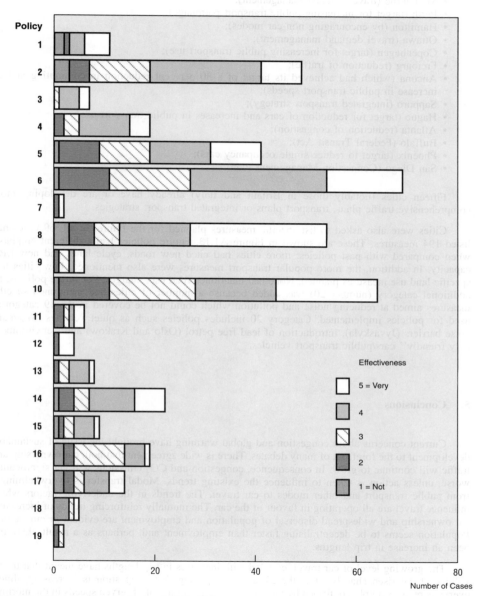

Policy

Effectiveness

- 5 = Very
- 4
- 3
- 2
- 1 = Not

Number of Cases

Note: Description of each policy is given in Table A1.9.

The cities which had listed the reduction of congestion or the management of demand as objectives and the methods they had listed are given below:

- Melbourne (travel demand management);
- Perth (target for increasing public transport patronage);
- Hamilton (by encouraging non-car modes);
- Ottawa (travel demand management);
- Copenhagen (target for increasing public transport use);
- Freiburg (reduction of traffic);
- Ancona (which had achieved its target of a 30 per cent reduction in commuting and an increase in public transport speeds);
- Sapporo (integrated transport strategy);
- Hague (target for reduction of cars and increases in public transport use);
- Atlanta (reduction of congestion);
- Buffalo (Federal Transit Act);
- Phoenix (target to reduce single occupancy cars);
- San Diego (Congestion Management Plan).

Fifteen cities (notably those in Britain and Italy) already have or are developing more comprehensive traffic plans, transport plans or integrated transport strategies.

Cities were also asked to list specific measures planned for the future. In all, 69 cities had listed 194 measures. These are shown in Figure A1.13. Future policies had a different emphasis when compared with past policies: more cities had cited new roads, cycle lanes and new LRT capacity. In addition, the more popular transport measures were also mentioned. Few cities had specific land use measures planned. None had mentioned road user charges. For future policies, an additional category (number 20) was added because a number of cities had mentioned specific measures aimed at reducing noise and pollution which could not be covered in the 19 categories used for policies implemented. Category 20 includes policies such as quiet vehicles (Weimar), noise barriers (Jyvaskyla), introduction of lead free petrol (Oslo and Krakow) and "environmentally friendly" cars/public transport vehicles.

5. Conclusions

Current concerns about congestion and global warming have brought the issue of sustainable development to the forefront of many debates. There is wide agreement that both car ownership and traffic will continue to grow. In consequence, congestion and CO_2 emissions will get significantly worse, unless action is taken to influence the existing trends. Modal transfer is overwhelmingly from public transport and other modes to car travel. The trends in the underlying factors which influence travel are all operating in favour of the car. The mutually reinforcing trends of increasing car ownership and widespread dispersal of population and employment are evident in most cities. Population seems to be decentralising faster than employment and, perhaps as a result, there has been an increase in trip lengths.

The growing level of car travel, coupled with increases in trip lengths have meant that traffic volumes have risen sharply. It is therefore not surprising that congestion is increasing almost everywhere, as is amply confirmed by the universal deterioration of observed speeds in the morning and inter-peak periods in the Central Business District (CBD) as well as in residential areas.

Figure A1.13. **Future measures planned**

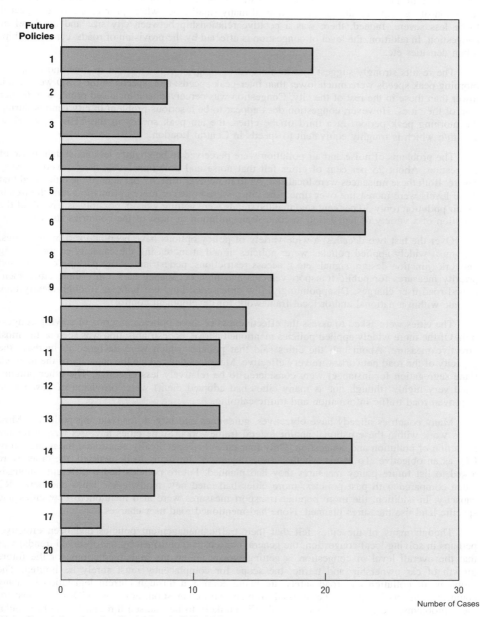

Note: Description of each policy is given in Table A1.9.

Even though the majority (68 per cent) of the cities felt that congestion was getting worse over time, only a third of the cities perceived congestion to be a severe or very severe problem. This is a reflection of the fact that the sample contained many small cities where problems can be expected to be less severe. Indeed, there was a positive relationship between city size and the level of congestion. In addition, the level of congestion is affected by the provision of roads, car ownership, urban densities etc.

The results strongly suggest that in most cities congestion is localised in time and in space: morning peak speeds were much lower than inter-peak speeds; and, speeds in the CBD were much lower than those in the rest of the city. Congestion was perceived as a localised problem in 60 per cent of the cities. However, congestion does appear to be a serious problem in city centres during the morning peak period. In a third of the cities, the am peak speeds in the CBD were below 19 km/h which is roughly equivalent to speeds in Central London.

The problems of noise and air pollution were perceived to be slightly less acute than those of congestion. About 25 per cent of cities felt that noise and pollution levels were severe or very severe. Both these nuisances were localised. As to trend over time, 47 per cent of the cities said that noise levels were increasing over time. The cities were however more optimistic about the trends for air pollution (only 30 per cent said that the trends were getting worse), possibly as a result of the adoption of a variety of legislation to control air pollution in most of the countries studied.

Over the last two decades, a wide variety of policy options have been adopted by the cities. The most widely applied policies were: policies aimed at increasing the capacity of the existing network (junction design, signals etc.); access restrictions; pedestrianisation; parking control; and priority measures for public transport vehicles and high occupancy cars. Only three cities mentioned road user charges. Disappointingly, few cities cited land use policies (though clearly they operate within a national and/or local framework for development control).

The cities were asked to assess the effectiveness of these policies in terms of solving congestion. Of the more widely applied policies mentioned above, pedestrianisation was seen as the most effective measure. About half the cities said that policies which were designed to increase the capacity of the road network were very effective. Measures that reduce the capacity of the network (lane segregation for instance) were considered to be relatively less effective. The other policies rated very highly (though not as many cities had adopted them) were: provision of new roads; improved road traffic information and traffic calming.

Many countries already have objectives, guidelines and targets for reducing pollution. Most cities work within these national and/or federal frameworks. Some cities have set targets for the reduction of pollution and congestion. Only four cities had specifically mentioned the reduction of CO_2 as an objective. To assess whether these objectives are likely to be realised, the cities were asked to list future policy measures they had planned. Future policies had a different emphasis when compared with past policies: more cities had cited new roads, cycle lanes and new LRT capacity. In addition, the more popular transport measures were also mentioned. Few cities had specific land use measures planned. None had mentioned road user charges.

Though many of the cities felt that their traffic management policies had been effective, perhaps in solving local congestion, the general consensus (confirmed by the observed trends) was that the overall level of congestion is getting worse. Given the high predictions for the future growth of car ownership and traffic, the scope for complacency must surely be limited. The problems of pollution and road safety are being addressed through current legislation in many countries, but this leaves a large residual problem with congestion, noise and CO_2 emissions: for these problems, the concept of sustainability is unlikely to be realised through the more popular policies adopted currently.

SUMMARY OF NATIONAL STRATEGIC PLANNING POLICIES

1. Introduction

Each country taking part in this project was asked to prepare an overview of national policies on urban travel and urban development in order to provide a broad picture of what is happening in each of the countries, what problems have been experienced and what measures have been taken to combat them, and with what success. They were also asked to indicate the type of plans which are being made, or could be made, in order to make cities safer and more pleasant places in which to live, work, shop and socialise, while at the same time reducing the harmful effects of travel. The point of bringing these National Overviews together and summarising the main findings is to see how much common ground there is between countries in their policies and their approaches and what successes have been achieved so that each may learn from the experiences of the others.

Even when brought together, the Overviews were not intended to provide a complete picture of urban travel and its consequent problems. They form just one part, a very important part, of the data base for the study, alongside the Questionnaire results, the Case Studies and the papers of the Basle (Frey and Langloh, 1992) and Dusseldorf conferences (OECD, 1993*b*).

Most of the information given in the Overviews has been included in the main body of the report. This annex contains brief descriptions only of overall policy for each of the countries concerned, together with a summary of the main conclusions drawn from analysing all the information given in the Overviews in a similar and consistent way.

2. Main aspects of policy of participating countries

The overall policies of countries are considered in alphabetical order.

Australia

Traditionally State and Local governments in Australia have had the responsibility for urban transport, land-use planning and environmental issues, but there have also been initiatives by the Commonwealth government to combat problems associated with urban travel. The Australian Design Rule System, backed by law, controls the design of vehicles to meet air pollution, noise and safety standards – these rules are currently being revised. The Building Better Cities programme is part of a long-term strategy to create more efficient, equitable, ecologically sustainable and liveable cities by promoting better integrated urban development, urban consolidation and urban renewal and is based on a partnership with the Federal, State and Local governments. It will provide

A$ 816 million (ECU 506 million) over the next 5 years. The funding and operation of urban public transport is primarily a State government responsibility but the Commonwealth government has made resources available for this purpose since 1983. Current funding of A$ 200 million (ECU 124 million) over 3 years to 1993 has been targeted to the outer urban areas which tend to have the poorest public transport facilities.

Following comment on a Commonwealth Government Discussion paper on Ecologically Sustainable Development, several working groups were established to formulate strategies to encourage the integration of environmental considerations into decision making in Australia's major industrial sectors. A number of recommendations on urban planning, transport infrastructure investment, traffic restraint, traffic control, urban freight, emission control and issues of social equity have followed from these studies. The Commonwealth government has adopted a planning target to stabilise those greenhouse gases not controlled by the Montreal Protocol (which referred to Ozone depleting substances) at 1988 levels by the year 2000 and reducing these emissions by 20 per cent by the year 2005.

Austria

The primary objectives of the Austrian urban and transport policies are to stem the growth of private transport and relieve pressure on the environment, mainly through improvements to the local public transport system and more stringent parking policies. The Federal government's contributions are mainly, but not entirely, financial. Since 1975 investment in the Austrian Railways urban network serving the major cities has amounted to A$ 20 billion (ECU 1.5 billion).

Canada

Canada is a diverse country, with many jurisdictions involved in transportation and planning. In a study of the sustainability of urban travel, an assessment has been made of the likely impacts of 25 major types of initiatives, which were considered to be capable of improving sustainability. These were assessed against a number of objectives concerned with reducing the need to travel, conserving energy and improving the environment. This assessment is summarised in Table A2.1. Powerful measures, like congestion pricing, compact and mixed land uses, HOV (high occupancy vehicles) facilities, rapid transit/commuter rail networks and pedestrian/bicycle ways were considered to be the most effective devices.

An examination was made of the current urban transportation activities in the eight largest urban regions of the country to determine the extent to which the 25 initiatives were being undertaken in each. This suggested that in urban Canada, most initiatives to improve the sustainability of transportation have advanced beyond the talking stage to concrete planning (32 per cent) or actual implementation (28 per cent). Thus, a start has been made in Canada in addressing the long-term problems of urban transportation.

Denmark

Denmark has set up a national transport action plan, "Traffic 2005", which expresses a number of objectives concerning energy consumption, air pollution and noise, to be achieved in the coming years. For energy consumption and air pollution, the objectives are: a stabilisation of the energy consumption and CO_2 emissions before 2005 and a 25 per cent reduction before 2030; a reduction of the NO_x and HC emissions of 40 per cent before 2000 and 60 per cent before 2030; a

Table A2.1. **Canadian assessment study of sustainable urban travel: initiatives and interactions**

Measures of more sustainable urban travel / Major types of initiatives	Reduced vehicular travel effort				Greater conservation of resources		Improved environmental quality		Improved economic efficiency		Enhanced quality of life		Broadened lifestyle choices	
	Shorter trips	More walking	More transit	More cycling	Fossil fuels	Farm-land	Air emissions	Water runoff	Less congestion	Lower transport costs	Greater safety	People places	Housing types	Travel modes
Urban structure/ design policies														
• Compact mixed land use	+++	+++	+++	+++	+++	+++	++	++	++	++	+++	+++	+++	+++
• Pedestrian-friendly streets	+	+++	+++	+++	+++	++	++	++	+	+	+++	+++	+	++
• Joint transportation/land use planning	++	+++	+++	+++	+++	+++	+++	+++	+++	+++	++	+++	++	+++
• Dev. nodes and intermodal transfer nodes	+	++	+++	+	++	++	++	++	+++	++	++	+++	+++	+++
• Parking supply management	+	++	+++	++	++	++	++	++	+++	++	+	++	+	+
Transportation infrastructure														
• Continuous, multi-modal arterial roads	++	++	+++	++	+		++		+++	+	+	++		++
• High occupancy vehicle (HOV) facilities	+	++	+++	++	+++	++	+++	+++	+++	+++	+++	+++	+	+++
• Rapid transit and commuter rail networks	+	++	+++	+	+++		+++	+++	+++	++	+++	+++	++	+++
• Local transit improvements	+	++	+++	+	++	+	+++	+++	+	+	+++	+++	+	+++
• Cycle and pedestrian ways	+++	+++	++	+++	+++	++	+++	+++	+++	++	+++	+++	+	++
Demand management practices														
• Parking price management	+	++	+++	++	++	++	++	++	+++	++	+	++	+	+
• Congestion pricing for road use	+++	+++	+++	+++	+++	++	+++	+++	+++	++	+++	+++	+	++
• Alternative work schedules	+++	++	++	+	++		++	++	+++	++	+	+		++
• Ridesharing		+			++		++	+	+++	+++	+	+	+	++
• Telecommuting	+++	++	+	++	+++	++	+++	+++	+++	++	++	++	++	+

199

Table A2.1. **Canadian assessment study of sustainable urban travel: initiatives and interactions** (*cont'd*)

Measures of more sustainable urban travel / Major types of initiatives	Reduced vehicular travel effort				Greater conservation of resources		Improved environmental quality		Improved economic efficiency		Enhanced quality of life		Broadened lifestyle choices	
	Shorter trips	More walking	More transit	More cycling	Fossil fuels	Farm-land	Air emissions	Water runoff	Less congestion	Lower transport costs	Greater safety	People places	Housing types	Travel modes
Transit management practices														
• Fare integration and schedule coordination		+	+++		++	++	+++	+++	+++	+++	+++	+++		+++
• Transit priority		+	++		++	++	++	++	++	++	++	++		++
• Traveller information systems	+	+	++	+	++	+	+	+	++	++	+	+		+
Traffic management practices														
• Advanced traffic management systems	++	+	+++		+		+++	++	+++	++	++	+	+	
• Driver information systems	+	+	++	+	++		++	+	++	+	+++			+
• Traffic calming		+	+++	+	++				++		+++	+++		
Cleaner vehicle technology development														
• Low-emission vehicles			++		++		+++	+++				+		++
• Energy-efficient vehicles			++		+++		++	++						++
• Emissions monitoring/testing programmes					+++		+++				+			
Public outreach and awareness programmes	++	++	++	++	++	++	++	++	++	++	++	++	++	++

Notes: Anticipated impact of initiative in helping to achieve Sustainable Urban Travel:
  +++ Large impact;
  ++ Moderate impact;
  + Modest impact.
Source: Canadian Overview.

200

50 per cent reduction of solid particle pollution before 2010 and a further reduction in the years after. The objective for noise is that not more than 50 000 homes should be subject to noise levels greater than 65 dB(A) by 2010 (corresponding roughly to a 65 per cent reduction).

These objectives are to be achieved by:

- influencing transport demand and modal split;
- improving the alternatives to car transport;
- reducing pollution problems;
- reorientation of transport investment plans;
- improving planning and research in traffic.

A separate action plan has been made for road safety, the objective of which is to reduce the number of casualties in the period 1988-2000 by 40-45 per cent.

To reduce the environmental impact of traffic in Danish cities, local councils are encouraged to make local action plans for traffic and the environment. The objectives of these action plans should relate to national objectives and include additional goals for reducing visual intrusion and severance caused by traffic. The Danish Environmental Protection Agency gives professional advice and financial support to local councils.

Finland

Transport policy in Finland, and especially in Helsinki, has favoured public transport since the early 1970s, mainly through the improvement of public transport services and the control of car parking in the central areas. Standards for noise and pollution have been set and all new major transport projects are subject to an environmental impact assessment which will be backed by law when the necessary legislation has been passed.

France

In France a partnership between the planning and transport authorities was set up as a result of the 1982 Transport Act which affirmed the need for a single authority at city level to be responsible for urban travel. This body is required to produce urban travel plans for transport, traffic and parking ensuring that pedestrians, cyclists and public transport users are properly catered for. Operational programmes, subsidised by government, are now being established and have as their aims to reduce travel, improve the environment, upgrade city life, enhance security and protect the environment.

Germany

Experience in Germany indicates that technical solutions on their own (road and rail construction, for example) have only a limited chance of influencing traffic conditions in cities. Urban and transportation planning will in future focus on the objectives of urban development, environmental improvement and urban quality. Each individual measure will be considered with respect to the contribution it makes towards improving the co-operation between the different modes of transport. Research in the field of urban development and transportation is being carried out by the Federal Ministry for Housing, Building and Urban Development using theoretical models to study the impacts of integrated policy approaches. Avoidance of additional traffic will be a necessary condition for all new development and must be taken into account at the planning stages of new settlement structures, whether using existing or new transportation routes. The concept of traffic avoidance will be supported by legal, fiscal and technical measures, as well as by those which influence traffic behaviour.

Italy

An information programme on environmental planning is being set up in Italy to disseminate new concepts on town planning to promote measures which are more environmentally sensitive. Technical measures concerning controls on emissions have already been implemented and now environmental planning programmes are being set up for specified areas of cities: these will define the main planning guidelines and will aim to create new districts with especially good urban amenities so as to offset the tendency to concentrate all such amenities in the main historic centres. This strategy of alternative districts will be closely associated with improvements in public transport and basic services.

Japan

Local governments have the primary administrative responsibility for urban planning in Japan but central government is in charge of the construction and maintenance of roads and the overall administration of railways. Comprehensive urban transport plans based on person-trip surveys have been periodically updated. Public transport by rail, both within and between cities, is extremely efficient, comprehensive and well used. Perhaps because of this there seems to be no obvious attempts to reduce car travel. In fact urban road investment has been increasing rapidly quite recently. Because of the size of the major Japanese cities and the excessive amount of time spent travelling, more emphasis is placed on decentralisation of activities and increasing mobility than in most other countries.

Luxembourg

Public transport has been improved considerably since 1990 by increasing train capacity by some 40 per cent, by adjusting bus services in Luxembourg-city and by creating a fares structure which allows free interchange throughout the country. Commuters are discouraged from using their cars by restricting the parking supply. A new system allowing regional trains to come closer to the city centre is under consideration.

The Netherlands

In the Netherlands, the Dutch government is pursuing a policy designed to restrain mobility without undermining the relatively large contribution that the transport sector makes to the national income. A location policy for businesses and services ''The right business in the right place'' is aimed at cutting down on the avoidable use of cars by siting new enterprises where transport needs can, where possible, be met by public transport and bicycle. They aim to limit the increase in traffic between 1986 and 2010 to only 35 per cent, reduce CO_2 emissions by at least 10 per cent, reduce emissions of NO_x and unburned hydrocarbons by road vehicles by 75 per cent, halve the number of homes whose external walls are exposed to noise levels in excess of 55 dB(A), halve the number of fatalities and injuries and reverse the fragmentation of the countryside and the natural environment. A variety of policy measures are proposed to achieve these results. Dutch policy lays special emphasis on promoting public transport, cycling and walking in place of the use of the private car.

Norway

Norwegian policy to reduce environmental impacts from transport is considered in the context of a national environmental policy with cost-efficiency as the guiding principle. This means that global and regional problems should be tackled using economic instruments applied to all emissions which contribute to the same problems. The use of such instruments should be harmonised both at the national and international level. These instruments will also have an effect on local problems, but additional measures will be required in many urban areas to reduce local air pollution and noise to an acceptable level.

Within the overall policy, a mixture of instruments is employed, of which economic and regulatory measures take precedence. In 1991, a CO_2 tax was introduced. Norwegian emission standards are mainly the same as those of the EU in this field. As a result of the EEA-agreement, Norway will have to implement future EU directives on emissions standards.

The Pollution Control Act will soon be applied to the transport sector. New provisions under the Act will set environmental quality standards concerning local air pollution and noise. If these standards are exceeded, the responsible polluter, or polluters (for instance, the owners of transport infrastructure, industry and heating plants) must take measures to reduce pollution or noise below the prescribed limits. According to the Building and Planning Act, city authorities and municipal authorities at county level are obliged to co-ordinate all land-use planning, road building and traffic planning. National guidelines conveying national policy in this field have recently been adopted by the government. Impact assessment reports are required as a basis for decisions on long-term development of the land-use and transport system.

Poland

Urban transport policy in Poland has for decades stressed the leading role of public transport. Ambitious comprehensive land-use/transportation plans have been produced, in which single function areas (residential, commercial, industrial, etc.) are linked with public transport provision (metros, light railways, rapid tramway, etc.). Different zones of cities are given different treatment with regard to public and private transport facilities. Because of lack of resources, however, only a fraction of these plans has been implemented, partly because they were over-ambitious and partly because of political and economic reforms during the last few years, which brought about a rapid growth of motorisation. In Warsaw, for example, there are now more than 300 passenger cars per thousand inhabitants. The transition from a centrally-controlled system to a market-based economy has affected urban public transport, which is now suffering a decline. New urban transport policy is being formulated at both local and central levels to cope with rapid growing traffic congestion and emerging economic and environmental problems.

Sweden

In Sweden, environmental aspects are actively incorporated within the transport sector, in order to find solutions which satisfy both the need for mobility and transportation and the need for reducing the external effects from traffic. Each year, the National Road, Rail, Sea and Air Transport Administrations produce a statement of the impact of their traffic mode regarding air emissions, noise, congestion, etc. Included in these ''environmental reports'' is a forecast of the future situation, and recommendations for action that is required to reach the environmental targets set by Parliament. The Ministry of Environment and Natural Resources and its agencies has a strategic planning and auditing role in this process, setting and monitoring the targets. General policy for reducing the impact from CO_2 emissions in the transport sector comprises the following: increased use of biofuels, use of economic instruments, improvements in public transport systems and improved efficiency in vehicle energy consumption.

In 1988, the Swedish Parliament introduced measures to internalise the external costs of travel and implement the "polluter pays" principle. In 1991, a system of environmental categories and taxes for Diesel oil was introduced. The differentiation is based on the contents of sulphur and aromatic hydrocarbons. This has proved to be an effective way of encouraging the use of cleaner fuels and lower emissions from buses, trucks and tractors. Now 80 per cent of Diesel traffic uses cleaner fuels and standard Diesel oil is disappearing from the market. Tax reduction on cleaner Diesel oil was the crucial factor in this rapid transition. The Swedish Government introduced a CO_2 tax in 1991 which is currently set at SKr 0.74 (ECU 0.08) per litre of petrol and SKr 0.92 (ECU 0.1) per litre of Diesel oil. Environmental classes on new cars were introduced in 1993 and on heavy vehicles in 1994.

In 1990 the Swedish government appointed special negotiators to consider radical solutions for the cities of Stockholm, Gothenburg and Malmo. They are required to consult with planners at the regional and municipal levels and to draw up a programme of measures for the improvement of traffic and the environment. The measures will include road and rail investment, charges levied on users, measures to reduce noise and improve the street environment, and new controls on vehicle emissions. The government is allocating SKr 5 500 million (ECU 575 million) as a contribution towards these measures, which will also be financed by the national road and rail administrations, the county councils and from vehicle tolls. In total some SKr 36 000 million (ECU 3 750 million) will be invested in this way during the 1990s.

Switzerland

Transport policy in Switzerland has for many years been dominated by environmental issues. The Federal government has set targets for air quality which local authorities must try to meet. If they are not met, the appropriate authorities are required to draw up a set of measures, but tensions have arisen between cantons and communes on the division of responsibility for environmental management. Federal requirements for transport policy include a number of measures to encourage the use of cycling, walking and public transport. A national research programme on urban and transport issues for the period 1990 to 1994 is investigating measures for reducing road traffic in cities and is examining policies which would make travellers bear the external costs of their journeys and, in consequence, reduce pollution levels.

Turkey

Policies proposed by local authorities in Turkey, and supported by central government, aim to shift the demand from cars to public transport through financing and pricing measures and the provision of new LRT and Underground systems, though increases in the existing road capacity are proposed mainly through traffic management and control measures and the construction of new orbital roads in order to reduce through traffic in the main cities. The policy also proposes physical planning measures to transfer traffic-generating activities to peripheral locations.

United Kingdom

The Government recognises that forecast levels of traffic growth, especially in urban areas, cannot be met in full. In urban areas it is acknowledged that road building may be physically impossible or environmentally unacceptable. It has adopted a policy of not building new roads to facilitate commuting by car into congested urban areas, and accepts that demand needs to be managed, alternatives to the private car be promoted and that land uses need to be planned and located in ways which will reduce the need to travel. The Government is committed to increasing the real level of duty on fuel by at least 5 per cent per year and is exploring the practicality of congestion charging for roads in urban areas, especially London.

In 1990 the Government published its Environment White Paper. This set out commitments to adopt measures to reduce CO_2 emissions and adopt planning policies which would reduce the need for car travel. The Departments of Environment and Transport have co-operated on research to develop planning policies and complementary transport policies to reduce the need to travel by car. As a result land-use planning policies have been adopted to influence the pattern of development and the location of major travel-generating land uses. New policy has been adopted for the location of employment uses and shopping, with a strong emphasis on locating in existing town centres, rather than out of town.

Investment in urban transport infrastructure has moved away from urban road building, although there are still proposals for bypasses of smaller towns with the objective of securing environmental improvements. Road investment is now mainly in inter-urban roads. Within urban areas, there has been a shift in emphasis toward public transport, with several major projects for improving the rail and underground network in London, and a number of light rapid transit schemes in provincial cities, such as Manchester and Sheffield. The Government recognises the need for a balanced approach, including roads, public transport investment, bus priority and cycling measures. In addition, the Government is seeking greater private investment, through public-private partnerships and through deregulation of bus services.

To secure improvements in urban travel, the Government has set targets, for example, to reduce accidents by a third by 2000, compared to levels in the mid 1980s. As yet no targets have been set for traffic or air pollution levels.

United States

Of the 3.6 trillion annual passenger miles travelled in the USA, car accounted for 89 per cent, aviation 10 per cent and all other modes approximately 1 per cent. In 1983, 75 per cent of the nation's 224 million daily passenger trips were made in metropolitan areas. Of these 81 per cent were made by car and only 3 per cent by public transport. Mass transport, however, constitutes a significant proportion of daily work trips in a few of the larger metropolitan areas with dense employment and residential cores.

Since the Clean Air Act Amendments considerable progress has been made in reducing air pollution, despite a 24 per cent increase in vehicular travel, but most of this was due to improved vehicle technology. Even so, 98 areas in 1991 failed to meet national ambient air quality standard (NAAQS) for ozone and more than half the population lives in non-attainment areas.

The USA has been seeking new ways to provide transportation in a cost-effective manner consistent with environmental goals. Alternatives to the use of cars (*e.g.* transit) and ways of managing them to make more efficient use of the available road capacity (*e.g.* through car-pooling) have been used, but widespread congestion and pollution remain. The Clean Air Act Amendments of 1990 and the Intermodal Surface Transportation Efficiency Act (ISTEA) of 1991, are both expected to have a major impact on the provision of transportation facilities and environmental quality. The former requires urban areas to meet specific national ambient air quality standards, sets a timetable for meeting them and outlines the steps that need to be taken if they are not met and the sanctions for not meeting them. The second of the two acts (ISTEA, 1991) offers greater flexibility for State and local agencies to fashion solutions to best suit their particular needs. It authorises $151 billion (ECU 124 billion) over six years for highways, mass transit and safety programmes and has created a Surface Transportation Programme with flexible funding.

These two Acts require integrated land use/transport planning with the goal of reducing congestion and air pollution while meeting the economic requirements of the region for mobility.

3. Summary and conclusions of Overviews analysis

All the countries taking part in this project are experiencing the same types of problems; congestion, road casualties, deteriorating public transport, high levels of vehicle emissions, noise, visual intrusion and barriers to pedestrian movement. Few, if any, have been able to reduce general congestion levels in cities, however much they have invested in the road network, though specific black spots have been improved. Few, if any, have been able (or willing) to reduce car travel either in cities or elsewhere, so that CO_2 levels have been rising everywhere and are expected to continue to rise in the future, unless more drastic policies are introduced.

With notable exceptions, the environmentally-friendly modes of cycling and walking have tended to decline in most countries. Urban public transport use has fallen in some countries and risen in others, though in almost all countries the share of all travel by public transport has fallen as trips have shifted to more peripheral areas of the city which are harder to serve by mass transit. Improvements to public transport have benefited the users and helped to attract and retain commercial activity in the city centres, but they have failed to attract car drivers in sufficient numbers to reduce car travel. Significant improvements, however, have been made in the fight against road casualties, despite a continuing increase in motorised travel, but much more needs to be done.

Progress has been made in lowering noxious fumes, lead and particulates from vehicles and there is every reason to believe that these will be brought down in the future to acceptable levels. Traffic noise, on the other hand, has tended to get worse in many countries, despite progress in reducing engine noise of individual vehicles. Some progress has been made on making particular areas of cities more compatible with the needs of people, but in general motorised traffic still seems to dominate cities to the detriment of those living, working and socialising there. Setting standards and targets for achievement by particular dates appears promising and has introduced a measure of harmonisation and collaboration between countries.

With regard to the future, the Overviews indicate that all the countries have proposed measures to try to combat the various problems experienced and some have set themselves overall targets for reduction of noise, pollution and casualties by specific dates. Some have also set targets for reducing the overall levels of car-km and CO_2 emissions by specific dates. Greater integration of transport and land-use policies is held by many countries to be the way forward, particularly linking new development with public transport provision. Land-use proposals affecting the location of homes, shops, offices, educational establishments, hospitals, etc., to try to reduce the need for travel are also very much under discussion. Measures to foster cycling and walking and improvements to public transport to make it a more attractive alternative to the private car are also favoured. Making travellers pay the full external costs of their journeys is now widely acclaimed and the techniques are already there, but whether the political will to put theory into practice is there remains to be seen.

There was a general awareness in the Overviews that, while some measures may be in conflict with each other, others may have limited scope if implemented on their own. For example, public transport improvements and land-use changes which place all the activities households require in close proximity to homes will be much more effective if combined with policies which increase the cost of using cars. An interesting example of combining measures was given in the Danish action plan in which they calculated that a particular mix of initiatives could reduce energy consumption (and therefore CO_2) by a quarter, NO_x and SO_2 by more than half, HC and particulates by three quarters and CO by over 85 per cent. While the programme of measures is ambitious, it is not unrealistically so.

SUMMARY OF CASE STUDIES

1. Introduction

Twelve case studies were commissioned by the Project Group to investigate the effectiveness of measures taken to deal with congestion and environmental problems in a variety of cities. The metropolitan regions of the cities selected had populations ranging from approximately half a million to over 30 million:

Tokyo	(32 million)	Berlin	(4.3 million)	Portland	(1.4 million)
Seoul	(18 million)	Milan	(4.0 million)	Helsinki	(0.8 million)
London	(12 million)	Hiroshima	(1.6 million)	Zurich	(0.8 million)
Paris	(11 million)	Stockholm	(1.6 million)	Grenoble	(0.6 million)

The information from the Case Studies has formed an important part of the data source used for the main investigation described in this report. It has complemented the information provided by the delegates in their National Overviews of policies (Annex 2), the results of the Questionnaire sent to 132 cities (Annex 1) and the papers presented to the Basle [Frey and Langloh (eds.), 1992] and Dusseldorf conferences (OECD, 1993*b*) organised by OECD and ECMT. This annex contains short summaries of the authors' original reports, one for each of the cities studied, highlighting the main policies chosen and their effectiveness. Each summary includes a small amount of background information to put the results into perspective. These summaries are presented in Section 2 of this annex, while Section 3 draws together the main findings from the individual studies. Section 4 indicates what lessons can be learned from the many approaches that have been tried and presents the main conclusions.

2. Case Study summaries

Tokyo case study

Background

Tokyo is one of the largest cities in the world with 32 million people in the Metropolitan Region and is expected to continue growing. It is served by a dense network of railways with the result that 60 per cent of the 21 billion mechanised trips per year are made by rail. Rail is holding its share of the market whereas bus travel has fallen by two thirds over the last 20 years and is now the main mode for commuting journeys in only 3 per cent of cases. Car travel has doubled over the same period, mainly at the expense of walking and cycling.

The huge size of Tokyo and its economic prosperity are at the heart of most of the problems suffered by workers, visitors and residents: soaring land prices, exceptionally high residential and commercial densities, overcrowding on both road and rail systems, waste disposal problems and high noise and pollution levels. Most of these problems are getting worse as the city expands and car ownership increases.

Policy impacts

Past policies have been mainly concerned with coping with the growth in activities and in travel – by building more roads and railways and setting up new business centres within the Metropolitan Region. They have not been geared specifically at reducing pollution levels, though the use of low polluting cars is now being promoted in a number of schemes. Very little has been done to reduce urban travel as a whole, and car travel in particular, with the result that congestion, pollution and CO_2 emissions have continued to grow.

While more road and rail investment is planned, the main plank of future policy seems to be to shift some urban activity from Tokyo itself to growth points outside the city but mainly within the Metropolitan Region. This will allow population to move back into the more central areas as businesses move out. The policy relies on the use of zoning measures, maximum floor area ratios and fiscal measures (both inducements and restraints through taxation) to achieve the desired results. How successful they will be in bringing homes and jobs closer together remains to be seen, but they should reduce the pressure on the central city and improve the general attractiveness of the region. They should also reduce the numbers of people travelling exceptionally long distances to work, though they might make it easier for travellers to use their own cars in the more peripheral areas. It is doubtful whether such measures on their own will reduce car use though mechanised urban travel as a whole might be reduced. Levels of congestion, noise, pollution and CO_2 emissions are unlikely to fall however.

Seoul case study

Background

Over 10 million people live in Seoul, the capital of Korea, (more than four times as many as in 1960) and over 40 per cent of all Koreans live in the Seoul metropolitan region. Car ownership at 63 per 1 000 persons is low by Western standards, but is growing rapidly. Almost half of all journeys are made by bus at present, but Underground rail is becoming a more dominant mode as the network develops. Gains to car and Underground have been at the expense of bus and walk.

Policy impacts

The rapid expansion of the Korean economy has led to an over-concentration of population and employment in Seoul at the expense of other cities and rural areas. Land and house prices have soared and intolerable demands have been placed on the transport system, resulting in severe congestion, parking problems, overcrowding on public transport, high accident rates, noise and air pollution.

The main thrust of policy during the last 30 years has been to foster development in areas away from Seoul, to control growth in Seoul itself and to transform the metropolitan area into a multi-centric region with a more balanced development pattern and improved accessibility. New Towns and industrial estates have been set up and green belts created. Zoning regulations, relocation orders and fiscal measures (both incentives and disincentives) have been used to guide development. These planning measures have been complemented by an extensive programme of Underground rail construction, combined with some road building, traffic management, bus priority on a large scale and other measures to improve traffic flow. Novel methods to restrain car ownership and use (see Section 3) have been tried.

The growth of the metropolitan region has undoubtedly been slowed down, but is still capturing an increasing share of the country's economic activity. The policies have, however, been successful in generating a multi-centre structure for the region, with more attractive amenities and improved transport facilities, but congestion, noise and pollution have not been noticeably reduced. The new Underground rail system, while providing an attractive alternative to car travel for journeys to the centre, captured a smaller proportion of travellers than expected and, with higher car ownership and more dispersed patterns of activity in the future, the new lines under construction might not do any better, unless more drastic policies to restrain the use of the car are imposed. Even if such measures are able to reduce congestion, noise and pollution levels, there is so much travel by rail and other mechanised modes that CO_2 emissions are unlikely to be reduced to any extent over the foreseeable future.

London case study

Background

London was once the largest city in the world with a population of 7 million – due largely to the development of the railways. It has now stabilised at 6.4 million and forms part of a metropolitan region of 12.3 million. Of the 3.9 million jobs in London, 1.2 million are in the central area, to which over a million workers commute each day, 84 per cent by public transport (mainly rail). Over 60 per cent of households own a car (only 43 per cent in Inner London) and two-thirds of all mechanised trips are made by car. Average journey lengths have increased by more than 10 per cent over the last 20 years, and journeys to work by 40 per cent.

Policy impacts

Planning policies have attempted to limit the spread of London, encourage the growth of strategic centres within the metropolitan region and strike a balance between the Capital's growth and that of other cities in the UK, without jeopardising London's position as a world city. The creation of a Green Belt and a series of New Towns helped to stem London's growth and ease local problems, though they probably encouraged a greater reliance on the car. Constraints on office and industrial development in London over a period of half a century had eventually to be relaxed when employment levels started to fall. The regeneration of London's Docklands under the Government's Urban Programme exceeded all expectations, though it has placed heavy demands on the transport system (now being addressed). Resisting peripheral development, such as out-of-town shopping centres, has benefited established centres and shifting the emphasis from the overcrowded west to the less-developed east has improved the balance of activities and eased local problems. However, with virtually no control on the overall level of office development in London, competition between different locations has led to a considerable over-supply.

Improving mobility and reducing congestion were the primary aims of most of the transport policies: none were pursued with the specific intention of reducing urban travel, though the relatively low level of investment in London's roads, together with restrictions on parking supply, has helped to restrain car use and bolster public transport. Reducing public transport subsidies has encouraged car use, but the planned year-by-year increases in fuel prices should help to redress the balance. Traffic management measures have tended to encourage car use at the expense of the more

211

environmentally-friendly modes. Despite all attempts to reduce congestion it has spread in both time and space. Noise levels have increased and any improvement in air quality from cleaner vehicles has tended to be offset by more traffic. On the other hand, safety has improved marginally (but still has a long way to go), public transport has remained buoyant and London has continued to function as a world city. But without severe restraint on the use of the private car, there will be no substantial impact on congestion and CO_2 emissions: moreover planning measures which bring homes and jobs closer together and public transport improvements will be unable to achieve their full potential. Since the structure of London has changed little over the last 60 years when public transport, cycling and walking served almost all of its needs, there seems to be no fundamental reason why London should not function as well in the future if policies are implemented which greatly reduce car travel in the interests of the urban environment, safety and pedestrian movement.

Paris case study

Background

The main Paris region (Ile-de-France) has a population of 10.7 million with 5.1 million jobs; both are rising. The central area (bounded by the old city walls) has 2.1 million people and 1.2 million jobs: both are declining slowly as decentralisation takes place. Paris is well served by the Metro and other rail services, with the result that 60 per cent of the 7 million motorised trips/day are made by public transport. Of the 33 million motorised trips/day in the Paris region, 30 per cent are made by public transport, but only 15 per cent of intra-suburban journeys. Public transport use is relatively static, but car travel is increasing. Average trip distances by both car and rail have been increasing steadily over the years. Goods traffic has increased sharply. Like most major cities, Paris suffers from chronic congestion, accidents, noise, pollution and inconvenience to pedestrians from heavy traffic.

Policy impacts

Co-ordination between land-use and transport planning has been at the forefront of policy for years, with the result that new development has tended to go hand in hand with the provision of good public transport, mainly rail. Decentralisation of functions and activities away from the Paris region has taken some of the pressure away from Paris without compromising its competitive position as a world city. The establishment of preferential axes for development, with new growth centres and five New Towns, all with good rail connections to Paris, have been generally success-ful, though the hoped-for close juxtaposition between homes and jobs in the New Towns was not achieved – a high level of interaction between these towns and Paris remained.

Improving public transport has been the main weapon in the attempt to achieve a more favourable modal split with lower levels of congestion and pollution. There has been little invest-ment in the road network in Paris itself, most of it being in the outer areas. High levels of operating subsidy have made the Paris system easy and cheap to use. These policies have prevented the decline in patronage which most other major cities have experienced, but they have not affected car use to any noticeable extent, nor have they reduced congestion. The net effect has probably been an increase in mechanised travel, but the policies were not aimed at reducing travel demand, but at improving mobility. Attempts to improve the urban environment have seemingly had little effect on noise and pollution (most reductions in noxious emissions have arisen from improvements in vehicle design). Efforts to make public transport attractive were not matched by any serious attempts to restrain traffic, even through the parking mechanism. Without severe restraint on the use of cars, the package of public transport improvements and planning measures will not achieve the desired reductions in congestion, noise and pollution.

Berlin case study

Background

After the re-unification of East and West Berlin, the city's population was 3.4 million and that of the whole metropolitan area, 4.3 million. With 300 cars per 1 000 persons, the degree of motorisation is below the level of other large cities in Germany (Hamburg 391, Frankfurt 477). Thirty-eight per cent of the journeys in the region are made by car, 26 per cent on foot, 6 per cent by bicycle and 30 per cent by public transport.

The metropolitan area has a polycentric structure with eight settlement axes served by the main radial urban railway lines. These settlements stretch from the central city, with its two centres developed during partition, to the outer metropolitan area. Inner and outer urban railways, inter-regional railways, road and motorway rings provide cross-links. Newer settlements on the urban fringe are geared much more towards the cell-shaped street network than to the railway network.

Policy impacts

For 45 years traffic policy in Berlin was determined by the division of the city into East and West.

In West Berlin, the traffic development plan of 1977 contained for the first time traffic policies with aims which were compatible with urban development and environmental objectives. This plan, sought to concentrate new settlements near the express rail transit lines; coordinate new housing and traffic routes; and increase the attractiveness of public transport by extending the rapid transit network, allocating priority to buses, increasing travel comfort with new rolling stock and improving transport interchanges. The plan also undertook to improve traffic conditions through traffic restraint and regulatory measures, pedestrianisation, parking control and park-and-ride facilities.

Prior to 1989, the public transport network was extended in order to avoid a predicted passenger loss of between 10 and 15 per cent. With regard to road traffic, however, the aim was still to expand the network and employ traffic management techniques to ensure free-flowing traffic. At that time, traffic jams were rare in West Berlin. When the Wall came down, there was an unprecedented increase in traffic volume, and traffic planning was confronted with new tasks.

In East Berlin, public transport was of greater importance because car ownership had grown more slowly than in the West. Rail-based transit, which had developed despite the critical economic situation took the main share in commuter travel. Its expansion had been determined by the development of new housing estates, such as Marzahn and Hohenschonhausen. In order to provide the new settlements with adequate services, the tram routes were extended as well. Passenger flows were exceptionally high at times (*e.g.,* up to 9 000 passengers per peak hour at Leninallee). Even so, the tram system in East Berlin came under threat and it was not until 1972 that it was decided that trams were the most effective and safest means of transport to meet the demands of East German cities: their existence was thus secured.

The East Berlin tram network of today, however, is characterised by a multiplicity of lines with diverse, uncoordinated frequencies and a high proportion of obsolete cars. Many of the lines are in places where there is no longer much demand so that some lines are greatly under-utilised while others, especially in peak hours, are overcrowded. After re-unification it was no longer possible, because of the Road Traffic Act, to give trams priority over other traffic in the way that it had been done in East Berlin.

The most important element of future policy for a reunited Berlin geared towards reducing traffic, is to control the settlement structure, a view which is also held by the wider Berlin-Brandenburg regional authority. The main planning directive favours the development of seven areas situated at a distance of 45-110 km round Berlin. Three of these are Brandenburg, Frankfurt/Oder (each with about 90 000 inhabitants) and Cottbus (with 126 000 inhabitants) and the others are towns or groups of towns with between 27 000 and 54 000 inhabitants each. These development areas will be linked to Berlin by regional rail rapid transit.

Nearer the centre land is being developed alongside old railway lines in a star-shaped pattern. In Brandenburg, this will take the form of settlement islands, strung on the railway line like a necklace, with green areas in between. The areas between the development axes, on the other hand, will remain undeveloped. The purpose of the settlement structure is to connect the green areas rather than the settlements. The existing core areas will be at higher densities than those further out.

The plan for the whole city is to provide a compact and functionally mixed settlement structure. To this end a set of potential growth points between the city core and the outer region are balanced both functionally and spatially. Further areas will be zoned as building land between the city and the hinterland becomes available.

Milan case study

Background

The city of Milan, with a population of 1.45 million, is at the centre of a metropolitan region of 4 million. While the region has had a fairly static population for many years, there has been a steady transfer of people from the city itself to the outer areas. Employment has been growing at about 1 per cent p.a. and it too has been moving outwards, though the centre has retained its share of administrative, cultural, financial and specialised services. Public transport has remained buoyant, though its share of the total travel market has declined, particularly for in-commuting and suburban travel, where car use has grown significantly.

Policy impacts

The main problems are increasing congestion (now affecting the suburbs during peak periods), pollution (exacerbated by Milan's climatic conditions) and illegal parking (some 400 000 cars are parked each day in public areas in the city centre).

The main plank of an integrated transport and urban development programme is the improvement and extension of public transport services to encourage present car users to switch to public transport. The measures involve the construction of new rail lines and improvements to the existing system to make it faster and more user-friendly. Most of the improvements to the rail network set out in the transport plan have already been completed. Extensions to the system have been approved and agreement reached on new light rail systems, including a fully automatic system to connect with the outer areas. To complement these measures, vehicle access to the historic centre of Milan was restricted in 1985 to halve the number of vehicles entering daily. New off-street car parks in the city centre are being built to allow streets and public places to be freed of parked cars and some industries which cause undue congestion are to be transferred to outer areas. Reductions in congestion and pollution resulting from these measures, however, are likely to be short-lived because of traffic growth.

An emergency measure to improve air quality was introduced in 1990. Under this measure, vehicle use (and domestic heating) is forcibly restricted when the level of pollution in the city exceeds a pre-determined reference level. If a second reference level is exceeded vehicle use is prohibited altogether. So far, vehicles have only been restricted to alternate day use, but this has kept pollution levels below the upper bound.

The policies being adopted are providing Milan with a highly efficient public transport service and by restricting access to sensitive areas, tackling the parking problem, and improving traffic flow in general, they will make the city more pleasant and efficient. Congestion may be eased by these policies and pollution contained within tolerable limits, but car use, the amount of mechanised travel and CO_2 emissions are unlikely to be reduced.

Hiroshima case study

Background

The Hiroshima Urban Region, consisting of five cities (of which Hiroshima is the most important) and five towns, has a population of 1.6 million, having grown from 1.1 million in 1965. Because Hiroshima is mono-centric and located on a delta surrounded by mountains, rivers and the sea, it has more serious congestion and greater pollution than most other Japanese cities of similar size. Travel within the urban region is mainly by car, motor cycle (a surprising 21 per cent) and on foot, with public transport (mainly bus and tram) accounting for only 13.4 per cent of journeys.

Policy impacts

The main concerns of increasing congestion, pollution (from both traffic and industry), noise and a decaying urban fabric are being addressed in three ways: – by transforming Hiroshima from a mono-centric city to a multi-centre region; by improving roads and parking supply to keep pace with increasing motorisation; and by improving public transport to capture some of the present car and motor cycle users. In addition to the construction of a new town, a new port and other specialised centres within the delta area of Hiroshima, other towns and cities in the wider urban region are being strengthened to take some of the pressure off Hiroshima itself. The road improvements are expected to take through traffic away from the city streets and to provide better communication between the new centres. The new off-street parking facilities will free the streets of at least some of the parked vehicles (new development will by law have to include a certain minimum number of parking spaces for which developers will receive a subsidy). It is hoped that these policies will reduce the proportion of the road network with severe congestion from 23 per cent to almost zero. The improvements to public transport (including a new guided-bus line) are intended to reduce average travel time on public transport by 5 minutes, despite the extra distance travelled as activities become more spread out.

While these policies will, no doubt, bring economic benefit to the whole region and some relief from congestion to particular areas, they are unlikely to increase public transport's share of travel, which has halved during the last 20 years, while car and motor cycle use has doubled to 60 per cent of all trips. In fact, the improved road network, together with a greater supply of off-street parking, is likely to encourage a further shift to car and motor cycle, so that noise and pollution may well increase over time, unless measures geared more specifically to reducing them, are adopted.

Stockholm case study

Background

Stockholm is a city of 700 000 population in an urban region of 1.6 million. Car ownership is high at 366 cars per thousand persons and car travel is expected to rise by over 80 per cent by the year 2020. The growth in road traffic has caused widespread congestion and environmental problems, particularly within the inner area of the city and on the main approaches. Public transport accounts for 42 per cent of all mechanised travel in the region (70 per cent during the peak), but its share is declining as car travel grows.

Development in Stockholm has been based largely on the "beads on a string" principle, in which the main districts and satellite towns are located on the main radial routes and connected to each other and to the city centre by good roads and relatively high speed public transport systems. These radial corridors are separated from each other by green wedges which allow much of the resident population to have relatively easy access to open country. Providing cheap public transport of high quality has always been a priority in Stockholm and a very comprehensive rail system has been built up as a result. Fares have remained low, but subsidies have risen dramatically. With rising car ownership and more and more people moving to lower density suburban areas, urban policy has become more sharply focused on ways to deal with this growth in car travel to the centre.

Policy impacts

In 1991, the signing of the so-called *Dennis Agreement* committed the authorities to "ameliorating the environmental and congestion problems of the region and enhancing the potential for economic development". It contained the most comprehensive transport package ever contemplated in the Stockholm region, involving a financial commitment of SKr 36 billion (ECU 3.7 billion) over a 15 year period, divided roughly equally between roads and public transport. The plan provides for more regional rail lines, track improvements, better co-ordination between services and more park-and-ride facilities. The metro system will be completely modernised and a new rapid tram line constructed round the inner city. A core network of services will be allocated exclusive street space, where practicable, and given priority at signals. Only environmentally-friendly vehicles will be allowed to operate in the core network. Services will be gradually increased as car travel is reduced.

The highway proposals, financed by state guaranteed loans are designed to improve accessibility while reducing car traffic in the inner city. They consist of a ring-road round the inner area and an outer cross-link for north-south traffic, with the more sensitive sections built in tunnel. As the various segments are completed, a system of tolls, using sophisticated electronic equipment, will be used to steer traffic on to peripheral routes and away from sensitive areas. The fees collected will be used to repay the loans. The street environment will be improved using pedestrianisation, noise reduction and other measures.

Impact studies made after the agreement suggest that by 2005, there will be a slight reduction in overall traffic growth of 5-10 per cent (the actual growth will be 15-30 per cent) compared to a situation in which the package is not launched. The largest benefits will arise in the inner areas of Stockholm, where traffic will be down by 25 per cent, mainly as a result of the tolls. Air pollutants, largely due to cleaner engines, will be down by about 50 per cent, while CO_2 emissions will remain about the same. Noise levels will be lower in the inner areas of Stockholm, but will be greater in the outer areas, especially in the green areas crossed by the outer cross-link. Other important effects of the package, however, have not been sufficiently analysed, in particular, secondary effects of the package, and the longer-term consequences for development patterns and transport. Thus, land-use planning has not been fully integrated with transport and traffic planning.

The *Dennis Agreement* is an agreement between the three leading political parties on the layout and economy of a developed traffic system in the Stockholm region. Due to environmental requirements, there is a risk that the project will turn out to be more expensive than originally planned. New calculations by the National Road Administration show that the cost for the road building part of the package is likely to rise by about 20-25 per cent due to technical reasons. Even

216

if the expected effects are somewhat indistinct, demonstrating that restraint measures can be made palatable is an achievement in itself and this opens the way to the possibility of more significant reductions in car use and greater improvements to the urban environment. However, the experiences from the *Dennis Agreement* so far, show that the process of constructing a package of measures of this type has to be handled carefully. Being a political compromise, the *Dennis Agreement* is rather fragile, since a change in the package might wreck the whole agreement. It is criticised for being an example of undemocratic decision-taking and not giving sufficient consideration to its environmental and structural aspects. To facilitate the implementation of such a package, it is necessary to create a broad acceptance in society for the proposed measures by showing that the measures really can achieve the commonly-accepted goals.

Portland case study

Background

Portland, USA, is part of a greater metropolitan region of 1.4 million people, containing numerous cities and counties. Decentralisation of both population and employment during the 1960s and 1970s led to sprawling suburbs, decaying buildings, derelict land sites and social problems on a large scale. Heavy dependence on the private car increased levels of congestion, noise and pollution. The decentralisation trend has now been halted and public transport improved, but, with almost two cars per household, car is still the dominant mode.

Policy impacts

To reduce reliance on the car, conserve energy and protect rural areas from urban sprawl, the state authorities set up a commission with special powers to tackle these problems. Cities and counties were obliged to adopt comprehensive plans and the Commission was given jurisdiction over land use permits with powers to refuse state grants if there was non-compliance. The cities themselves were left to deal with transport problems in their own way.

In downtown Portland, high-density housing was provided to increase the resident population and measures introduced to make the area more attractive and pedestrian-friendly, including the conversion of a riverside freeway into an esplanade. Coupled with more stringent parking regulations and a free downtown transit service, these measures have transformed the area into a living, vibrant place with 30 000 more jobs and with 40 per cent of commuters using transit. Road schemes have been scrapped in favour of new transit lines and residential densities in transit corridors are being increased to bring more people into the catchment area. Present policy is to have no more freeways within the city limits, but six new light rail lines and a central area trolley circulation system. By contrast, Hillsboro, 32 km west of downtown Portland, adopted a less environmentally-oriented approach and now has vast, low-density residential and industrial areas, congestion, air pollution and a decaying city centre, with 92 per cent of trips being made by car. Unlike Portland, congestion has increased and air quality deteriorated.

A proposal to build a bypass to the west of Portland brought about intense opposition, which provoked the authorities into a re-appraisal of the scheme. As a result, new guidelines for transport and land-use planning have been issued which are geared to reducing the reliance on car travel and achieving reductions in environmental nuisances. In addition, a proposal has been made by a conservation group for a land-use alternative to the bypass for a particular part of the metropolitan area. This development pattern is estimated to be capable of accommodating 65 per cent of new households and 78 per cent of new jobs within walking distance of the transit lines. With complementary transport measures, it is estimated that veh-km travelled could be reduced by up to

14 per cent, compared with the bypass proposal. Public transport share would be 50 per cent higher and car use 4 per cent lower and in the transit corridors cycle and pedestrian use would be doubled. This alternative will be evaluated alongside other possibilities and holds out the hope that what has been achieved in downtown Portland could be repeated in the suburban centres too. However, even if initiatives like this succeed, travel in the metropolitan region as a whole would still be mainly by car, with all the attendant problems associated with motorised travel. Nevertheless, it does seem that a package of land-use and transport measures which locate homes and jobs closer to each other and to high-quality transit routes, combined with public transport improvements and better facilities for pedestrians and cyclists, can achieve a reduction in car use, albeit a modest one.

Helsinki case study

Background

Helsinki is a medium-sized capital city of half a million inhabitants within a metropolitan region of over three-quarters of a million. Like most cities at the present time both population and employment are decentralising and car ownership, trip lengths and the amount of commuting into and out of the region are all increasing. Unlike some cities, however, public transport usage (mainly bus and tram) is holding its own, though its share of total travel is diminishing. Moreover, the city centre remains strong, though with a smaller proportion of the total jobs within the CBD.

Policy impacts

Maintaining a high use of public transport in those areas where public transport is particularly effective (along the main radial corridors and in the city centre itself) and investing in roads to keep up with the growth in car ownership in other areas, seem to be at the heart of policy decisions. Measures to promote public transport include:

- generous subsidies to keep fares low (only half of the operating costs are covered from the fare box);
- segregated bus and tram lanes with priority at traffic signals;
- improved rail service and extensions to the metro system;
- ticketing and information systems which make it easier to use the system.

Controls on parking in the city centre complement these measures.

All in all, the policies have enabled public transport to remain the predominant mode of travel for journeys to and from the city centre. They have benefited existing public transport users and have provided car drivers with a more attractive alternative to car travel for particular types of journeys. They have helped to retain the strength and compactness of the city centre and made it more attractive. While decentralisation of employment is still continuing, the city centre has been able to retain a relatively high proportion of jobs.

Investing in new roads to facilitate orbital movements in the outer areas, which are not well served by public transport, will inevitably pose some threat to public transport use in general. Moreover, land-use changes, influenced at least partly by these road improvements, could eventually result in a decline in both city-centre activities and subsequently in public transport use.

Since measures are being employed which improve *both* public transport and the road system, the total amount of mechanised travel will undoubtedly increase to the detriment of the more environmentally friendly modes.

Zurich case study

Background

The city of Zurich, with over a third of a million inhabitants, is part of a conurbation of nearly a million people. While population within the city has tended to fall over the years, employment has increased appreciably, particularly office and retail activities. Car ownership at 380 cars per 1 000 persons is considerably lower than in the rest of the canton, reflecting both the difficulties in parking and the high quality of public transport, which captures nearly 40 per cent of all trips within the city and 76 per cent of work and shopping trips to the central area. A new metro system has recently been introduced, but trams still form the backbone of the system.

Policy impacts

The main policy aims in Zurich are to improve mobility while curbing the use of the private car, enhance the image of the city, improve the quality of urban life and reduce air pollution and noise, while still catering for the needs of industry and commerce. The means of achieving these aims are mainly through public transport improvements – the use of dedicated tram tracks and bus lanes; preferential treatment at traffic signals; new metro lines and a central transport authority to co-ordinate all public transport services. Parking constraints and traffic control to limit vehicle entry when the automatic monitoring system indicates that congestion levels have become unacceptably high complement the public transport measures. The number of public parking spaces in the city centre has been reduced and attempts are being made to cut down on the number of private spaces (these have trebled over the last 20 years). The thrust of planning policy is to encourage new development along existing populated corridors which are well-served by public transport and to channel as much traffic as possible on to the main road network, leaving residential areas relatively free from traffic. Extensive 30 km/h speed limit zones have been introduced in selected residential areas and it is hoped to implement similar schemes in other such areas of the city by 1995.

With over 300 million passengers a year, public transport has retained its role as the predominant mode of travel in Zurich. From 1985 to 1990 (when the metro was opened) ridership on municipal transport services alone increased by over 30 per cent to a level of 470 public passenger transport trips per inhabitant per year (about twice the level of that in most comparable cities). The authorities intend not only to maintain this high level of usage, but to raise ridership by a further 1 per cent per year through continued improvements to the system. The improvement of public transport was not, however, an end in itself, but was intended to increase mobility within the region and to combat the growth in car trip-making, in order to reduce some of the more damaging effects caused by road traffic. The policy has certainly improved mobility, but despite everything that has been done, there has been no change in the volume of car traffic in Zurich itself, nor in any of the radial corridors along which the new metro lines run. Car traffic has remained constant during peak hours since the mid-1980s and has actually risen during off-peak hours. In the canton generally, as well as in the neighbouring districts, car traffic has been increasing steadily over the years.

Grenoble case study

Background

Grenoble, a city of 400 thousand people in a metropolitan area of 550 thousand, has a constricted location with little space left for further development. Population and employment are both decentralising, though 90 per cent of the jobs within the metropolitan region are still within the city boundaries. There are over 400 cars per 1 000 persons and the car is used for half of all trips. Its share is increasing, as is public transport's, but the latter accounts for only 12 per cent of trips, though it is the predominant mode for journeys to the centre. While over a third of trips are still made on foot, only a few per cent are on bicycles. Suburb-to-suburb trips now outnumber journeys to the central area.

Policy impacts

Intense urban development took place within the city during the 1950s and 1960s, when the population of Grenoble trebled. The growth was mainly in the outer areas of the metropolitan region while employment remained largely in Grenoble itself. This caused the imbalance between homes and work places to increase and journeys to lengthen. Congestion spread to all parts of the city and pollution was made worse by the constricted layout of the city and its topography. New zoning laws were introduced to facilitate the growth of important sub-centres and green belts were set up to preserve existing natural areas between the various townships.

Ambitious highway plans were formulated, but were subsequently scaled down as the emphasis shifted towards a more integrated approach to transport, with better public transport and more facilities for pedestrians and cyclists. Special lanes for buses were designated, pedestrian precincts established (with extending fingers, where necessary, to facilitate access by residents) and an extensive programme of (mainly suburban) cycleways introduced. A new tramway system on dedicated tracks was brought into operation and accompanied by a number of complementary measures to restrict parking, improve traffic circulation and increase the city's general attractiveness. Combined tram and pedestrian streets were created. New public transport connections were set up in low density areas and park-and-ride facilities improved. The controlled parking zone in the city centre was extended, new parking garages constructed and measures introduced to remove illegally parked vehicles from the streets. The number of parking spaces for shoppers was maintained, but the number for commuters reduced substantially.

Special arrangements were set up between the city and central government to increase public transport capacity, improve the service and increase productivity. Fares were raised in an attempt to reduce the substantial deficits.

To help finance the public transport system, use was made of the transport contribution tax, a tax which, at the discretion of the local authority, can be levied on all firms with more than nine employees in towns with over 20 000 population. The earlier hopes of bringing homes and work places closer together by developing activities outside the city were not fulfilled. The imbalance between the main employment areas and the housing estates persisted and travel distances increased. New roads and by-passes brought economic benefits, as new firms were attracted to the region, but there were severance problems and no lasting relief from congestion.

The implementation of the tramway and the complementary measures affecting parking and pedestrianisation were generally successful and good for the environment. The earlier target to increase the share of public transport use from 13 per cent in 1970 to 30 per cent in 1985 was not achieved and this was later revised. Public transport use has increased substantially as the city has grown, but its modal share has increased only modestly, and then mainly as a result of a shift from cycling and walking, and not from former car drivers. The tramway system has helped to reduce noise and pollution levels in the city, though increases in road traffic are tending to erode these benefits.

3. Overall results

This section brings together all the results of the individual reports to see what can be learned about the impacts of different policies, bearing in mind the basic differences in the cities examined.

Characteristics of the cities studied

Table A3.1 compares the main travel and geographic parameters of the cities studied. It can be seen that the populations vary in size from less than half a million to over 10 million and the metropolitan regions in which they are situated from just over half a million to over 30 million. In practically all cases population and employment have been decentralising over several decades. Even in cities in which the number of jobs in the central area has been increasing, the number in the outer areas has been increasing at a greater rate.

Car ownership, which varies from a very low level in Seoul to a very high level in Portland, USA, is increasing in all cities and, as a result, more and more trips are being made by car at the expense of all the other modes, though in some cities public transport is managing to hold its own. The larger cities depend heavily on rail transport, while the smaller ones depend much more on bus and tram. For trips to the Central Business District (CBD), the proportion of commuters using public transport is remarkably high, reaching 70 or 80 per cent in some cities, but for all trips in the metropolitan region car travel is the predominant mode (generally between 40 and 60 per cent), except in Tokyo and Seoul, where it accounts for only about a quarter of trips. The figures for the proportion of trips on foot and by bicycle are unfortunately not as reliable as those for the motorised modes because of the way these types of trips are recorded in travel surveys.

Average journey distances have been increasing steadily in all cities over the years, because of the increase in car ownership, the widening separation between homes and jobs and the increasing concentration of retail, leisure and health facilities in out-of-town areas.

Problems encountered

Table A3.2 gives an indication of the sorts of problems which cities are facing and how severe they perceive these problems to be. Congestion, pollution and parking were clearly the problems of most concern, particularly in the larger cities. The imbalance between population and employment facilities and over-concentration of activities in central areas (leading to exceptionally high land prices) were severe problems in the two largest cities (Tokyo and Seoul) and in Hiroshima. Even such large cities as London and Paris were not greatly concerned by problems of this nature and smaller cities hardly at all. Berlin, on the other hand, due to its special circumstances, has suffered from escalating land prices. While all the cities were suffering to some extent from a spreading of activities, only in Portland, USA had urban sprawl become a really serious issue, resulting in a severe deterioration of the city itself and a decaying town centre.

There is a tendency in most of the cities for public transport to lose its market share to the private car, though the absolute numbers of passengers have been fairly steady in most cases as a result of the intense efforts made over the years to bolster public transport by whatever means possible: in so doing, other problems, in particular, that of financial solvency, have often been made worse.

When carrying out these case studies, the cities were not presented with a list of potential problems, so it is possible that they might have overlooked some problems. For example, visual intrusion, hindrance to pedestrians caused by traffic flows and the general domination of cities by

Table A3.1. Basic characteristics of cities

	Population (millions)		Employment (millions)		Cars per head	Trips/day (m) in MR	% of all trips in MR by:			Commuting to CBD	
	MR	City	CBD	MR			car/taxi	PT	W/C	% PT	Main mode
Tokyo	31.8	8.2	6.7[a]	16.5	–	74	22	56	22	–	rail
Seoul	18.0	10.6	–	–	0.06	23	25	63	12	–	bus
London	12.3	6.4	1.2	3.9	0.35	–	41	20	39	84	rail
Paris	10.7	2.1	1.2	5.1	0.37	33	43	20	37	75[d]	rail
Berlin	4.3	3.4	0.8	2.0	0.30	11	38	30	32	–	rail
Milan	4.0	1.5	0.8	1.6	0.49	5.3	–	39	–	–	bus/rail
Hiroshima	1.6	1.0	–	–	0.25	3.8	59[b]	13	28	–	bus/tram
Stockholm	1.6	0.7	–	–	0.37	–	58	42	–	70	rail
Portland	1.4	–	–	–	0.75	–	84	8	8	40	bus
Helsinki	0.8	0.5	0.2	0.5	0.35	2.2	46	32	22	70	bus
Zurich	0.8	0.4	0.3	0.5	0.38	–	28[c]	38[c]	34[c]	76	tram
Grenoble	0.6	0.4	–	–	0.40	–	52	12	36	–	bus

a) Tokyo Ward Area (larger than CBD).
b) Includes motor cycle (21%).
c) Refers to city, not the MR.
d) Estimated.

Notes: m   millions
MR.   Metropolitan Region
CBD Central Business District
PT   Public Transport
W/C Walk/Cycle

Table A3.2. Severity of problems as perceived by cities

Type of problem	Tokyo	Seoul	London	Paris	Berlin	Milan	Hiroshima	Stockholm	Portland	Helsinki	Zurich	Grenoble
Planning aspects												
Imbalance between people and jobs	+++	+++	+	+		+	++		++	+		+
Over-concentration of people and jobs	++	+++	+	++		+	++		++		+	+
High land prices	+++	++			++		+++		++			
Decaying urban fabric			+		+		+		++	+		
Urban sprawl out-of-town facilities			+	+	+				++			
Road traffic												
Congestion	++	++	++	++	++	++	++		++	+	+	+
Parking	+	++	+	++	++	++	++	++	++		+	+
Accidents		+++	+	+								
Public transport												
Poor quality service	+		+	+	+	+	++		++	++		+
Declining market share			+	++	+				++	++		++
Financial burden	++	+++			++		++					
Overcrowding												
Environmental issues												
City dominated by traffic	++		++	++	++	++	++		++	+	+	+
Noise	++	+	++	+++	++	+	++		++	+	+	++
Pollution		++						+				
CO₂ emissions								+				

Note: + to +++ denotes severity of problem.

the motor car are regularly condemned by planners and public alike, but less than half the Case Study reports referred to these. Similarly, road accidents which feature constantly in newspapers and on the radio and television were mentioned in only three of the Case Study reports. Despite surveys indicating that people found traffic noise to be more irritating than almost any other aspect of urban living, noise nuisance was given only a passing mention in several of the reports.

Policies and measures tried

The main planning and transport measures taken by the various cities are shown in Table A3.3, together with an indication of how important the particular types of measures appeared to be from the reports. Strategic land use/transport planning can be seen to have been a feature of policy in all the cities, though the extent to which this type of planning has shaped the development of the cities may vary considerably. In most cases the essential element of the strategic plan has been the linking of new development to the provision of public transport, though new road construction and existing rail and road infrastructure must have played a part also. Strategic planning has been no less important in the medium and smaller cities than in the larger cities. In London, where there has been no strategic planning authority for a number of years, this type of planning has been in less prominence recently and what there has been, has been under the direction of central government. Strategic planning, however, played a major role in London's growth a century ago, when development was closely linked to the expansion of the rail network, and since, with the development of electric tram and bus networks and later with mass car ownership.

Regional policy has been mainly concerned with securing a better balance of activities between competing cities. This has meant introducing measures to curtail growth of the dominant city (often a capital city) and encouraging it in other cities through fiscal inducements or even by compulsory transfer of particular employment groups *e.g.* government departments. Naturally, such measures have been appropriate to only the largest of the cities studied and usually as a result of extremely rapid growth (this was the case in Seoul). In London and Paris, on the other hand, any constraints on growth had to be managed with care to allow these cities to still function as world cities. In London in particular, policies to encourage the transfer of activities to other cities had to be curtailed when London was hit by recession. Encouraging economic activity to locate in New Towns or designated growth areas within the metropolitan region has been a popular policy of all except some of the smaller cities studied. While almost all cities have been constantly regenerating their central areas, replacing older industries by modern office and service activities and renewing the infrastructure accordingly, only Portland has undertaken the task of completely renewing its downtown area, which had been allowed to fall into a serious state of neglect and decay.

On the transport side, improvements to public transport have been the most popular policies over recent decades, with a tendency for rail construction to feature most in the larger cities and service improvements most in the smaller cities. Whereas road construction had been thought to be the way forward some decades ago, the emphasis changed towards public transport provision later when it was realised that road construction was not achieving the desired results. Nevertheless, there has been a need for some road improvements in selected places on both environmental and traffic flow grounds. Traffic management, park-and-ride and priority to buses and trams have been applied across the whole range of cities and parking controls have been the main means of restraining car traffic, though other measures have additionally been used in some cities. Cycleways, pedestrianisation and traffic calming measures are referred to in some of the Case Study reports, but surprisingly little is said about these measures, especially traffic calming (perhaps this is because it is a relatively new measure).

Table A3.3. **Main policies and measures tried**

Policies and measures	Tokyo	Seoul	London	Paris	Berlin	Milan	Hiroshima	Stockholm	Portland	Helsinki	Zurich	Grenoble
Planning aspects												
Strategic land use/transport planning[a]	+++	++	+	+++	+++	+++		+++	+++	++		+
Regional policy[b]	+	+++	++	++	++		++					+
Restraint on central city growth	+++	+++	++	+	++		+					
Designated growth areas and new towns	+++	+++	+++	+++	+	+			+++			++
Regeneration of city centre	+	+		+	+	+			+++			
Relocation of employment groups	+	++	++	++				+				
Fiscal inducements to relocate	+	+			+	+		++		++	++	
Zoning regulations	+	++	++	++	+	+		++		++	++	++
Green belts	+	+	+		+	+	++	+			+	+
Transport												
Road construction	++	+	+	+	+	+	++	++	++	+	+	+
Rail construction	+++	+++	+	+++	++	++	+	+++	+++	+++	++	++
Improved service/lower fares			+++	+++	+	+++	+	+++	+++	+++	+++	++
Traffic management			+	++	+++	++	+	++	++	+	+++	++
Bus/tram priority		++	+++	++	+++	++	+	+	+	+++	+++	+++
Toll charges/road pricing		+				+	+					
Parking controls		++	++	++	++	++		+	++	++	++	+
Park-and-ride			+		+	+		++		+	+	+
Car restraint		+				+		+			+	
Cycle priority								+	+		+	+
Pedestrian priority			++		+	+		+	+	+	+	++
Traffic calming					++					++	++	++
Car pooling		+			+	+		+	+		+	
Standards for noise/pollution												

Note: x to +++: denotes importance of measures tried.
a) e.g. new developments linked to provision of public transport.
b) e.g. employment encouraged to move to other parts of the country.

Some of the cities have shown great initiative and boldness in introducing new measures and the more novel of these are listed in Table A3.4, which also gives some appreciation of how successful they have been (where this could be ascertained from the Case Study reports). Seoul and Milan have shown particular ingenuity: perhaps in the case of Seoul, the extremely rapid growth in population and activities forced the authorities to think boldly. Most of the measures shown in Table A3.4 are concerned with restraining private car ownership and use – a tax on households with two or more cars; a ban on households owning a car if they have nowhere to garage it; and a number of measures limiting when and where cars can be used. A voluntary "no-car" day was tried in Tokyo, but was not very effective. Car use was limited to alternate days in Seoul and Milan, but drivers found ways round this limitation. In Milan, it was applied when pollution levels reached a certain threshold and was successful in keeping pollution below the level at which a complete ban on traffic would have become mandatory. Even though it worked satisfactorily, the consensus was that alternate day working is suitable only as an emergency measure.

Restricting access to sensitive areas by all vehicles, except particular types and those with permits, has been successfully tried in Milan and Berlin. Prohibiting the entry of goods vehicles to particular areas at certain times of the day has been tried in a number of cities. In Tokyo, specific areas have been designated as low-pollution areas: vehicles which do not satisfy the emission criteria will be increasingly prevented from entering such areas. Taxing employees for parking facilities provided by their firms is being tried in Zurich. The use of tolls to collect revenue (sometimes for road construction purposes) has been fairly common, but not for the purpose of restraining traffic: now there is widespread discussion on the merits of using tolls for this purpose.

Most of the remaining novel measures are concerned with ways of raising money for transport purposes (usually public transport) – a transport levy on property developers, a traffic generation fee on new buildings and a transport levy on local firms in relation to their payroll. The latter has been successfully tried in Paris and Grenoble and has been one of the main sources of funding for public transport. Perhaps the most novel of all the measures listed is the land-use alternative to a proposal to build a by-pass to the west of Portland. As yet, this alternative is only at the theoretical stage, but is being seriously considered by the authorities alongside the bypass scheme and several other alternatives. Calculations using a theoretical model suggest that this land-use alternative could reduce vehicle-kms travelled by up to 14 per cent compared with the bypass proposal (see Portland Case Study in Section 2 of this annex).

Impacts and achievements

Policies, whether on their own or as part of a package, are implemented with particular objectives in mind. Some of these were mentioned in the Case Study reports and a list of them is given in Table A3.5 under the main headings of planning, transport and environmental issues. Unfortunately, it is not easy to assess policy achievement, because it takes a long time for all the ramifications of a policy to work through the system (particularly where land-use changes are concerned), by which time the impacts may well have been modified by background changes unrelated to the policy in question. It is almost impossible to disentangle the impacts of the individual component policies of a package. Merely seeing whether a particular problem has been eased or not, does not give any indication of what would have happened had the policy not been implemented.

Nevertheless, it is useful to see what impacts the policies adopted by the cities have had against the objectives listed, even though these particular objectives might not have been the ones the cities themselves would have selected at the time. On this basis, Table A3.5 was constructed: looking at what has happened in this way helps to give some insight into what appears to be working in the right direction and what does not.

226

Table A3.4. **Novel measures tried and their success**

Novel measures	Tokyo	Seoul	London	Paris	Berlin	Milan	Hiroshima	Stockholm	Portland	Helsinki	Zurich	Grenoble
Tax on households with two or more cars		+										
Ban on households owning a car if they have nowhere to garage it		+										
Voluntary "no-car" day	+											
Car use limited to alternate days		+				++						
Traffic restrictions:												
• to sensitive areas					+	+++		0				
• when pollution is bad					++	++						
• when congestion bad											+	
• to goods vehicles			+			+		0			0	
• to all except low-polluting vehicles	++	+						0				
User tax on employee parking								0			0	
Tolls		+										
Transport levy on:												
• property developers						+						
• new buildings		+										
• firms				+++								+++
Differential fees and quotas for schools and colleges		+										
Land-use alternative to road proposals									0			

Note: x to xxx: indicates measure of usefulness.
0: refers to measures under consideration or in the pipeline.

Table A3.5. Achievement of broad objectives

Objective	Tokyo	Seoul	London	Paris	Berlin	Milan	Hiroshima	Stockholm	Portland	Helsinki	Zurich	Grenoble
Planning aspects												
Constrain city's growth and encourage growth elsewhere	+	–		+			+					
Promote multi–centre structure	+++	+++	++	++			+++					
Make city centre more attractive	+		+	+	++	++	+	++	+++	+	+	+
Bring homes and jobs closer together	:	–	–	–					++			–
Encourage cycling and walking		+		+	+	+	+	+	+		+	
Restrain out–of–town facilities			++	–	–				+++	++		–
Transport												
Improve mobility and accessibility	+	++	+	+	+	+	++	+++	++	++	+++	+
Reduce road congestion	–	–	–	–	–	:	++	:	+	:	:	+
Improve parking arrangements		+	+	++	–	++	++	:	+	++	+	+
Reduce accidents		+	+	+				:	+	:	+	++
Improve public transport	++	+++	:	+++	+++	+++	+	+++	++	+++	+++	++
Encourage modal shift to public transport	:	+	–	+	+	+	–	+	++	+	++	+
Reduce financial burden of public transport			++	–				–	+	–		+
Reduce dependence on car	:	–	+	–	–	:	–	:	+	–	:	+
Reduce need for mechanised travel	–	–	–	–	–	–	–	–	–	–	–	–
Environmental issues												
Reduce noise levels	–	–	–	–	+	–	–	:	:	:	:	+
Reduce pollution	–	–	–	:	+	+	–	–	+	–	+	+
Reduce CO₂ emissions	–	–	–	:	+	–	–	–	–	–	–	–

$Notes:$ x to +++: indicates the strength of the impact.
– to — : denotes failure to achieve the objective.
.: denotes no effect.

On the planning side, constraining the growth of the central city and encouraging growth elsewhere was only partially successful in those cities which attempted to do this: in Seoul, for instance, growth continued despite all attempts to constrain it, whereas in London the policy worked so well it had to be reversed at a later stage. Promoting a multi-centre structure, however, was successful in all the cities which sought this type of land-use pattern and particularly in the mega-cities of Tokyo and Seoul. Attempting to make cities look more attractive has been a constant activity in all cities over many decades, but little mention was made of this in the Case Study reports, except for Portland, where the city had deteriorated to such an extent that something drastic had to happen. While great improvements were made to downtown Portland, some of the other parts of the metropolitan region remained in a very poor state.

It is not clear how serious were the attempts to bring homes and jobs closer together, despite all that has been said on this issue. Only in Portland was there convincing evidence that something on these lines had been achieved. In most of the other cities, journeys to work (and to other activities also) have been lengthening consistently over several decades. With regard to the slow modes, there have been some minor achievements in the provision of localised cycling and walking facilities in some of the cities, but overall the tendency has been for these modes to lose out to mechanised modes. The trend towards larger concentrations of shops, leisure and health facilities and industrial and business parks in out-of-town areas is partly responsible for urban sprawl and more car use. While the spread of these activities has not stopped, some notable successes in constraining such developments have been obtained, particularly in London, Portland and Helsinki.

On the transport side, most of the efforts have been directed towards improving people's mobility and this has automatically made work places, shops and other activities more accessible to those with cars and those able to use the improved public transport facilities. Those on foot or on two wheels, however, may not have benefited to the same extent, though some improvements to the facilities offered to cyclists and pedestrians have been made in some cities, as noted above. Table A3.3 showed that improving public transport has been the main plank of transport policy in these cities and Table A3.5 shows that they have, on the whole, been most successful in these endeavours, though the financial burden, in the form of large subsidies, has not been eased in most cases. Despite the massive investment in public transport improvements, the modal share has changed little and where public transport has increased its share, it has generally been at the expense of walk and cycle. As a result, the policy has done little to ease congestion levels in these cities. Parking policy has probably done more than anything else to keep congestion levels at bay and according to the reports seemed an acceptable tool. In almost all of the cities, dependence on the private car has increased, despite all that has been done to foster public transport. The improvements to public transport have increased dependence on mechanised modes even more.

With regard to environmental issues, none of the measures discussed above seem to have brought about any significant improvement to noise levels in these cities, though some improvement in Grenoble and Berlin was noted. The situation is a little better with regard to pollution where noticeable improvements were observed in selected areas of some of the cities. Greenhouse gases were not even mentioned in most of the Case Study reports and no policies appear to have been implemented with the express intention of reducing CO_2 emissions.

4. Concluding remarks

The general conclusions of the Case Studies are similar to those which emerged from an inspection of the National Overviews (Annex 2). All cities seem to be suffering from the same sorts of problems; congestion, casualties, a worsening urban environment in one way or another and inaccessibility for those without access to a car. All have attempted to solve the problems in much the same way, though different emphasis has been placed on different policies by cities of different size and type.

Some aspects of policy stand out, in particular, the shift over the years from road based solutions to those depending on the provision of high quality public transport. But despite all the efforts made, road congestion has not been reduced to any extent in any of the cities (though how much worse it would have been had the measures not been taken is difficult to say). Noise levels and traffic domination are just as troublesome as they were, except in those areas where entry restrictions have severely reduced traffic levels. And there have been an increasing number of such areas in recent years, thanks partly to some innovative measures. Air pollution in general seems now to be on a downward trend, though this probably came too late to be reflected in the findings of the Case Studies. There were, however, noticeable improvements in particular areas of some of the Case Study cities, where selective action to improve air quality had been taken.

Mobility has increased through improved public transport services and by more and more people buying cars, but for those without a car and not able to take advantage of the improved transit services, conditions have got worse. Only now are policies being formulated to lessen society's dependence on the car and reduce urban travel in total (and not just the *growth* in travel). While none of the Case Studies suggested that serious thought had been given to reducing the wider environmental effects of mechanised travel through CO_2 emissions, this too seems now to be on the agenda.

BIBLIOGRAPHY

ACEA (1993), *Trucks and Their Environment: The Road Ahead,* Association des constructeurs européens d'automobiles, Brussels.

ALLEN, G. (1981), "Highway Noise, Noise Mitigation and Residential Property Values", *Journal of TRR, 812,* pp. 21-26.

BARTHOLOMEW, K.A. (1993), "A Tale of Two Cities", Portland, Oregon, Case Study report submitted to OECD/ECMT Project Group on Urban Travel and Sustainable Development, *1 000 Friends of Oregon,* Portland, USA.

BEHBEHANI, R., V.S. PENDAKUR and A.T. ARMSTRONG-WRIGHT (1984), *Singapore Area Licensing Scheme: A Review of the Impact,* World Bank Water Supply and Urban Development Department, Washington DC.

BLAND, B.H. (1984), "Effect of Fuel Price on Fuel Use and Travel Patterns", *TRRL Laboratory Report 1114,* Transport and Road Research Laboratory, Crowthorne, Berkshire, UK.

BREHENY, M.J. (Forthcoming). "Counter-urbanisation and Sustainable Urban Forms", In J. Brotchie, M. Batty, P. Hall and P. Newton (eds.), *Cities in Competition: The Emergence of Productive and Sustainable Cities for the 21st Century.*

BREHENY, M.J. (1990), "Towards Sustainable Development", In A. Mannion and S. Bowlby (eds.), *Environmental Issues in the 1990s.* Open University Press, London.

BREHENY, M.J., T. GENT and D. LOCK, (1993), *Alternative Development Patterns: New Settlements,* Department of the Environment, HMSO, London.

BROWN, W. (1994), "Dying From Too Much Dust", *New Scientist,* 12 March 1994.

CERVERO, R. (1991), "Congestion Relief: The Land Use Alternative", *Journal of Planning Education and Research,* Vol. 10, Part 2.

CMHC (1993), *Urban Travel and Sustainable Development: The Canadian Experience,* Canada Mortgage and Housing Corporation, Ottawa, Canada.

COLWILL, D.M., C.J. PETERS and R. PERRY (1984), "Water Quality of Motorway Runoff". *Transport and Road Research Laboratory Supplementary Report SR832,* Department of Transport, Crowthorne, Berkshire, UK.

DASGUPTA, M. (1993), "Urban Problems and Urban Policies: OECD/ECMT Study of 132 Cities", International Conference on "Travel in the City – Making it Sustainable", June 1993, Dusseldorf, OECD, Paris.

DAWSON, J.A.L. and I. CATLING (1986), "Electronic Road Pricing in Hong Kong", *Transportation Research 20A: pp. 129-34.*

DELSEY, J. (1991), *Nuisances from Heavy Goods Vehicles,* European Conference of Ministers of Transport (ECMT), OECD, Paris.

DOLDISSON, A. (1988), "Environmental Traffic Management – The German Inter-ministerial Research Programme", *Environmental Issues,* pp. 71-85.

ECMT (1994), *Trends in the Transport Sector 1970-1992,* European Conference of Ministers of Transport (ECMT), OECD, Paris.

ECMT (1990), *Transport Policy and the Environment,* European Conference of Ministers of Transport (ECMT), OECD, Paris.

ERTI (1992), *The Efficient Use of Energy: Looking in the Future,* European Round Table of Industrialists, ERT, Brussels.

EU GREEN PAPER (1992), *The Impact of Transport on the Environment: A Community Strategy for "sustainable mobility",* COM (92) 46 final, Commission of the European Union, Brussels.

EU GREEN PAPER (1990), *Communication from the Commission to the Council and Parliament,* COM(90)218 final, Commission of the European Union, Brussels.

FEDERAL COUNCIL OF SWITZERLAND (1986), *Ordonnance sur la protection de l'air (OPair),* Government Printing Office, Berne.

FOURACRE, P.R., R.J. ALLPORT and J.M. THOMSON (1990), "The Performance and Impact of Rail Mass Transit in Developing Countries", *TRL Research Report RR 278,* Transport Research Laboratory, Crowthorne, Berkshire, UK.

FREY, R.L. and P.M. LANGLOH (eds.) (1992), "The Use of Economic Instruments in Urban Travel Management", *WWZ, Report No. 37,* University of Basel, Basel, Switzerland.

GOODWIN, P.B. (1992), "A Review of New Demand Elasticities with Special Reference to Short and Long Run Effects of Price Changes", *Journal of Transport Economics and Policy,* 26 May 1992, pp. 155-170.

GS EVED (1993), *Grundlagen zur Kostenwahrheit im Verkehr,* General Secretariat of the Energy and Transport Ministry, Berne, Switzerland.

HALL, P. and C. HASS-KLAU (1985), "Can Rail Save the City? The Impacts of Rail Rapid Transit and Pedestrianisation on British and German Cities", Gower Publishing Company.

HASS-KLAU, C. (1993), "Impact of Pedestrianisation and Traffic Calming on Retailing: A Review of Evidence from Germany and the UK", *Transport Policy,* Vol. 1, No. 1, Butterworth-Heinemann.

HILLMAN, M. (1992), "The Role of Walking and Cycling in Public Policy", *Consumer Policy Review,* Vol. 2, No. 2.

HILLMAN, M. (1991), *One False Move...: A Study of Children's Independent Mobility,* Policy Studies Institute, London.

HILLMAN, M. and J. ADAMS (1992), "Safer Driving – Safer for Whom?". Conference on "Eurosafe: Safer Driving in Europe", July 1992. The Association of London Borough Road Safety Officers.

HOPKIN, J.M., T. ROBSON and S.W. TOWN (1978), "The Mobility of Old People: A Study in Guildford", *Transport and Road Research Laboratory Report LR850,* Department of Transport, Crowthorne, Berkshire, UK.

IIUE (1992), *Towards Sustainable Traffic and Transport,* International Institute for the Urban Environment, Delft.

IPCC (1990), *Climate Change, the IPCC Scientific Assessment,* Intergovernmental Panel on Climate Change, Cambridge University Press, New York.

JANSSEN, L.J. (1993), "Blue zone Munich", Conference on "Travel in the City – Making it Sustainable", June 1993, Dusseldorf. OECD, Paris.

JORGENSEN, G. (1993), *Ecological Land-use Patterns – Which Strategies for Redevelopment?*, OECD Expert Meeting on the Ecological City, 12 May 1993, OECD, Paris.

KENWORTHY, J. and P. NEWMAN (1989), *Cities and Automobile Dependence: An International Sourcebook*, Gower Technical, Aldershot, UK.

KETCHAM, B. (1991), "Making Transportation Choices Based on Real Costs (Revised)", Paper given at the Transportation 2000 Conference on "Making Transportation a National Priority", Snowmass, Colorado, USA.

KRAG, T. (1993), *Cycling in Urban Areas*, European Cyclists' Federation, February 1993, OECD, Paris.

KREIBICH, V. (1978), "The Successful Transportation System and the Regional Planning Problem: An Evaluation of the Munich Rapid Transit System in the Context of Urban and Regional Planning Policy". *Transportation*, Vol. 7.

LANG, J. (1987), "Protecting the Community from Transportation Noise", *Proceedings of the 54th Annual Conference of the National Society for Clean Air*, Brighton, UK.

LARKINSON, J. (1992), "Research into Road Pricing: The UK Department of Transport's Programme". In R.L. Frey and P.M. Langloh (eds.), *The Use of Economic Instruments in Urban Travel Management, WWZ, Report No. 37*. University of Basel, Basel.

LRC, (1993). *London Area Travel Survey Initial Results*, London Research Centre, London.

MACKENZIE, J.J., R.C. DOWER and D.D.T. CHEN (1992), "The Going Rate: What it Really Costs to Drive", World Resources Institute, Washington DC, USA.

McLAREN, D. (1992), "Compact or dispersed? Dilution is no solution", *Built Environment*, Vol. 18, No. 4.

MAIBACH, M., R. ITEN and S. MAUCH (1992), *Internalisieren der externen Kosten des Verkehrs*, Zurich, Switzerland.

MALMSTEN, B. (1993), "Using Charges to Manage Traffic and Parking, The Dennis Plan", Conference on "Travel in the City – Making it Sustainable", June 1993, Dusseldorf, OECD, Paris.

MASSER I., O. SVIDEN and M. WEGENER (1992), "The geography of Europe's futures", Belhaven Press, London.

MAURIN, M., J. LAMBERT and A. ALANZET (1988), "Enquête nationale sur le bruit des transports en France", *INRETS Report 71*, Institut National de Recherche sur les Transports et leur Sécurité, Arcueil, France.

MENR (1992), *Ecocycles: The Basis of Sustainable Urban Development*, Ministry of the Environment and Natural Resources, Environmental Advisory Council, Stockholm (Almanna Forlaget).

MITCHELL, C.G.B. (1991), "Road Transport and the Environment – A Brief Overview", University of Bradford Silver Jubilee Conference, September 1991, UK.

MITCHELL, C.G.B. and A.J. HICKMAN (1990), "Air Pollution and Noise from Road Vehicles", *Transport Policy and the Environment*, ECMT Ministerial Session, European Conference of Ministers of Transport, OECD, Paris.

MORTON-WILLIAMS, J., B. HEDGES and E. FERNANDO (1978), "Road Traffic and the Environment", *SCPR Report*, p. 390, Social and Community Planning Research, London.

NEWMAN, P. (1992), "An Australian Perspective", *Built Environment,* Vol. 18, No. 4.

NIURR (1993), "Transport Energy in Towns and Commuting Regions. An Investigation Based on Swedish Data", Norwegian Institute for Urban and Regional Research, *NIURR Planning Report 2,* Oslo.

NL (1991), *Fourth Report on Physical Planning,* The Hague, Netherlands.

NL MOH, P.P. and E. (1991), *The Right Business in the Right Place,* National Physical Planning Agency, The Hague, Netherlands.

OECD (1994), *Reducing Motor Vehicle Emissions in the Long Term,* Paris.

OECD (1993a), *OECD Environmental Data, Compendium 1993,* Paris.

OECD (1993b), International Conference on "Travel in the City – Making it Sustainable", June 1993, Dusseldorf, Paris.

OECD (1992), International Conference on "The Economic, Social and Environmental Problems of Cities", 18-20 November 1992, OECD, Paris.

OECD (1988a), *Transport and the Environment,* Paris.

OECD (1988b), *Cities and Transport,* Paris.

OECD (1986), *Fighting Noise,* Paris.

OLDRIDGE, B. (1992), "Congestion Metering in Cambridge City", In R.L. Frey and P.M. Langloh (eds.), *The Use of Economic Instruments in Urban Travel Management, WWZ, Report No. 37,* University of Basel, Basel.

OPCS (1993), *Growth of One Parent Families 1971-1991,* Office of Population and censuses, HMSO, London.

ORFEUIL, J.P. (1992), "Prospects for Travel Behaviour and Travel Behaviour Research", *Journal of International Association of Traffic and Safety Sciences,* Vol. 16, No. 2, IATSS, Tokyo.

OWENS, S. and P. RICKABY (1992), "Settlements and Energy Revisited", *Built Environment,* Vol. 18, No. 4.

PAPAYANNOS, T. and Associates (1992), *Environmental Perspectives and the Quality of Life, 1995-2010,* Greek Case Study for European Foundation on Living and Working Conditions.

QUINET, E. (1994), "The Social costs of transport: evaluation and links with international policies". Published by OECD as *Internalising the social costs of transport,* Paris.

SAMARAS and ZIEROCK (1992), *Assessment of the Effect in EU Member States of the Implementation of Policy Measures for CO_2 Reduction in the Transport Sector,* EU, Brussels.

SERAGELDIN, I. (1993), "Environmentally Sustainable Urban Transport, Defining a Global Policy", *Public Transport International,* Vol. 2, 1993.

SERC (1993), *Cities and Sustainability,* Science and Engineering Research Council: AFRC-SERC Clean Technology Unit, Swindon, UK.

STEADMAN, P. and M. BARRETT (1990), *The Potential Role of Town and Country Planning in Reducing Carbon Dioxide Emissions,* The Open University, Milton Keynes, UK.

T&E (1993), *EU 1996/97 Emission Limit Values for Cars – A Response to the Commission's Proposals,* European Federation for Transport and the Environment (EFT&E), Brussels.

TASCHNER, K. (1992), *Car Use and Fiscal Instruments in the European Community,* European Environmental Bureau, Brussels.

TEIK, L.C. (1993), "Full-day ALS from January Next Year", article in *Straits Times,* 16 April 1993, Singapore.

TESSITORE, M. (1993), "Limiting Car Use in Milan", Conference on "Travel in the City – Making it Sustainable", June 1993, Dusseldorf, OECD, Paris.

UK CSO (1993), *Expenditure and Resources,* Central Statistical Office, HMSO, London.

UK DOE (1994), *Planning Policy Guidance PPG13: Transport,* Department of the Environment, HMSO, London.

UK DOE (1993), *Planning Policy Guidance PPG6: Town Centres and Retail Developments,* Department of the Environment, HMSO, London.

UK DOE/DOT (1993), *Reducing Transport Emissions through Planning,* Department of the Environment, Department of Transport, Ecotec Research and Consulting Ltd., HMSO, London.

UK DOT (1993), *London Area Traffic Survey,* HMSO, London.

UK DOT (1991*a*), *Transport Statistics Great Britain 1980-1990,* Department of Transport, HMSO, London.

UK DOT (1991*b*), *Road Accidents, Great Britain 1990: The Casualty Report,* Department of Transport, HMSO, London.

UK DOT (1991*c*), *Transport and the Environment,* Department of Transport, HMSO, London.

UN (1993), *Statistics of Road Traffic Accidents in Europe,* Vol. xxxviii, United Nations, New York.

US DOT (1993), *Transportation Implications of Telecommuting,* US Department of Transportation, Federal Highway Administration, Washington DC.

US DOT (1992*a*), "Edge City and ISTEA – Examining the Transportation Implications of Suburban Development Patterns", *Searching for Solutions, a Policy Discussion Series,* No. 7, US Department of Transportation, Federal Highway Administration, Washington DC.

US DOT (1992*b*), *Air Quality Programs and Provisions of the Intermodal Surface Transportation Efficiency Act of 1991 (A Summary),* US Department of Transportation, Washington DC.

US DOT (1992*c*), *Summary of Transportation Programs and Provisions of the Clean Air Act Amendments of 1990,* Federal Highway Administration, US Department of Transportation, Washington DC.

VIRLEY, S. (1993), "The Effect of Fuel Price Increases on Road Transport CO_2 Emissions", *Transport Policy, Vol. 1, No. 1,* (Butterworth-Heinnemann).

WACHS, M. (1993), "Lessons from Los Angeles: Transportation, Urban Form and Air Quality", *Transportation, Vol. 20, No. 4.*

WALMSLEY, D.A. and K.E. PERRETT (1992), "The Effects of Rapid Transit on Public Transport and Urban Development", *TRL State of the Art Report SOAR 6,* Transport Research Laboratory, Crowthorne, Berkshire, UK.

WALMSLEY, D.A. and M.W. PICKETT (1992), "The Costs and Patronage of Rapid Transit Systems Compared with Forecasts", *TRL Research Report RR352,* Transport Research Laboratory, Crowthorne Berkshire, UK.

WATERS, M.H.L. (1990), "UK Road Transport's Contribution to Greenhouse Gases: A Review of TRRL and Other Research", *Transport and Road Research Laboratory Contractor Report CR223,* Department of Transport, Crowthorne, Berkshire, UK.

WEBSTER, F.V., P.H. BLY and N.J. PAULLEY, eds. (1988), *Urban Land-use and Transport Interaction: Policies and Models,* Report of the International Study Group on Land-Use Transport Interaction (ISGLUTI), Avebury, Aldershot, UK.

235

WEBSTER, F.V., P.H. BLY, R.H. JOHNSTON, N. PAULLEY and M. DASGUPTA (1985), *Changing Patterns of Urban Travel,* European Conference of Ministers of Transport (ECMT), OECD, Paris.

WHITELEGG, J., A. GATRELL and P. NAUMANN (1993), *Traffic and Health,* Environmental Epidemiology Research Unit, University of Lancaster, Lancaster, UK.

WIT de, T. (1993), "Overview of Traffic Calming", Conference on "Travel in the City – Making it Sustainable", June 1993, Dusseldorf, OECD, Paris.

WOOTTON, J. (1993), "Local Transport Solutions with 20/20 Vision", in *Local Transport Today and Tomorrow,* Local Transport Today, London.

WORLD ENERGY COUNCIL (1993), *Energy for Tomorrow's World.*

DEFINITIONS AND ABBREVIATIONS

Country Aggregates

ECMT
(with abbreviations): Austria (A), Belgium (B), Bulgaria (BG), Croatia (HR), the Czech Republic (CZ), Denmark (DK), Estonia (EW), Finland (FIN), France (F), Germany (D), Greece (GR), Hungary (H), Ireland (IRL), Italy (I), Latvia (LV), Lithuania (LT), Luxembourg (L), the Netherlands (NL), Norway (N), Poland (PL), Portugal (P), Romania (RO), the Slovak Republic (SK), Slovenia (SLO), Spain (E), Sweden (S), Switzerland (CH), Turkey (TR) and the United Kingdom (UK).

EU: Countries of the European Union, *i.e.* Belgium, Denmark, France, Germany, Greece, Ireland, Italy, Luxembourg, the Netherlands, Portugal, Spain and the United Kingdom.

OECD Europe: All European Member countries of the OECD, *i.e.* countries of the European Union (EU) plus Austria, Finland, Norway, Sweden, Switzerland and Turkey.

OECD: All Member countries of the OECD, *i.e.* the countries of the OECD Europe plus Canada, United States, Japan, Australia and New Zealand (at the time of finalisation of this report, Mexico was not yet a full Member).

Note: All references to "Germany" concern the territory after 3 October 1990, *i.e.* "western Germany" plus "eastern Germany", though references to country aggregates, *i.e.* to OECD Europe or OECD, include western Germany only.

Currency

Monetary units: Costs are given in the countries' individual currencies, together with the equivalent number of ECUs.

237

Other abbreviations

UN: United Nations
GDP: Gross domestic product
CBD: Central business district
VKT: Vehicle kilometres travelled
LRT: Light rapid transit
HOV: High occupancy vehicle
CNG: Compressed natural gas
LPG: Liquefied petroleum gas
CO_2: Carbon dioxide
CO: Carbon monoxide
NO_x: Oxides of Nitrogen
SO_2: Sulphur dioxide
VOCs: Volatile organic compounds
HCs: Hydrocarbons
CFCs: Chloro fluoro carbons
dB(A): Decibels "A" weighted to correspond to the response of human beings
Bn: Billion (thousand million)

Cut-off Date

The statistical information presented in this report is based mainly on data collected prior to 31 December 1992.

238

MAIN SALES OUTLETS OF OECD PUBLICATIONS
PRINCIPAUX POINTS DE VENTE DES PUBLICATIONS DE L'OCDE

ARGENTINA – ARGENTINE
Carlos Hirsch S.R.L.
Galería Güemes, Florida 165, 4° Piso
1333 Buenos Aires   Tel. (1) 331.1787 y 331.2391
Telefax: (1) 331.1787

AUSTRALIA – AUSTRALIE
D.A. Information Services
648 Whitehorse Road, P.O.B 163
Mitcham, Victoria 3132   Tel. (03) 873.4411
Telefax: (03) 873.5679

AUSTRIA – AUTRICHE
Gerold & Co.
Graben 31
Wien I   Tel. (0222) 533.50.14

BELGIUM – BELGIQUE
Jean De Lannoy
Avenue du Roi 202
B-1060 Bruxelles   Tel. (02) 538.51.69/538.08.41
Telefax: (02) 538.08.41

CANADA
Renouf Publishing Company Ltd.
1294 Algoma Road
Ottawa, ON K1B 3W8   Tel. (613) 741.4333
Telefax: (613) 741.5439
Stores:
61 Sparks Street
Ottawa, ON K1P 5R1   Tel. (613) 238.8985
211 Yonge Street
Toronto, ON M5B 1M4   Tel. (416) 363.3171
Telefax: (416)363.59.63
Les Éditions La Liberté Inc.
3020 Chemin Sainte-Foy
Sainte-Foy, PQ G1X 3V6   Tel. (418) 658.3763
Telefax: (418) 658.3763

Federal Publications Inc.
165 University Avenue, Suite 701
Toronto, ON M5H 3B8   Tel. (416) 860.1611
Telefax: (416) 860.1608
Les Publications Fédérales
1185 Université
Montréal, QC H3B 3A7   Tel. (514) 954.1633
Telefax : (514) 954.1635

CHINA – CHINE
China National Publications Import
Export Corporation (CNPIEC)
16 Gongti E. Road, Chaoyang District
P.O. Box 88 or 50
Beijing 100704 PR   Tel. (01) 506.6688
Telefax: (01) 506.3101

CZECH REPUBLIC – RÉPUBLIQUE TCHÈQUE
Artia Pegas Press Ltd.
Narodni Trida 25
POB 825
111 21 Praha 1   Tel. 26.65.68
Telefax: 26.20.81

DENMARK – DANEMARK
Munksgaard Book and Subscription Service
35, Nørre Søgade, P.O. Box 2148
DK-1016 København K   Tel. (33) 12.85.70
Telefax: (33) 12.93.87

EGYPT – ÉGYPTE
Middle East Observer
41 Sherif Street
Cairo   Tel. 392.6919
Telefax: 360-6804

FINLAND – FINLANDE
Akateeminen Kirjakauppa
Keskuskatu 1, P.O. Box 128
00100 Helsinki
Subscription Services/Agence d'abonnements :
P.O. Box 23
00371 Helsinki   Tel. (358 0) 12141
Telefax: (358 0) 121.4450

FRANCE
OECD/OCDE
Mail Orders/Commandes par correspondance:
2, rue André-Pascal
75775 Paris Cedex 16   Tel. (33-1) 45.24.82.00
Telefax: (33-1) 49.10.42.76
Telex: 640048 OCDE
Orders via Minitel, France only/
Commandes par Minitel, France exclusivement :
36 15 OCDE

OECD Bookshop/Librairie de l'OCDE :
33, rue Octave-Feuillet
75016 Paris   Tel. (33-1) 45.24.81.67
(33-1) 45.24.81.81
Documentation Française
29, quai Voltaire
75007 Paris   Tel. 40.15.70.00
Gibert Jeune (Droit-Économie)
6, place Saint-Michel
75006 Paris   Tel. 43.25.91.19
Librairie du Commerce International
10, avenue d'Iéna
75016 Paris   Tel. 40.73.34.60
Librairie Dunod
Université Paris-Dauphine
Place du Maréchal de Lattre de Tassigny
75016 Paris   Tel. (1) 44.05.40.13
Librairie Lavoisier
11, rue Lavoisier
75008 Paris   Tel. 42.65.39.95
Librairie L.G.D.J. - Montchrestien
20, rue Soufflot
75005 Paris   Tel. 46.33.89.85
Librairie des Sciences Politiques
30, rue Saint-Guillaume
75007 Paris   Tel. 45.48.36.02
P.U.F.
49, boulevard Saint-Michel
75005 Paris   Tel. 43.25.83.40
Librairie de l'Université
12a, rue Nazareth
13100 Aix-en-Provence   Tel. (16) 42.26.18.08
Documentation Française
165, rue Garibaldi
69003 Lyon   Tel. (16) 78.63.32.23
Librairie Decitre
29, place Bellecour
69002 Lyon   Tel. (16) 72.40.54.54

GERMANY – ALLEMAGNE
OECD Publications and Information Centre
August-Bebel-Allee 6
D-53175 Bonn   Tel. (0228) 959.120
Telefax: (0228) 959.12.17

GREECE – GRÈCE
Librairie Kauffmann
Mavrokordatou 9
106 78 Athens   Tel. (01) 32.55.321
Telefax: (01) 36.33.967

HONG-KONG
Swindon Book Co. Ltd.
13–15 Lock Road
Kowloon, Hong Kong   Tel. 2376.2062
Telefax: 2376.0685

HUNGARY – HONGRIE
Euro Info Service
Margitsziget, Európa Ház
1138 Budapest   Tel. (1) 111.62.16
Telefax : (1) 111.60.61

ICELAND – ISLANDE
Mál Mog Menning
Laugavegi 18, Pósthólf 392
121 Reykjavik   Tel. 162.35.23

INDIA – INDE
Oxford Book and Stationery Co.
Scindia House
New Delhi 110001   Tel.(11) 331.5896/5308
Telefax: (11) 332.5993
17 Park Street
Calcutta 700016   Tel. 240832

INDONESIA – INDONÉSIE
Pdii-Lipi
P.O. Box 4298
Jakarta 12042   Tel. (21) 573.34.67
Telefax: (21) 573.34.67

IRELAND – IRLANDE
Government Supplies Agency
Publications Section
4/5 Harcourt Road
Dublin 2   Tel. 661.31.11
Telefax: 478.06.45

ISRAEL
Praedicta
5 Shatner Street
P.O. Box 34030
Jerusalem 91430   Tel. (2) 52.84.90/1/2
Telefax: (2) 52.84.93
R.O.Y.
P.O. Box 13056
Tel Aviv 61130   Tél. (3) 49.61.08
Telefax (3) 544.60.39

ITALY – ITALIE
Libreria Commissionaria Sansoni
Via Duca di Calabria 1/1
50125 Firenze   Tel. (055) 64.54.15
Telefax: (055) 64.12.57
Via Bartolini 29
20155 Milano   Tel. (02) 36.50.83
Editrice e Libreria Herder
Piazza Montecitorio 120
00186 Roma   Tel. 679.46.28
Telefax: 678.47.51
Libreria Hoepli
Via Hoepli 5
20121 Milano   Tel. (02) 86.54.46
Telefax: (02) 805.28.86
Libreria Scientifica
Dott. Lucio de Biasio 'Aeiou'
Via Coronelli, 6
20146 Milano   Tel. (02) 48.95.45.52
Telefax: (02) 48.95.45.48

JAPAN – JAPON
OECD Publications and Information Centre
Landic Akasaka Building
2-3-4 Akasaka, Minato-ku
Tokyo 107   Tel. (81.3) 3586.2016
Telefax: (81.3) 3584.7929

KOREA – CORÉE
Kyobo Book Centre Co. Ltd.
P.O. Box 1658, Kwang Hwa Moon
Seoul   Tel. 730.78.91
Telefax: 735.00.30

MALAYSIA – MALAISIE
University of Malaya Bookshop
University of Malaya
P.O. Box 1127, Jalan Pantai Baru
59700 Kuala Lumpur
Malaysia   Tel. 756.5000/756.5425
Telefax: 756.3246

MEXICO – MEXIQUE
Revistas y Periodicos Internacionales S.A. de C.V.
Florencia 57 - 1004
Mexico, D.F. 06600   Tel. 207.81.00
Telefax : 208.39.79

OECD PUBLICATIONS, 2 rue André-Pascal, 75775 PARIS CEDEX 16
PRINTED IN FRANCE
(97 95 04 1) ISBN 92-64-14370-X – No. 47241 1995